Private Confederacies

CIVIL WAR AMERICA

Peter S. Carmichael, Caroline E. Janney, and Aaron Sheehan-Dean, editors

This landmark series interprets broadly the history and culture of the Civil War era through the long nineteenth century and beyond. Drawing on diverse approaches and methods, the series publishes historical works that explore all aspects of the war, biographies of leading commanders, and tactical and campaign studies, along with select editions of primary sources. Together, these books shed new light on an era that remains central to our understanding of American and world history.

Private Confederacies
The Emotional Worlds of Southern Men as Citizens and Soldiers

James J. Broomall

University of North Carolina Press CHAPEL HILL

© 2019 The University of North Carolina Press
All rights reserved
Set in Merope Basic by Westchester Publishing Services

The University of North Carolina Press has been a member of the
Green Press Initiative since 2003.

Library of Congress Cataloging-in-Publication Data
Names: Broomall, James J., author.
Title: Private confederacies : the emotional worlds of southern men
   as citizens and soldiers / James J. Broomall.
Other titles: Civil War America (Series)
Description: Chapel Hill : University of North Carolina Press, [2019] |
   Series: Civil War America | Includes bibliographical references and index.
Identifiers: LCCN 2018020212| ISBN 9781469649757 (cloth : alk. paper) |
   ISBN 9781469651989 (pbk. : alk. paper) | ISBN 9781469649764 (ebook)
Subjects: LCSH: Masculinity—Southern States—19th century—History. |
   Men—Southern States—Social life and customs—19th century.
Classification: LCC BF692.5 .B755 2019 | DDC 155.3/32097509034—dc23
   LC record available at https://lccn.loc.gov/2018020212

Cover illustration: Detail from photograph of Henry J. Walker and Levi Jasper
Walker, 1887. American Civil War Museum, under the management of
Virginia Museum of History & Culture (FIC 2013.00272).

This book incorporates previously published material from "We Are a Band of
Brothers: Manhood and Community in Confederate Camps and Beyond," *Civil
War History* 60, no. 3 (2014): 270-309 (used here with the permission of Kent State
University Press); and "Personal Reconstructions: Southern Men as Soldiers and
Citizens in the Post-Civil War South," in *Creating Citizenship in the Nineteenth-
Century South*, ed. William A. Link et al. (Gainesville: University Press of Florida,
2013), 111-33 (used here with permission).

To Bill and Pete,
mentors, friends, and colleagues

Contents

Acknowledgments xi

Introduction 1

CHAPTER ONE
Words 12

CHAPTER TWO
Soldiers 32

CHAPTER THREE
Battle 61

CHAPTER FOUR
Demobilization 86

CHAPTER FIVE
Reconstructions 108

CHAPTER SIX
Violence 131

Conclusion 153

Notes 157
Bibliography 199
Index 223

Illustrations

Three Confederate prisoners at Gettysburg 41

Confederate Camp during the Late American War
by Conrad Wise Chapman 56

The Fifty-Ninth Virginia Infantry — Wise's Brigade
by Conrad Wise Chapman 57

Wise Brigade by John J. Omenhauser 59

Ku Klux Klan costumes in North Carolina, 1870 136

Acknowledgments

As any author knows, a book is only possible because of other people. I have been incredibly fortunate in my professional and personal lives to be surrounded by supportive friends and family. Because of family's precedence in my life, I shall begin by acknowledging those closest and dearest to me. My parents have generously sacrificed vacations to accompany me on research trips, have kindly offered quiet spaces when I needed a place to write, and have supported my passion for history since I was a child. Their love provides me with a constant guide. During my first year in graduate school at the University of North Carolina, Greensboro, while pursuing a degree in museum studies, I met Tish Wiggs. Fifteen years and several states later, she remains my constant companion, my best friend, and my beloved wife. She and our beautiful children, Simon, Henry, and Addy are the most important people in my life. Tish and our children give me unparalleled joy and delayed the book's completion in the most wonderful ways. My in-laws, Sefton and Cheryl, have always given us a warm home to visit and lavished me with support. Cheryl, in particular, has lent her considerable editorial talents to helping me polish and refine this project.

Good friends have provided support over the years and helped form many of the ideas underpinning this work during long, meandering conversations. I am happy to acknowledge them: Rob Burdick, Mike Clarke, Rich Condon, Troy Cool, Jeff Curry, Ernie Dollar, Mike Galloway, Chris Graham, Gary Keefer, John McMillan, Chris Meekins, Kevin Pawlak, Dana Shoaf, David Southern, Peter Thomas, Matt Williamson, and Steve Wismer. Through graduate school, academic conferences, and other venues, I have benefited from conversations with and the comments of Kevin Adams, Aaron Astor, Joe Beatty, Joel Black, Brian Bredehoeft, Andrew Canady, Catherine Clinton, Clay Cooper, Jason Daniels, Laura Davis, Angela Diaz, Adam Domby, Greg Downs, Angela Elder, Andrew Fialka, Katie Fialka, Jim Flook, Allison Fredette, Dennis Frye, Lesley Gordon, Matt Hall, Scott Huffard, Jim Knight, Peter Luebke, Jenn Lyon, Ben Miller, Steve Noll, Taylor Patterson, Jason Phillips, Chris Ruehlen, Dan Simone, Jay Smith, Roger Smith, Diane Sommerville, Dave Thomson, Ben Wise, and Angie Zombek. Sean Adams, Bill Blair, Matt Gallman, Jon Sensbach, and Sevan Terzian each read earlier iterations of this project from start to finish. Each of them therefore made an indelible mark on this book—my sincerest thanks for taking the time to read my work and for caring enough to offer tough commentary. More recently, Aaron Sheehan-Dean read this project in its entirety and offered an extremely thoughtful and useful comment for which I am most grateful. At the University of North Carolina Press, first David Perry and, later, Mark Simpson-Vos shepherded me through the process of making my thoughts into this book project. Finally, I would like to acknowledge the anonymous readers from UNC Press. I spent a lot of time responding to the readers' reports because they pushed me to write a better book. Thank you for the trenchant criticism and insightful commentary.

During a one-year teaching appointment at Virginia Tech, Mark Barrow, Joe Forte, Dennis Hidalgo, Marian Mollin, Matt Saionz, Dan Thorp, and Peter Wallenstein provided support and help when I needed it. Over the years, at sundry conferences or at my request, Paul Anderson, Joe Beilein, Stephen Berry, David Brown, Lisa Cardyn, Paul Cimbala, William Davis, Barb Gannon, Lorri Glover, Matt Hulbert, Brian Luskey, Jeff McClurken, Sarah Meacham, Megan Kate Nelson, Rachel Shelden, David Silkenat, Andy Slap, Trae Welborn, LeeAnn Whites, Tim Williams, and Michael Woods provided either formal or informal comments on this work that greatly advanced my thinking. Portions of this project have been presented before audiences at the Southern Historical Association, the Organization of American Historians, the American Historical Association, the University of Georgia's Southern Roundtable Forum, the Symposium for the Civil War Sesquicentennial Committee of the North Carolina Department of Cultural Resources, the Conference of Florida Historians, the University of North Florida's Past to Present lecture series, Shepherd University's Research Faculty Forum, and various Civil War roundtables—thank you to these many audiences for their thoughtful suggestions.

I held my first tenure-track job at the University of North Florida. The department chair, Charles Closmann, provided a supportive environment and made sure I was not overwhelmed by committee work as a junior faculty member; additionally, office manager Marianne Roberts helped me with sundry tasks linked to this project. Greg Domber, David Sheffler, and Dan Watkins became good friends and intellectual companions during my time in Jacksonville. I presented portions of this project before members of UNF's History Department and acknowledge the helpful commentary of Denise Bossy, Alison Bruey, David Courtwright, Denice Fett, Chau Kelly, and Harry Rothschild. I have since moved to Shepherd University, where I serve in the History Department and act as director of the George Tyler Moore Center for the Study of the Civil War. Jennifer Alarcon, the center's program assistant, helped with the final stages of book production and always provided laughter when I needed it most. My colleagues Keith Alexander, Sally Brasher, David Gordon, Liz Perego, and Julia Sandy have made and make Shepherd an incredible home. My students in the Civil War and nineteenth-century America concentration have made teaching and mentoring an enjoyable, even joyful, experience. Our dean, Dow Benedict, is a model leader. And my colleague Ben Bankhurst makes life in Shepherdstown, West Virginia, fun, interesting, and intellectually stimulating.

This book is dedicated to William A. Link and Peter S. Carmichael. Bill and Pete have been with me since the beginning of graduate school and believed in me when others did not. Because of their trust and through their support I have become a scholar and an author. Perhaps more importantly, though, because of their friendship I have become a better person. They are individuals of untold generosity, charity, and goodwill. They and their wives, Susannah Link and Beth Getz Carmichael, have opened their homes and lives to me in ways usually reserved for family. Bill and Pete have read virtually every word I have written since graduate school. And both always lavished support when appropriate and criticisms when necessary. This dedication is a small but important gesture. Working with Bill and Pete in graduate school was a pleasure. Becoming their friend and colleague is a privilege.

In researching this project and writing this book, I benefited greatly from generous outside support. I would like to formally acknowledge both these institutions and the awards they granted: the Louisiana History Research Fellowship awarded by the Louisiana State University Libraries' Special Collections; the Research Appointment Fellowship awarded by the Institute for Southern Studies, University of South Carolina; and the Archie K. Davis Fellowship awarded by the North Caroliniana Society, University of North Carolina, Chapel Hill. The University of Florida's History Department, its College of Liberal Arts and Sciences, the Richard J. Milbauer Chair, the University of North Florida's Faculty Development Research Grant, and Shepherd University's Professional Development Grant provided generous support for conferences, research, and travel over the years. The Kent State University Press and the University Press of Florida allowed me to reprint portions of previous publications in this book.

Introduction

On June 20, 1863, Commissary Sergeant Harrison Wells of the Thirteenth Georgia Infantry Regiment encamped along the banks of the Potomac River near the small hamlet of Shepherdstown, West Virginia. Part of Confederate general Robert E. Lee's invading Army of Northern Virginia, he was preparing to cross the "Rubicon," positioned on the "brink of the Union." He did not miss the moment's gravity. Writing to his fiancée, May "Mollie" Long, Wells reflected, "I think that we will certainly have the best of success this time; and I am pretty certain that this will be a glorious campaign for us." Despite his optimism, Wells was tired. Deprived of his "loved one's society at home" and desperate for news, he had seen "many hardships and dangers" since he last wrote Mollie. Hard marches and sharp fights had defined the Pennsylvania Campaign for the rank and file. Wells's position in the army meant that he did not have to fight; some charged that commissaries were cowards. But he had joined the fray to do his "whole duty" to his country, benefit his "fellow soldiers as much as possible, and if not lighten, at least share some of their hardships."[1]

Race, class, and gender defined white Southern masculinity.[2] Wells's June letter places these markers of identity in stark relief. Worried about his public honor, he left the safety of the commissary stores for the uncertainty of the front lines. Grounded by his family, he desperately yearned for their comforting correspondence. Reared in a slaveholding society, he maintained that the Confederate raiders should return from Pennsylvania with slaves. And as a soldier in Lee's army, he pledged fealty to nation. Nothing about Wells's sentiments is surprising, even if the letter itself is revealing. His words demonstrate what scholars have long argued about the centrality of honor, manhood, and ideology to the Confederate soldier's war.[3] Yet Wells's letter also points to something less commonly observed by historians of the Civil War era: his choice of expression.[4] When he received news from home, he felt loved. He recounted his soldiery comportment in prideful terms. Expectations for an upcoming battle and subsequent victory evoked excitement. The rigorous campaigning had tired him. And he embraced his fellow soldiers as beloved comrades. Harrison Wells *felt* the experience of war.

The emotions and feelings it engendered became both a means of understanding and a model for self-expression.

This book seeks to understand the emotional worlds and gender identities of white Southern men in the Civil War-era South. Ethnography and argument are equally important to this project.[5] I argue that Confederate men, raised in an antebellum Southern culture that demanded self-control, struggled to understand their wartime experiences. They responded by creating emotional communities composed of fellow soldiers who crafted a common language of uncertainty. Soldiers relied on each other for psychological support, physical comfort, and personal security. Descriptive letters home related the range of emotions engendered by a conflict that had undermined white Southerners' self-assuredness and left many grasping for comprehension. During the Reconstruction era, whites resurrected their wartime communities during veteran reunions but also in paramilitary groups. Nostalgic over the past and angry at the present, white Southerners intended to restore a social order undone by emancipation and war and created a mythology to explain their lost cause.

The white Southern men who became Confederate soldiers seceded from the Union in order to establish an independent nation founded on slavery. To secure this goal, they provoked a war that destroyed the institutions they and their leaders had intended to preserve. This story is well known, and the white South's defeat became, in historian C. Vann Woodward's phrase, "the burden of southern history."[6] Scholars are less secure in their knowledge about *how* these events personally affected Southerners over the course of time. Historians have debated the extent of change prompted by civil war and social reconstruction and how, in turn, individuals reacted to and were transformed by these events. Several prominent scholars of the postbellum South have charged that Southerners remembered the war but that its pains and its consequences were eventually forgotten. The conflict did not decisively change Southerners' intellectual frameworks, excepting the readjustment to emancipation.[7] Conversely, cultural and intellectual historians have posited that the forces of war and emancipation forever shifted white mind-sets and came at great personal costs. Former Confederates' war of defiance continued into the years of Reconstruction and beyond, and many veterans struggled with long-term traumas sustained during their military service.[8] *Private Confederacies* engages these debates and seeks to understand how the American Civil War, emancipation, and Reconstruction affected the personal lives, emotional expressions, and gender identities of white Southern men. By so doing, this project shifts the locus of inquiry and expresses the significance of emotion and gender to cultural evaluation, charts the shifting contours of relations among men and between men and their families, explores the association between private feelings and public acts, and reexamines nineteenth-century Southern history through an exploration of personal narratives that are inseparable from broader sociopolitical developments.

Close-grain studies of white Southerners' psychological suffering as a result of the conflict and its impact on the collective household have illustrated the Civil War's long shadow.[9] The emerging picture is tragic and illustrates the Civil War's human costs.[10] Although this scholarship has influenced *Private Confederacies*, this project also heeds recent warnings that have pushed back against the "dark turn" in Civil War-era studies.[11] As historian Frances M. Clarke has charged, Victorian Americans found redemption in the war's carnage and believed that suffering positively influenced personal character and society.[12] *Private Confederacies* mediates between these historiographical camps, demonstrating that white Southerners grappled with personal demons while also readjusting to wartime and postbellum life. It is only by considering the dialectic between public and private experiences that the depth of Southerners' lives can be plumbed. This work, therefore, focuses on the external expression of emotion and an examination of thoughts and feelings that reveal Confederates' inner experiences.[13]

In the antebellum South, slaveholders relied on public "masks" to confer power and construct a particular vision of self.[14] More broadly and among different classes, self-mastery signaled a man's control over himself and an elevation above slaves, women, and children—individuals who became defining "others."[15] Once in Confederate armies, men sought to gain control over an authoritarian and often unpleasant life, for an individual's behavior, as viewed from the outside, dictated public reputation.[16] Few men went to war realizing the rigors of campaign or the terrors of combat. Some soldiers endured the contest well—emphasizing the necessity of personal sacrifice for family and country—whereas others succumbed to depression and found little meaning in the struggle.[17] Within these broader camps, individuals could and did change their feelings over time, thereby demonstrating fluidity in their personal responses to war.[18] Ambiguous reactions to the Civil War should come as no surprise, given the scale of human loss and suffering.

Confederates' range of reactions to war and reconstruction is best understood and accessed through the study of individuals—a methodological approach underpinning this project. The example of William J. Clarke is illustrative. In 1865 Clarke returned to his North Carolina home, restoring family relations and renewing friendships; however, he could not easily rebuild his prewar life. Four years earlier, Clarke had left his wife, Mary Bayard, and their children for war. He had promised to acquit himself "as becomes the husband of a heroic woman" and to leave their children a noble heritage if he should fall in battle.[19] Having received the rank of colonel and been recognized for his gallantry, Clarke had fulfilled his promises. But upon his return, he suffered physically from battle wounds, which confined him to bed, where he turned to a journal as his confessor. To the public, he self-consciously projected the image of the proud Southern warrior. In his small, leather-bound book, however, he recorded his inescapable physical and emotional pains: "suffered a good deal," "feeling very badly," and "my wounds [have] been painful" are just a few lines denoting his considerable anguish.[20] Uneven financial fortunes and an uncertain future compounded these traumas and left Clarke depressed and prone to excessive drinking. His feelings and behavior disrupted hopes for a seamless family reunion, as Mary Bayard struggled to maintain the public veneer of domestic tranquility and the personal happiness of her children. Clarke's inner demons and Mary Bayard's outward facade demonstrate the tangled relationship between private experience and public expression in Southern culture.

Clarke at first appears to be just one of the thousands of traumatized veterans who had no hope of financial success or personal redemption in the postbellum South. But this portrait is incomplete. A graduate of the University of North Carolina, Clarke had studied law in the antebellum era and served as a lawyer in Raleigh. This training and experience aided him during the political tumult of the Reconstruction era. He and his family eventually moved to New Bern, North Carolina, where he served as a trustee and then principal of New Bern Academy. Later, after declaring himself a Republican, Clarke served on the state senate, oversaw the publication of the weekly newspaper the *Signal*, and acted as a political agitator. At the height of Ku Klux Klan violence in North Carolina, Governor William W. Holden appointed him commander of the First North Carolina State Troops. In July 1874 Clarke declared himself "no bolter—no disorganizer" but instead a citizen seeking to "purify the temple, not destroy it."[21] Although his opinions and politics upset many Democrats in the region, Clarke became a prominent public figure in post-Civil War North Carolina as he assumed key political, military, and educational posts.[22]

Clarke was a disabled veteran, a state military officer, an educator, a political agitator, a husband, and a father. The Civil War had damaged him, but he also sought to change the world created by that conflict. Clarke's story illustrates the range of reactions to war, emancipation, and reconstruction and refuses to subscribe to neat categories. Instead, his example is instructive and opens a central question in Civil War–era studies: How did Confederates make meaning of their wartime experiences and reintegrate into civilian life after the war's close?

As Clarke had discovered, destruction and creation paradoxically marked the two faces of Southerners' civil wars. As veterans mustered out of the military, home as a haven was no longer so simple as many had hoped for and as people today might imagine. Instead, the fractured lives of Confederate veterans created fissures in the post–Civil War South's domestic and social arenas. Thousands of veterans returned home damaged, starkly revealing the conflict's human cost and enduring consequences. The Civil War also created new relationships, as manifested in how Southern men interacted with and perceived one another, interactions characterized by new levels of emotional disclosure, physical intimacy, and feelings of camaraderie that carried over into the postwar era.

Men are central to this story, but only with the explicit acknowledgment that women and children directly informed masculinity, for gender is socially constructed and the product of context, class, and place.[23] Antebellum white Southern men adhered to an honor-based culture that had fostered the creation of distinct expressions of Southern manliness based on Christian gentility, physical prowess, and ideological principles.[24] Strict lines of gender and racial hierarchy moderated and governed Southerners' public emotional expressions. Men commanded themselves and their feelings firmly, which bolstered an atmosphere of competition, erected barriers between men, and maintained a white social order. The crisis of war called this order into question and forced the reconfiguration of prewar behavior and expression as white Southerners, now Confederate soldiers, lived with and fought in military units that together experienced the strain of combat and the effects of want—all the while being separated from suffering families. The war created contradictions in men's emotional regimes as they came to rely on other men for support, learned of a family structure altered by the conflict's financial and emotional strains, and witnessed the abolition of slavery. With military defeat, whites questioned themselves as never before, sometimes suffering from self-doubt.[25] Civil war had necessitated new models of expression between veterans and among men and women. War caused men to express levels of emotionality and vulnerability that society once saw as the purview of women.[26] But white men also embraced a virulent, martial masculinity that they wielded during Reconstruction and beyond to suppress freed peoples and to restore white rule. Thus, in the wake of the Civil War, contrasting models of masculinity emerged from war and defeat.

Each of the men examined in this project served the Confederacy in some direct capacity—as an infantryman, as an officer, as a government official. The work connects people experientially, but only with a consideration of how age and life experience shaped reactions and ideas in sometimes starkly different ways: the view of a veteran of both the Mexican-American War and Civil War and the contrasting one of a twenty-two-year-old Confederate soldier. The project started out as an examination of the postwar lives of Confederate veterans. As the research progressed, questions reoccurred while particular sources came to dominate the answers. How, for example, could Southerners' reactions to military defeat be understood without uncovering their models of expression before and during the Civil War? In what terms did veterans understand and communicate their wartime experiences? In addressing these questions, a new framework emerged that included the prewar and wartime South as a way to reveal the complexities of the postwar era. Further, a narrow range of documents—notably, letters and diaries—became essential to addressing the project's questions, for this evidence offered a critical way to examine men's emotional lives.

Both the sources underpinning this study and the men and women examined herein limit the book's claims. The majority of the white Southerners discussed in *Private Confederacies* were slaveholders or members of slaveholding families who wrote extensively about their personal experiences; further, the project's study group is drawn largely, though not exclusively, from the Eastern Seaboard and Upper South.[27] This privileged group disproportionately turned out to fight because they were highly invested in and derived the most benefit from slavery. Social and economic class shaped their commitment to the Confederacy, and they willingly endured the physical and emotional hardships that came with military service because they had the most to gain or lose from the war's outcome.[28] The two chapters on the wartime era almost exclusively consider the war in the East and the Army of Northern Virginia. Rather than trying to find a "representative" sample of "typical" soldiers, this project started out with an entirely different premise that considered the exceptional importance of slaveholding Confederates as vital to the understanding of war and peace in the American South.[29] Wielding a disproportionate degree of power in the antebellum era, enlisting in extraordinarily high numbers during the Civil War, and spearheading extralegal resistance to Reconstruction, elite Southerners' words and actions reveal the varied personal and emotional reactions to the Civil War era.

Historians have mined similar evidentiary bases to understand how, in Drew Gilpin Faust's wording, white Southerners "wrote to explain—themselves to themselves, to each other, and to the wider world."[30] White elites projected a vision of filial piety that underpinned a public discourse integral to the South's hegemonic culture.[31] Untangling this imagery illuminates a constructed depiction of men in war and peace but also exposes an elusive unity because neither secession nor the Confederate cause received wholesale support.[32]

This work is most engaged with those scholars who write, in historian Jason Phillips's words, studies of "citizens at war."[33] Reid Mitchell and Joseph Glatthaar have been at the forefront of this methodology, crafting intimate views of how the rank and file understood and portrayed the Civil War. So, too, is the project indebted to Bell Irvin Wiley's groundbreaking scholarship on the common soldier and his world. The communities from which these soldiers came assume primacy in my analysis and demonstrate the integrity of home and battlefronts. As Glatthaar notes, "Soldiers brought cultural notions and values from home that shaped the way they felt and performed their duties as soldiers."[34] *Private Confederacies* follows the lead of this scholarship by first considering Southern men's prewar writings and social lives to reveal their models of self- and emotional expression during wartime. The project's emphasis on men's interior worlds has important consequences when considering their military experiences. Although soldier communities are well understood as sources for morale, historians have not fully appreciated them as networks of emotional support that were different from and deeper than antebellum male friendships. Battle rendered many men incapable of adequately communicating the experience of war to friends and family who remained at home, thereby heightening the sense of brotherhood they shared with other veterans. Once men reentered civilian society, the martial manhood and soldier communities forged in civil war were transformed into tools to suppress freed peoples through paramilitary organizations and the Ku Klux Klan.

Private Confederacies privileges individual stories, for people ultimately shaped both the personal and the emotional contours of Southern culture. By examining men between the antebellum and postbellum eras, the book seeks to understand Confederates' changing responses to other veterans and their families. A diverse range of scholarship over the past several decades has demonstrated how both social mores and expected patterns of behavior guide emotional expression and gender identity. Building on these approaches, this work primarily uses letters, diaries, memoirs, and public performances to illuminate Southerners' inner and outer worlds. Recorded words reveal how individuals both understood and gave meaning to war and reconstruction. As such, writers are quoted often and freely, as their words and the nuance of their expressions shed light on abstract thoughts, cultural forms, social conditions, and personal lives.[35] Further, primary source materials are used with little or no editing in order to preserve the integrity of original words and phrases; *sic* is not employed unless absolutely necessary. When writers' disparate words are examined together, broader cultural patterns are revealed. Although individuals underpin this study, *Private Confederacies* seeks to understand the culture that men and women continually shaped and reshaped in order to discern broader patterns. Coupling culture's ethos with an individual's sensibility can reveal, in Clifford Geertz's phrase, "a collective text."[36] Studying the intersections between private ideas and public acts allows this work to reach beyond the idiosyncrasies of individuals alone and make broader conclusions about Southerners' behavior. In important ways, hunting expeditions, military encampments, and the rituals of paramilitary organizations were cultural performances that served as public representations of social thought.

How white Southerners *experienced* maturation, death, soldiering, battle, camp, and reconstruction is accessed through their modes of expression. Beyond actions and words, this study also takes seriously men's emotional lives and is attentive to the language men employed to express themselves, which is illustrative of—to employ Barbara H. Rosenwein's conceptual instrument—an emotional community.[37] Although people in the twenty-first century cannot fully apprehend how nineteenth-century men *felt*, they can examine their models of emotional expression and the accompanying language that served as a mode for social communication.[38] Emotions helped men navigate and reflect on periods of transition such as the coming of war, the shock of battle, the environment fostered by the military, and the monumental shift of emancipation.[39] These experiences engendered a range of feelings including euphoria and sadness, certainty and ambivalence. *Private Confederacies* examines how men both perceived and portrayed these events and considers the spectrum of men's reactions.

The example of Confederate military defeat demonstrates how emotions history will be used in this study. In the spring and summer of 1865, the surrender of Confederate armies brought an end to men's martial lives.[40] How, though, did men interpret these events, and how did men's reactions to defeat influence their actions during Reconstruction? The majority of military engagements had taken place in the South, an extraordinarily high percentage of white Southerners had served and suffered, homes were destroyed, and the South lost.[41] Veterans were gripped by, and attempted to make sense of, feelings such as anxiety, depression, and isolation. So, too, were men overjoyed with the prospect of returning home, proud at having honorably served their state, and excited to resume their prewar occupations. Southerners' range of emotions—while timeless—must be rooted in historical context.[42] The experience of war had bound together Confederate veterans, and they often shared a conflicted language of defeat. The early tumult and contradictory feelings witnessed at the war's end morphed into an entrenched uncertainty about the future expressed by some as melancholy, or the "blues." Other soldiers, although happily ensconced within their families, missed the camaraderie of camp. Both groups reached out to other veterans with whom they could and did share their feelings. Veterans' communities assumed many forms in the postbellum era, ranging from the banal (social gatherings) to the sinister (participation in the Ku Klux Klan). Men found meaning in and gravitated to these communities because in them they expressed shared languages born from camp and campaign.

In the years after the Civil War, veterans' recorded words were often taut with emotion as they reflected on the war and its consequences. Men who had once defined their lives by an ancient code of honor and mobilized into armies believing in the righteous of their cause were now exposed to self-doubt, shame, and submission.[43] These emotions were transformative. Arguably, as never before, Southern men exposed themselves and their most inner feelings in the written word. Historian Stephen W. Berry has greatly advanced our understanding of Southern men's emotional lives in the antebellum period, but few scholars have followed his lead into the postwar years. Historians' neglect of Southern whites' emotions, Berry explains, is often rooted in limitations within source materials; for, as he writes, nineteenth-century men "were encouraged to cloak their hearts and stifle their doubts, to so carefully groom their public persona as to become it."[44] The self-doubt provoked by the prostration of the Confederate cause unmoored Southern men, leaving them to grapple with ideas of self and identity.

Private Confederacies is chronologically organized and attuned to change over time—understanding the Civil War's social and cultural impact requires a long view. The book explores the private lives and cultural expressions of white men and women living in the American South between the 1840s and 1870s and is in conversation with recent studies of nineteenth-century Southern history that are underpinned by broad periodization.[45] This expansive approach is used to reveal cultural change over time but also understands distinct periods in nineteenth-century Southern history and does not posit a "long Civil War."[46] The six chapters of this work are both thematically driven and chronologically organized to reveal cultural experience and to chart its changing expression.[47]

Chapter 1 is foundational to the project's broader claims because it establishes how antebellum men channeled and portrayed their emotions. It grows out of and contributes to a rich, if still burgeoning, body of literature that calls for an analysis of the men's gendered lives.[48] White Southerners' gender roles and emotional lives are critical to understanding how men perceived their maturation into manhood, their regional identity, and their thoughts and behavior. By chronicling diarists' ruminations, men's enthusiasm for nature and hunting, and college students' hopes and doubts, this chapter creates a layered portrait of white masculinity on the eve of the Civil War that stresses the interplay between men's public and private lives.

Military service tested independent Southern men. They responded to the army's discipline and order by continuing to embrace the flexible masculinities seen in the antebellum era. Most importantly, as revealed in chapter 2, soldiering thrust civilians into an entirely new physical setting composed of men with whom they ate, slept, and lived. Although this fraternity was initially disquieting, many soldiers came to embrace it, prompting them to form close bonds that proved essential to their mental and physical well-being once engaged in military campaigns. But men also bristled at military strictures. They struggled to maintain a degree of autonomy, as witnessed in their preference for uniform items from home and their selection of mess and tent mates.

Most Confederates entered military service entirely unprepared for the rigors of prolonged campaigning and the mounting casualties of Civil War battles. Chapter 3 documents how men responded to war with confused reactions and conflicted emotions. Southerners' reactions to war are not altogether surprising, given the self-doubt and anxieties revealed in the antebellum era. Just as prewar diarists searched for the best means of self-expression, so too did soldiers ponder how best to communicate their wartime experiences. Many veterans expressed their emotional reactions to the catastrophe of war; still, though, words often failed to capture the scope and scale of carnage. By considering the ordeal of combat and the battlefield's consequences through Southerners' visceral reactions, this chapter uses the lens of emotions history to craft a new narrative for a worn subject.

The American Civil War did not end tidily at Appomattox Court House as older studies once suggested. Instead, with war came a series of unintended outcomes that unsettled Southern veterans and left them grappling with themselves, their government, and their society, as explained in chapter 4. This chapter considers three entwined points: soldiers' personal traumas, veterans' initial shift from soldier to citizen, and fluctuating notions of manliness seen at the war's close. White Southern men had invested themselves completely in the cause of war but were unprepared for its consequences. How men attempted to resolve these difficulties is examined in chapter 5. Although many Confederates looked toward peace and the restoration of family life with great eagerness, the war had impacted their ability to function. Many veterans felt the pain of surrender and defeat for years after the Civil War's conclusion, and their temporary military service had come to define key elements of postwar life.

Chapter 6 explores white Southerners' fierce reaction to the collapse of the antebellum social and racial order and the possibility of black equality. The disfranchisement of some ex-Confederates and the simultaneous enfranchisement of African Americans incited fierce resistance as an affront to whites' honor. Across the South, therefore, white Southerners dismantled a federally ordered, postwar state through varied measures, with violence and terror serving as effective tools. The Ku Klux Klan is the most prominent example of white Southern violence. Deeply entrenched racism and acts of political insurgency propelled the Reconstruction-era Klan, which used contemporary forms of popular culture to create meaning and to communicate a virulent model of self-identity. The Klan's fragmented orders were connected by emotional expression born of racism and defeat.

At its heart, *Private Confederacies* is an exploration of the American Civil War's meanings over time. The shift from civil war to civic peace was not only a national transformation but also a personal process. The forces of war transformed and then underpinned Southerners' notions of manliness and emotional lives. The book seeks not only to write the life stories of these veterans but also to interrogate the ways in which civil war and reconstruction were personal processes that shaped gender, emotions, and Southern identity in the mid- to late nineteenth century. Southerners' words and actions break down traditional periodization. Private letters and public acts construct a different portrait of men grappling with the war and isolate its fundamental meanings to their lives. Historians have come to better understand why soldiers fought but must now fully realize the results of that decision.[49]

CHAPTER ONE

Words

The diary's first page attempts to ward off prying eyes: "Dont read the contents of a page, For fear that you'll provoke my rage." A neatly penned sketch follows, replete with rifle, hunting bag, powder horn, and a cluster of slain birds.[1] So begins fifteen-year-old George Anderson Mercer's diary, a five-volume record spanning the antebellum and postbellum eras. His short sentence, coupled with the vibrant image, reveals a contrasting engagement with a personal world of self-reflection and an outer realm of action. Mercer's admonition demonstrates his desire to keep his personal record private, while his sketch conveys his public passions for hunting and nature.

Public duties and private dreams flowed together in the words and pages of Southerners' diaries, and their texts command attention as both performance and record.[2] Writers used the typically confidential pages of journals to express their feelings and assess their masculinity.[3] In the late summer of 1851, for example, Mercer recorded an entry that recounted the joys he derived from writing and walking. His "excursions in the wild woods" were essential to his maturation as an independent man, while the maintenance of a journal gave him a quiet pleasure that honed his writing and forced concentration.[4] Using Mercer's diaries as an entrée into a broader world of Southern manhood, this chapter considers written constructions of self-identity; hunting and natural inquiry as reflections of the control and release of feelings; and education and social life as formative to young men's social and intellectual development. Rather than adhering to a rigidly defined model of manliness, men such as Mercer demonstrated through action and word that they could be introspective and reclusive, aggressive and competitive.[5] White Southern men thus maintained overlapping models of behavior that were used at different times according to different needs. Understanding these complex layers of behavior is difficult; therefore, personal narratives guide this chapter, and Mercer will serve as a touchstone to reveal multiple masculinities.

Southerners' emotional lives were central to their expressive culture and suggest a reconsideration of W. J. Cash's oft-quoted observation that the Southern man "did not (typically speaking) think; he felt."[6] Critiques of Cash's anti-intellectual Southerner are rightly justified, but his monolithic portrait of masculinity also contains a core truth: emotions were a central piece of white masculinity. Southern men felt and expressed anxiety and anger, joy and depression. Throughout the antebellum era, intimate associations with women or private acts of keeping a journal confidentially channeled men's feelings. By so doing, men learned the emotional control vital to their public face. Southerners' emotional expressions are therefore elusive because they actively maintained public masks. Diaries offer an entry into these otherwise lost worlds and demonstrate that men thought about more than just honor and violence, however important these forces were to their public lives.[7]

Mercer's slaveholding family's wealth and accompanying power directly informed his writing and set his record apart from the majority of nonslaveholding whites. Such caveats offer necessary historical context about social class, rather than negating the source's relevance or broader meaning. Within the diary's folds, readers are exposed to internal contests between passion and restraint, models of self-understanding and introspection, self-reflection, and social commentary. These themes, ideas, and dilemmas were not unique to Mercer but rather filled the pages of many of his social contemporaries' personal journals as well. The diary's virtue as evidence also reveals its drawbacks: rather than revealing mass behavior, it instead captures an individual psyche.[8] Yet this type of source is almost incomparable in its revelation of consciousness, and it is an essential starting point for this broader study, for within the pages of these records, Southerners actively investigated themselves and their social and emotional lives. Such explanations, as linked to a broader drive for self-understanding, shaped personal narratives, stories underpinned by but also filtered through class and cultural expectations and prescriptions.[9]

Raised in wealth and privilege, the self-conscious and introspective Mercer recognized the responsibilities and obligations of manhood. Born in 1835, the Savannah, Georgia, native had been named after his mother's father, George Anderson, a prominent cotton merchant. His father, Hugh Mercer, a successful banker and graduate of the United States Military Academy—where he had befriended Robert E. Lee—held a prominent place in Savannah society. His great-grandfather General Hugh Mercer had fallen at the Battle of Princeton during the American Revolution.[10] Within his pre-Civil War volumes, Mercer chronicled hunting expeditions, nature walks, and student life. These experiences shaped daily life among white elites such as Mercer, while his reflections marked his maturation into adulthood, his changing station as a man, and his emotional world. These sentiments and sentences, examined in conjunction with his contemporaries, reveal how men perceived and experienced their world.

Diaries

Although the breadth and depth of Mercer's work mark it as unique, the thoughts and sentiments expressed therein are not. Recent scholarship has crafted a complex portrait of Southern masculinity based on the principles of Christian gentility, ideological expression, and emotional communication.[11] Mercer's personal diaries are replete with these themes, but the genre itself deserves further scrutiny. While journals have been thoroughly studied for explanatory quotes, the diary as a form of expression and a discrete type of evidence is seldom considered.[12] Diaries offered their writers a venue for free thought, self-expression, and interrogation.[13] Diaries allowed space for rumination and fostered personal monologues that often read more like conversations between writers and their journals. Unlike personal letters or public proclamations, diary entries could be boundless and were not dictated by queries or guided by narratives.

Writers pondered freely in the folds of their journals. Young Virginian and future member of the First Rockbridge Artillery Clement Daniel Fishburne, for example, ruminated in his diary, "[I do] not think in the English language. I make no language for my thoughts as I go along, but let them rush pell-mell over one another, so that no one of them leaves a distinct mark or impression of its own." Glimpses of these rambling thoughts often overtook his entries, revealing how diaries are truly narrative expressions.[14] As he reflected on his role as a teacher, Fishburne's thoughts wandered from the mundane to the grand. As he wrote, "I am here, a spectator as it were of the acts performing from day to day on a limited portion of the world's stage. . . . They only see me as one of a vast multitude, taking it for granted, that I contribute my mite toward the consummation of what each of them individually is laboring to accomplish. The world generally is selfish perhaps.—Not perhaps—it is. But so am I:—not less so than many others. The world drives on."[15] Fishburne's entry captures the inner workings of a young man's mind as he considered his occupation and place in society, as well as the wider workings of the world.

Diary writing and letter writing were different endeavors entirely. For the middle and upper classes, specific rules and etiquette dictated a letter's form and style. Punctuation and spelling mattered; content and mood were controlled.[16] Individuality defined the letter, as it was often part of a broader exchange. According to one advice manual, letters served as a message sent expressly on "an errand of kindness to ourselves."[17] Thus, the letter's intended audience shaped its content, as is especially noticeable in letters between men and women, which were careful orchestrations that often obscured as much as they revealed.[18] As will be examined later in this work, the experience of battle tested men's abilities to compose such studied correspondence. By contrast, diary entries, though shaped by many of the dictates of epistolary works, differed in function, giving hint to the content and form of Southerners' wartime writings. Diaries were confessionals for the expression of inner thoughts, feelings, and concerns; the volume's pages became a place to purge and ponder. Such records provide remarkable insights into how Southern men viewed themselves, their families, and their place in the world. Fishburne began his first attempt at maintaining a diary while he was teaching in Christiansburg, Virginia, in 1854. The diary's beginning includes an extended explanation of the volume's purpose. Fishburne described how many "men and women of distinction have been in the habit of daily writing out their thoughts and observations of passing events." Continued practice produced positive results. He therefore endeavored for similar outcomes through observation, reflection, and expression as fostered by the daily or weekly practice of writing.[19]

Nineteenth-century writers differed from their eighteenth-century counterparts; their expression of thoughts and feelings denoted a cultural shift.[20] Antebellum men and women craved emotional expression, and diaries served as an important medium. A century earlier, diarists had revealed little about personal motivations and feelings, typically recording only events and transactions. Colonial Americans had neither the inclination nor the ability to engage in recorded self-examination.[21] Only by the nineteenth century did journal writing become an important private ritual for the middle and upper classes, and an essential piece of emotional expression. By mid-century, approximately 80 percent of Southern whites and 95 percent of New Englanders were literate;[22] and a broader spectrum of the population picked up pen or pencil. Not all diarists proved introspective, however. Scores of white Southerners maintained journals to record debts, detail their farms' economies, or simply chronicle random thoughts. Moreover, diarists composed only a minority of Southern society who were privileged by race and class. Writers' proclivities, tastes, and lifestyles determined who would and who would not write. William J. Clarke, for example, although well educated and thoughtful, found writing tedious. He suffered financial difficulties and never joined the planter class. Clarke frequently wrote business letters and infrequently corresponded with family, except his wife and children, with whom he maintained regular correspondence. In writing to Frances Miller, his sister-in-law, Clarke drew from a comment his son had made. "Writing is a great bore," he declared, "tho' he would talk a great deal to the person he is addressing were they present."[23] A self-proclaimed talker, Clarke chose conversation rather than correspondence.

Diarists were typically well educated and taught to value and develop intellect. Entries often described what they were reading, contemplated their roles among family and within society, and betrayed personal doubts and quests for self-improvement. These topics transcended the concerns of many Southerners but are nevertheless reflective of what qualities some writers held dear. A typical series of entries representing Mercer's range of interests and commentaries may be found in his diaries from the autumn of 1859. He variously discussed William Makepeace Thackeray's *Newcomers* and his aversion to reading such novels because they furnished "feeble mental pabulum," commentary on how duels preserved "gentlemanly deportment," and the "insurrection at Harper's Ferry" led by the "mad, fanatical" John Brown.[24] In these entries, Mercer offered judgments that reflected both what he despised and what he valued. Worried about the deleterious effects of novels, he charted a course for self-improvement through the record of the plot and characters. Concerned by Northern denouncements of dueling, he contended that the "duel is not surely half so debauching in its tendency as those brutal prize fights that constantly occur at the north."[25] Fixated by the events surrounding Brown's raid and its attack on slavery, Mercer came to the South's defense: "The Virginians deserve great credit for the temperate manner in which they have proceeded. . . . If anything could justify lynch law, it would be the conduct of these assassins."[26] The diary afforded Mercer time for deliberation and contemplation; his observations and records both shaped and reflected his understanding of self, region, and nation. For the reader, this source renders a slice of one man's life in decipherable text, shedding light on the otherwise shadowed portions of his mind.

Although men and women were tied by a dedication to the craft of writing, nineteenth-century diaries reflect gendered differences. The majority of white women who were diarists used their journals as an avenue for religious contemplation. Female diarists examined their relationships with God and interrogated their earthly existence. Southern women, far more often than men, analyzed their religious ideals to help guide their daily lives.[27] Meditative writing fostered the creation of deeply personal religious experiences central to broader spiritual quests. For example, in a typical diary entry, Williamsburg, Virginia, resident Nanny C. Waller looked toward a kindly God and away from her worldly trials, striving for an afterlife "where sickness, sorrow, pain, and death are felt and feared no more."[28] Late eighteenth- and early nineteenth-century female diarists from New England followed a similar form, although their writings adhered to two specific trajectories: accounts of tasks that reflected a strongly Protestant tradition and explicit, often highly critical, self-examination.[29] For women in both regions, religion guided content. Although pious Southern men certainly considered their immortal souls within a journal's folds, their writings tended more toward the secular.[30] For men and women, journal writing reflected a nineteenth-century cultural emphasis on introspection and self-sacrifice.[31]

For men unwilling or unable to outwardly portray emotional frailty in public settings, writing served as a means of guarded release and reflected the stern requirements of white masculinity. Permitted few unrestricted disclosures and defined by guarded interactions, men's feelings were expressed privately among family or within their writings. Diaries served as venues for the exploration of emotions. Discussions of depression, for example, occurred regularly. Josiah Gorgas turned to his diary when he was feeling downcast. Although he could not isolate a reason for such feelings, his writing offered a means of release and room for rumination.[32] Similarly, George Mercer went to his diary while away at Princeton after his mother's death. He longed to pour his sorrows into his mother's "willing ears," to breathe her name "among the forests where she died."[33] His mother's death no longer allowed for such intimate exchanges, but he could still purge himself through pen and paper. Reflections on the passage of time, particularly noticeable during the shifting seasons, could also invoke feelings of despair. Edmund Kirby-Smith, an officer in the U.S. Army and future Confederate general, contemplated the passing of summer and the beginning of autumn in mid-November 1849. Describing the season as both sad and beautiful, he felt overwhelmed by his feelings and the accumulated weight of his afflictions.[34] Finally, Clement Fishburne tried to parse out his feelings as he felt overcome by the "blues" but was not sure if these feelings were "included under melancholy." He referred to *Webster's Dictionary* for one definition but thought it too general. He wanted to probe deeper: "I shall try and find it treated metaphysically if possible." With due course he wanted to compare his findings to those presented in Robert Burton's classic, *The Anatomy of Melancholy*. Regardless of terminology, endemic suffering profoundly affected Southerners' mind-sets and morale. Gorgas, Mercer, Kirby-Smith, and Fishburne each found release through writing, disclosing strong emotions that weighed heavily on their minds. And each man turned repeatedly to this medium for expression, often writing what might have otherwise gone unexpressed.

Men of the antebellum South felt deeply, but Southern culture demanded self-control and emotional moderation. Men adhered to this code because it deeply informed their self-understanding. Indeed, as historian Steven M. Stowe remarks, "a man's private sense of himself" was "bound up with public display."[35] White elites constructed elaborate guards and public masks to maintain and reinforce the South's power structure. Hegemonic control governed men's actions as they commanded mastery over those whom they deemed dependents. These displays, so integral to social constructions and self-understanding, produced divisions between men's private and public lives.[36] Nonetheless, strict adherence to codes of honor and restrained comportment did not completely silence men's vibrant emotions, which were expressed privately. Male diarists both bridged and bolstered such divides as they wrote about and pondered their public actions, personal relationships, and self-definitions.

Distinctions between public and private writings guided and framed content. Some authors wrote instructional and reflexive journals intended for personal consumption only—these works functioned as private vessels (the now-famous secret diaries of James Henry Hammond and William Byrd II exemplify this model).[37] Those authors who desired privacy penned written warnings to prying eyes. As noted in the chapter's beginning, the first page of Mercer's diary includes the admonishment, "Dont read the contents of a page, For fear that you'll provoke my rage." In a similar vein, John Burgwyn MacRae labeled his college journal, kept while attending the University of North Carolina, "strictly private," while Martin Witherspoon Gary warned in his notebook from South Carolina College, "Read no man's secrets without his consent."[38] Kirby-Smith desperately hoped that under divine influence he would never be "called upon to blush for the record" of his most "secret thoughts and actions."[39] Curious interlopers, and later historians, were unhindered by such warnings, but the sentiments reflected the authors' sincere attempts to guard and secure their innermost thoughts and feelings. Keeping private journals private is, of course, a timeless pursuit. But the tension between men's public and private lives in Southern society is clearly demonstrated in writers' desires to guard their sentiments. Secret diaries offered men a refuge, an unrestricted arena to explore themselves as well as their internal worlds and outer responsibilities. In their writings, men could expose themselves rather than hide behind poses. But the domain had to be secure.

Self-Improvement

The habit of writing fostered routines, and many men used diaries for personal development. Southerners' strides toward self-improvement were explicitly linked to public control, which manifested itself in the mastery men demanded over women, children, and the enslaved. The whites examined herein were members of the middle and upper classes. They valued education and initiative, strove for personal development, and looked toward future prospects; scholars have deemed this category of men the "Masculine Achiever."[40] Indeed, as historian Timothy J. Williams has argued, college-attending Southern men embraced an "intellectual manhood" that emphasized industry and perseverance, reflecting "middle-class" and "bourgeois" values—a strikingly modern man.[41] The ideals of both "intellectual manhood" and the "Masculine Achiever" dictated that hard work and persistence would result in self-advancement. Rather than being Northern characteristics, as scholars had maintained, self-reliance and industry also had roots in the South, as both Jan Lewis and Williams have demonstrated. In the wake of the American Revolution, a new language of individualism had appeared in whites' correspondence.[42] This trend continued into the 1840s and 1850s, as evidenced by the use of daily and weekly journals to assist in self-constructions—personal notations functioned as vehicles for upward mobility.

Southerners' reflective documents recorded accomplishments and noted admonishments. Gorgas created a personal record consciously for later use by his children; and upon his forty-third birthday, he pondered his achievements and failings. "May it bring forth better fruit than the past," he opined, though he hastily added, "I have not been absolutely idle."[43] Gorgas marked his recent efforts with notations on physical labor, family health, military duties, and intellectual development. In one sweeping sentence, Gorgas both extolled his virtues and revealed his self-doubt. By balancing his manly accomplishments with his promise to achieve more, Gorgas soothed his wounded pride with self-punishment. Kirby-Smith, then stationed as an instructor at West Point, similarly kept a journal with a desire for self-improvement and "a consciousness of many imperfections." Diligently recording names, dates, and passages from works he was reading, Kirby-Smith wanted to build his knowledge and improve his memory through writing. By now a veteran of the Mexican-American War, in which his older brother had been killed, Kirby-Smith began to use his diary as a confessional. Grieved and saddened by recent events, he eschewed others' company, using self-seclusion for rumination and betterment.[44] Diarists retreated within during periods of personal crisis. As a circumspect Fishburne contemplated his diary's function, for example, he warily embraced its potential utility. He contended, "If I knew exactly what course in life I am to pursue, I might make observations which would undoubtedly be of service to me. . . . As it is, however, *fancy* alone must dictate all these, for I know not yet what I may do."[45]

Men such as Mercer, Gorgas, Kirby-Smith, and Fishburne followed the values of professionals and an emerging middle class. Above all, they heeded the call of the slave South's desire to appear "progressive." Men used diaries to ensure better habits and to make themselves better men. Kirby-Smith used his time at West Point and his journal entries for personal advancement. "I am determined to make the most of my opportunities," he wrote, "and amongst other things, to begin a course of history, commencing with the ancients, and to record here a brief summary with such comments as may assist in stamping the subject on my memory."[46] Similarly, Gorgas, who strove constantly to obtain "self-command," made entries about his translations of French texts that he used to sharpen the mind and included prolonged considerations of the ill effects of overeating and drinking that damaged the body.[47] Diaries allowed these men to foster specific habits. Their actions, moreover, align with broader trends among Southern whites. Elizabeth Brown Pryor, discussing Robert E. Lee and other men of his class, maintains that the antebellum era placed an "emphasis on individual initiative, on education as a basis for upward mobility, on future prospects, and on the invention—or reinvention—of the self."[48] It is therefore not surprising that once Southern men became Confederate soldiers, they often viewed soldiering as part of their personal development; arduous campaigning offered men invaluable lessons about duty.[49]

The consequences of men's self-constructions are particularly powerful in the context of the slaveholding South, and each of the diarists studied was either a slaveholder or part of a slaveholding family (through lineage or marriage). Through the process of self-improvement, whites also bolstered their claims on hegemony. T. J. Jackson Lears's configuration of hegemonic theory posits ideology and economics as key to a historical bloc's successful control. By creating a worldview that appeals to a wide range of groups, "hegemonic culture is not merely an ideological mystification but serves the interests of ruling groups at the expense of subordinate ones."[50] The appealing values of thrift, industry, and self-improvement created the ideological mystification to which Lears alludes; and diaries advanced these goals by fostering education, initiative, economic success, and self-control. Southerners envisioned achievements as the products of personal perseverance without recognition of the privileges whiteness and gender afforded. Whites commanded themselves firmly and benefited from the South's system of patriarchy. That they accepted the benefits of this social order is undoubted. Rarely did any of the diarists examined in this study explicitly question or even consider their elevated status.

Diarists were attuned observers, if not always social commentators. Many examined not only how they interacted with society but, more importantly, how its requirements affected them. That white elites used their position for personal betterment is unquestionable. Men wielded an extraordinary amount of power in Southern society, and to say otherwise diminishes the lives of those caught within the folds of that power structure. But it is also clear that some men confronted their future public station with trepidation and anxiety. Writing offered a modicum of control over the vicissitudes of life, reflecting how men shaped their social interactions and perceptions. For such men, manhood was a responsibility not to be taken lightly; and the frailty of existence proved troubling. Diarists used their journals as devices to order time's passage and to lend meaning and purpose to their existence. While attending college in New Jersey, for example, Mercer thought of home and aging: "We are all hastening towards the grave: what my experience may be, God only knows. But advancing age shall not wholly rob me of childhoods pleasures."[51] While Mercer unhappily surrendered himself to change by seeking solace in his memories, Kirby-Smith dreamily wondered how omnipotence might feel: "What a strange thing it would be, if only for a brief period we could see at one glance, all the manifold operations that are going on around us, and are destined to effect the course of our life—to bring us weal or woe, to lead us right or wrong, to raise us to fortune or sink us to adversity."[52] Kirby-Smith's desire for all-powerfulness illustrated his need for control. Reflecting on maturation, he mourned how society had forced boys at an early age to leave home and cast "themselves into the arena of life." Once there, they must "strive to carve out their fortunes from amongst the struggling and ambitious crowd."[53] For both Mercer and Kirby-Smith, the diary's pages created an avenue for expression and a means of control. Duty demanded that both men embrace the rigors of public life, but both men also reflected on the effects and meaning of such experiences.

The authors of the foregoing passages wrote at particularly vulnerable moments in their lives—periods when they felt isolated and alone. Mercer was away at college; and Kirby-Smith, adrift at West Point. At his respective institution, each man interacted with the elite of his generation and prepared for the public station he would assume eventually while engaging in a rigorous life of learning. Both men found comfort in their writing and looked to nature and religion for solace. They needed, in essence, avenues of escape. Kirby-Smith charged, "From nature must we seek our most desirable pleasures. . . . Ever, ever appealing to the heart, and telling with a deep mysterious view of Gods goodness and excellence."[54] Similarly, Mercer, who had dedicated much of his first volume to his rambles around Savannah's countryside, maintained, "The woods and fields and flowers are mine till I die."[55] A divine presence bestowed such natural beauty. Upon his mother's death, Mercer envisioned "God's tender arm . . . stretched forth to gather her into his fold."[56]

Men's desire for self-improvement demonstrates the multifaceted facade of Southern masculinity. Expression, industry, and appearance shaped a social presence, which demanded self-governance and self-regulation.[57] Thus, men such as Mercer, Gorgas, and Kirby-Smith maintained records of what they read, what they had accomplished, and what they ate or drank to regulate and govern themselves. Yet such rigidity should not obscure men's real vulnerabilities and uncertainty. Southern men attempted to make sense of their social roles, private thoughts, and personal feelings through their diaries. Men commanded themselves and those around them firmly and allowed for few personal disclosures. But these same men also experienced doubt, expressed wonderment, and embraced a range of emotions, demonstrating the two different faces of Southern manhood: the public and the private.

Family and Friends

For all the insularity that autobiographical writing fostered, most diarists could not but help comment on loved ones or friends. Families were central to Victorian Americans' emotional lives, and writers used their journals to shape and to contemplate familial relationships. In the home, families experienced and explored a gamut of feelings, ranging from intense pleasure to taxing anxiety; and diaries offered a private venue to safely channel these mixed emotions. Entries echoed domestic exchanges and typically conformed to reigning gender inequalities.[58] Writing allowed men to explore the internal dynamics of family life, reinforced narratives of male-centered power and control, and fostered a detached adulation of women, who became subject and object on paper.

The winter of 1857 found Gorgas firmly ensconced within his family at a military post in Augusta, Maine. He continued his practice of journal writing, where he explored the possibilities of domestic bliss; but by so doing, he also exposed the limitations of gender equality. On January 28, huddled by a furnace, he noted the temperature to be thirty-six degrees below zero.[59] Perhaps the frigid air prompted Josiah and his wife, Amelia, to dream of purchasing a Southern plantation. Josiah reflected on these dreams in the folds of his journal. They would grow rich, he held, as Amelia became the "mistress of a hundred bales of cotton per annum and 40 or 50 ebony faces, whom she would make happy."[60] Although a playful—if racist—entry rooted in an intimate exchange between husband and wife, the writing reveals the broader gender inequalities shaping their marriage.[61] The Gorgas family continued to be uprooted—and stranded in Maine in 1857—because of Josiah's military career. Neither the northern climate nor its "uncongenial" people pleased the Gorgases, who pined for their old home in Mount Vernon, Alabama.[62] These moves must have been especially trying for Amelia, whose family had remained in the Deep South. Josiah recognized the strains of military life on both himself and his family: "My great regret is the wandering life we are obliged to lead."[63] Correspondence between Josiah and Amelia reveals the depth of their affection, but Amelia had dedicated herself to his contentment by sacrificing her personal happiness to maintain his military career.[64] And Josiah often enjoyed the comforts of domesticity without the same degree of self-sacrifice. His diaries reveal that he hoped to use the profits from his profession to create the domestic happiness of which he had deprived his wife.

Gorgas's focus on both career and family aligned with a broader nineteenth-century practice of "masculine domesticity" that allowed men to play a role in family without limiting professional pursuits.[65] Aldert Smedes, an Episcopal clergyman and founder of the Saint Mary's School for girls in Raleigh, North Carolina, distilled elements of this public discourse in a published sermon in 1851. A woman, he contended, should "endeavor to render the home of her husband a place of rest from the toils of business—of comforts amid the disappointments of life—of cheerful recreation amid its cares—it should be especially her effort to make it the residence of purity and piety."[66] The home became a woman's kingdom and her prison. In the nineteenth century, companionate marriage asked men to cultivate love and affection with their families and to share in their wives' domestic concerns.[67] But economic demands forced many men to leave their homes for extended periods, creating conflict.

Serving in the military and still single, Kirby-Smith rued the changes that came with the days of supposed "freedom and civilization." Boys, he argued, "must all at an early age, leave the homestead, and casting themselves into the arena of life, strive to carve out their fortunes from amongst the struggling and ambitious crowd." In deeply biased, gendered language, he conversely considered the proposition for girls who "marry and under the influence of the kind and pleasing tie, forget early associations and the claims of kindred and trusting in fond reliance upon the husband of their choice, follow the newfound object of affection off to distant lands."[68] Kirby-Smith had isolated a real theme: men had to negotiate the conflicting obligations of duty to work and duty to home. He felt wedded to a profession that separated him "from those [he] love[d] & the enjoyment of a home." Writing to an army friend while stationed in Fort Brown, Texas, he complained, "There is no home for me; a life in the wilds of Texas, the deserts of New Mexico or California perchance a death in the field of battle, the happiest lot to which I now aspire, may yet await me."[69]

The diary entries of Gorgas and Kirby-Smith, while idiosyncratic, also reflect the broader social shifts they experienced and tried to understand. Diarists' emotional disclosures were an essential part of a shifting sensibility in the early to mid-nineteenth century, for journal writing allowed men to ruminate on such changes. Marital success, once built on property, assets, and social standing, now rested on a foundation of mutual admiration, romantic love, and domestic stability.[70] Companionate marriage, however, was an ideal that did not always match a lived reality; and a wide gulf often separated the sexes.[71] Nonetheless, some men and women found ways to bridge such divides.[72] Newlywed Nanny Waller, for example, confided in her diary as she approached her one-year wedding anniversary that her husband, Charlie, had not once offered a hasty reply, nor had he ever shown her "anger in its mildest, and most unoffending garb," "when self in all of its partial views" had told her she "deserved rebuke. All others ha[d] been tart," but he remained an "affectionate . . . indulgent and devoted husband."[73] Men and women increasingly saw each other differently; and while marriage itself repressed her, the home still offered redemption.[74]

Diaries reinforced inequalities but also generated intense, raw emotions about friends and family. Indeed, as writers pored over their old journal entries, they became lost in nostalgia. While at college, Mercer read with "tearful pleasure" old entries for the better part of an hour.[75] Diaries evoked memories—both pleasurable and painful—and were central to the emotional lives of writers. Past writings could evoke sorrow or joyful remembrance.⁷⁶ Parents encouraged their sons publicly to stifle their emotions and exert self-control. Diaries offered an avenue for men to fulfill their parents' stern requirements while still satisfying their own emotional needs and expressions.⁷⁷

Life's uncertainty is a recurrent theme in the works of nineteenth-century writers, especially in diaries and letters among family. Frequent deaths among friends and relatives shaped the perspectives of the living. For some writers, mortality conjured up images of family, stark emotions, and deep thoughts. In dealing with death, writing offered solace. After his mother's passing, Mercer bid her farewell, recalled their joyful shared experiences, and wished her well in "a better, brighter land." Mercer's mourning caused him to consider human fragility and to contemplate life's course. He noticed the gray hairs on his father's head and how "Sisters, Brother, Cousins and all, [were] stealing from the sun-shine into the shadow of life."⁷⁸ Upon the birth of one of Gorgas's children, Gorgas remarked, "Since my last entry a daughter [Mamie] has been born to us. She is a nice plump looking little pet. Will she live to look over these pages which here record the opening of her book of life? Heaven grant it."⁷⁹ Hopeful for the future, though very much aware of potential pain, Gorgas deemed his daughter's prospects uncertain.

Reflections on death transcended the gendered differences witnessed in many nineteenth-century diaries. Although mourning rituals were highly gendered in form, the pain of loss knew no boundaries. All Southerners were aware that death severed earthly relationships, and many struggled to comprehend the loss. As North Carolina diarist Cornelia Phillips Spencer pored over her husband's handwriting years after his death, she tenderly wrote in her journal, "When I look at these—look at the well-known beloved handwriting—think of what he was when he wrote them—how full of life & strength & hope & happiness, & think of how he died—Oh Magnus my heart swells with bitterness & anguish. I am afraid I never shall become *reconciled* to my husband's death, never at least in this life."⁸⁰ Spencer's hint at an afterlife is a recurring theme in nineteenth-century writing. Letters of condolence reassured mourners that their loved ones were now in a better place while the bereaved often looked forward to a heavenly meeting.⁸¹ The death of a cousin's son was what prompted Waller to think about religion. Tab's death produced much sorrow and provoked her to draft a letter of condolence in the pages of her diary. Like Spencer, she took solace in the belief that he now rested "in the bosom of his father, where sickness, sorrow pain or death are felt and feared no more." Yet the mournful event also provoked careful examination. Waller's strict reading of Christian doctrine directed her to comment, "The Idol of his Mother's heart Take warning all ye who have disobeyed that first and often violated command!! Thou shall have none other God than me, For mark the penalty. . . . God forbid I should have any other Idol, then the great Jehovah."[82] This doctrinal language did not appear in the letter to her cousin, but the diary's freedom and secrecy allowed Waller to contemplate fully what duty to God and duty to family meant.

On the Hunt

Just as Southerners used journals to discuss family, so too do their records reflect an engagement with the outside world. Mercer's diary demonstrates a key dimension to Southern manhood: passion and restraint as revealed by an engagement with the natural world. Throughout his childhood, Mercer had wandered the fields and woods outside Savannah, often accompanied by family slaves. On some occasions, he quietly consumed nature, inspired by its beauty. On other trips, though, with his trusty gun Sweet Lips, he tracked prey—mostly birds and small game—and amassed hundreds of kills throughout the 1850s. His youthful walks in the woods inspired his lifelong writing habit, as evidenced throughout the pages of his childhood journal, where Mercer enumerated kills, sketched wildlife, and chronicled his expeditions: "Having determined to go coon hunting that night, half a dozen negroes were soon collected, together with several dogs." Once darkness cloaked the woods, "the merry winding of the bugle announced that we had started . . . and many a merry laugh was heard ringing through the forests as we passed along."[83] Mercer's entry unconsciously portrays the power and place of which he was part as he transformed the enslaved into "sable friends" and marched merrily across the South's bountiful lands.

A generation or more of scholarship has looked to hunting as a demonstration of men's pugnacity and their potential for violence.[84] As Rod Andrew writes, "By combining the virtues of prowess, self-control, and various elements of mastery, hunting became a display of that white masculinity and mastery."[85] Less documented, though, is how men also exhibited curiosity for natural wonder and splendor and in what ways hunting connected to emotional control and release. Trips into the forest loosened cruelty, hatred, and violence but also engendered admiration, passion, and respect.[86] Hunting symbolized white Southerners' internal contests between passion and restraint, piety and aggression.[87] Most explicitly, hunting privileged and rewarded bellicosity. In field and forest, men channeled unrestrained passion and unchecked aggression into the pursuit of game, an activity socially sanctioned and approved. The feelings unleashed on the hunt did not ebb quickly. The pursuit of wildlife instilled pugnacity and bloodlust, and in a culture arguably predisposed to violence, hunting only increased militancy.[88] But for all their brutality and violence, trips into the woods also allowed men to ponder nature's wonders, enjoy the conservation of close friends, and escape from the demands of daily life. Some Southern hunters even used the sport for scientific inquiry.

Trips into the natural world were expressive forms of culture through which men symbolically illustrated their assumptions about the world.[89] In the fields and on the hunt, men were removed from the trappings and traditions of ordinary society. By the mid-nineteenth century, both American and English women were participating in fox hunts, a sport of the genteel and elite. But many hunts remained an all-male arena in which hunters constructed and enacted rituals and rites, creating a uniquely homosocial culture.[90] Consequential elements of male sensibility were derived from hunting excursions. Significantly, too, such activities presaged men's entry into Confederate military service and its fraternity of soldiers.

The South's vast forests and abundant wildlife consistently awed the region's visitors and made firearms important for recreation and hunting.[91] Yet blacks and whites never had equal access to the panoply of flora and fauna. Southern men of all classes and backgrounds went hunting and fishing with some frequency; however, their motivations and models of behavior differed. Poor whites, generally without their own hogs, chickens, or cows, used hunting and fishing to supplement their meager grain- and corn-based diets.[92] Enslaved and freed blacks, too, relied on game for protein, but because of the expense of rifles and shotguns, as well as laws prohibiting slaves from gun ownership, traps and dogs were commonly employed to capture game.[93] For white Southern planters, hunting was a sport—an elite ritual that distinguished them from those who hunted for subsistence, or "pot-hunters," as they were derisively known.[94] Elite Southerners used the hunt to evoke their connections, real and constructed, to the Old World aristocracy.[95] For hunters of every class, gaming and its spoils reinforced men's claims to patriarchal authority, despite substantial differences in purpose and practice.[96]

More ritualistic than practical, the pageantry associated with planters' hunts bolstered social prestige and reinforced class hierarchies.[97] Imaginative and aggressive white planters created vast personal kingdoms, and planters' improved lands precluded access to anyone but the landowners themselves and their invited guests. Such men of wealth defined their social standing through manners, dress, demeanor, conversational style, and hunting customs. Hunting clubs attended by enslaved blacks allowed fiercely independent white men to represent freedom from want, subjection, and subordination.[98] Planters' commitment to the preservation of hunting as an elite ritual ignited conflict with those who claimed common rights to land and resources. (Planters often gifted the spoils of their hunt to signal their authority to perceived social inferiors and reinforce dependence.)[99] As a result, in the early to mid-nineteenth century, wealthy whites engaged in court disputes and called for legal regulations to codify their positions.[100] But the lack of substantial enabling legislation resulted in the nullification of most hunting laws in the antebellum South. Only in the final years of the antebellum era were proponents of conservation-minded hunting successful in creating protective laws, but class biases tinged these acts.[101] Hunting, its customs and its character, thus reflected planters' command of resources, control of time, and conquest of nature. Such elements instilled hunting with a model of intellectualism, distancing it from its more primeval roots.

Young men were welcomed into this fraternity through ritual. A son met his father's friends, perhaps enjoyed a nip from a communal flask, and experienced the excitement, sweat, fear, and triumph of the hunt. While a deeply emotional experience, hunting helped men learn mastery over self, society, and nature.[102] For the elite, hunting parties were supported by drivers, typically enslaved blacks, who beat thickets and tracked game with packs of seasoned dogs, often of English and Irish blood.[103] Mounted hunters traversed open terrain, patiently waiting until opportunity or chance allowed them a shot. The hunt banded together men of agreeable dispositions who wanted to enjoy the companionship of congenial neighbors, kin, or even strangers—men who shared a similar image of masculinity.[104] Some rituals marked the novice's successful first kill. William Elliott explained how a senior hunter would slit the dead animal's throat and then bathe the neophyte's face in blood—not a typical practice but highly suggestive nonetheless. This blood symbolically joined the hunter to the hunted and to a fellowship of sportsmen.[105] In Elliott's telling of one man's entry into this brotherhood, the man's face remained "glaring like an Indian chief's in all the splendor of war-paint." In the evening, he returned home to his wife, who heartily welcomed her husband after seeing the "stains of victory" on his face.[106] In this not-so-subtle vignette, the hunter becomes the provider of food and the conqueror of the forest, and he is associated with the imagined fierceness and savagery of Native Americans. Hunting evoked man's civilized and primal nature and functioned as a rite of passage into manhood.

The pursuit and conquest of game created a stage on which hunters enacted their own masculine dramas and explored their emotions and fears. In an explosive and dangerous atmosphere, men reveled in the passion and intensity engendered by the pursuit of game. Elliott's poetic description of a hunt captures the range of sensations: "'There they go! Look! for the hedge! Rowser leads—he leaps the hedge—ha! he has overrun the track. Black has caught it up—it is all right! There they go—look at them!—listen to them! . . . Does it not make your pulse quicken. Is there not a thrill of pleasure shooting through your frame? Can you tell your name? Have you a wife? a child? *Have you a neck?*' If you can, at such a moment, answer questions such as these, you do not feel your position and are but half a sportsman!"[107] While written partly for effect, Elliott's account evinces the hunt's exhilaration, confusion, and anticipation, as well as the hunter's focus, delight, and quickened pulse. In these moments, the pursuit, capture, and conquest of the quarry were all that mattered in a man's world. Indeed, in the thrill of the hunt, men cast aside their worldly duties, only reinforcing how rigorously masculine hunting proved to be.

Southerners showcased their rifles and shotguns and presented deft displays of marksmanship. Hunting was a contest not simply with nature but also among men, and sporting called forth men's ideals and fears. Hunting and its accruements were definitively masculine symbols. Men formed close bonds with their rifles, even naming them. Mercer recalled, for example, "Never, shall I forget the day when first a gun was mine. It stands out brightly among the brightest scenes of my boyhood. I could not compute my happiness—my gun . . . was a treasure without a price."[108] Similarly, Edward Porter Alexander—future Confederate general and expert artillerist—wrote that during his youth his gun was the "dearest possession on earth."[109] Rates of gun ownership in the South were higher than in any other region of the country and reinforced white supremacy and male patriarchy; planters, especially, regarded firearms as necessary components of the machinery of control.[110]

The hunt's violence and stimulation created an irrepressible appetite in Southern men. A "ruling passion" for the hunt still gripped an aged and infirm hunter who was unable to do much besides dream of past glories.[111] This quality spilled over into many aspects of Southern life, creating men with grand visions and lofty, self-appointed positions.[112] In its extreme, hunting and its culture of violence schooled Southerners in the art of war. Elliott observed, "Assuredly, there is no such preparatory school for war; and the expert hunter will, I doubt not, show himself the superior in the field to another, every other way his equal, yet wanting this experience!"[113] Elliott's words were not mere hyperbole. Hunting explicitly demonstrated men's dominance over nature and suggested their mastery over women and slaves. Moreover, hunting's horses, guns, and killing echoed the rigors of combat.[114] While not contributing directly to war, like slave patrols, dueling, excessive drinking, and contests of political honor, hunting increased Southern violence.

Toward Civil War

In the summer of 1859, Virginian and future Confederate officer John Warwick Daniel stepped before a body of students at Lynchburg College. In his speech titled "Orations on the Illustrious Dead," Daniel entwined personal feelings and public service, and by so doing called for his youthful audience to look within themselves and discover something bigger. Taking his listeners to the "time honored arches of Westminster abbey," Daniel conjured Britain's dead: the poet, the orator, and the soldier. Together, they rested in immortal slumber not forgotten but still honored by their country. Statesmen, soldiers, and sages traveled to visit the fallen hero, shedding "tears for his lamented genius, & departed worth." Only through service to country, Daniel contended, were the dead recognized.[115] Thus, his speech attached special honor to those whom duty drove and who elided distinctions between society and self. These attributes were of great importance to an audience that war would soon mobilize. Indeed, appealing to students' emotions and ambitions, Daniel looked to the contemporary political strife as an opportunity for young men to make their marks and to prove that duty to the community trumped individual ambitions. "The old ship of state is riding rudderless o'er the waves of oceans," he contended, "the waters of disunion are rolling around her, and in the dim distance, we behold a dark abyss yawning to close over her forever."[116] The spirit that animated the "illustrious dead," Daniel charged, must now inspire the citizenry to action, even to arms.

Significantly, Daniel's speech prominently featured the citizen's role as soldier, reminding his audience, "Tho Grecian glory has indeed vanished . . . the mighty Alexander who led her legions o'er the brow of the dark Caucasus, still lives." For the young men at Lynchburg College who were transitioning from adolescence into adulthood, the military offered an affirming passage into the realm of men. And through service to country, they believed, men would find their immortality. Daniel evoked the image of the slumbering, timeless warrior "with his sword at his side, and his martial cloak around him."[117] Young men across the South, such as Daniel and the students at Lynchburg College, excitedly, if naively, looked to war as an opportunity for greatness. The exigencies of the 1850s had prepared many for the possibility of conflict; however, no one could fathom what would come.[118]

The young men in Daniel's audience were not unlike George Mercer, Edmund Kirby-Smith, and Clement Fishburne. For the young Southern men "waiting for something dramatic to happen[,] . . . the wait was over" with the coming of civil war, writes Stephen Berry.[119] How men initially responded to civil war is suggested in the folds of their antebellum journals. Men's writings immediately reinforce the image of the ready-made warrior that has captivated generations of scholars.[120] The pugilism exhibited while hunting, the competition witnessed between men, and the fierce desire for independence reflected a martial masculinity tailored for soldiering. Historians have frequently commented on these qualities, concluding that Southerners' efforts never to lose face resulted in contests of honor between men and the suppression of self-examination.[121] Yet Southern men's diaries also expose the overriding importance of inquiry and intellect, which revealed writers who suffered from self-doubt, agonized over an unknowable future, and approached manhood with a degree of trepidation. Men accordingly went to war less secure and more uncertain than their public personas suggested. Significantly, though, the Southerners examined herein embraced *both* restrained and martial masculinities, demonstrating a flexible model of manhood that proved essential to surviving the rigors of military service and the vicissitudes of war.

CHAPTER TWO

Soldiers

In early January 1862, Confederate private Ruffin Thomson composed a letter to his father, a physician and small planter in Mississippi, introducing him to army life. Moving from the material to the ethereal, he described the equipment, environment, and uncertainty that came with soldiering. He first noted how all the necessities of life were stowed away in a recently issued knapsack. The bag "holds our clothes—a good deal can be packed into one of them"; further, it could be deployed as an ersatz desk, as Thomson found out while writing his letter. The knapsack signaled an independence from excessive material items but also a dependence on equipment that could become burdensome on long marches. He next described the winnowing that inevitably came with war: "We got ride of six of [our] company since coming up here—not suitable for soldiers." Confederates who remained in the ranks formed tightly knit fraternities that became critical to their wartime self-identities. Thomson then went on to re-create his environment for his father. His tent brimmed with men. One man had a fiddle, to the great amusement of some, while others enjoyed hymns; an exceedingly noisy setting, he decided. Finally, he spoke of soldiering's ambiguities. Thomson's regiment had been ordered to cook three days' worth of rations—typical before a battle. Anticipation mingled with uncertainty as the troops looked toward an upcoming fight that might never come.[1]

When explaining his life as a Confederate soldier, Thomson focused on the materials of war and the milieu of camp because these elements were so foreign to his family and so essential to his perceptions of army life. The letter thus provided a way of explaining how Southern civilians became Confederate soldiers. This chapter follows Thomson's lead by focusing on how material culture and military encampments were central to Confederates' wartime self-identities and fostered emotional exchanges among soldiers.[2] Despite some excellent, albeit short, descriptive references to Confederates' appearance, few studies have considered seriously how soldiers' uniforms shaped and displayed men's values, ideas, and attitudes.[3] Moreover, the camps and fields where Confederate soldiers spent the vast majority of their military lives have garnered little scholarly attention.[4] "It is odd," notes historian Michael DeGruccio, "that Civil War historians have mostly steered clear of the boom in material culture studies of the last three or four decades."[5] But to nineteenth-century Americans, material mattered.

Military attire distinguished soldiers from citizens and established visible bonds among troops.[6] Despite being clad in a variety of colors and materials, the South maintained conventional uniforms throughout the war that were easily identified by cut and style.[7] Yet the overt purpose of military clothing should not obscure the deeper meaning soldiers invested in it. In the early years of the conflict, when government manufacturing remained a nascent industry, soldiers were largely supplied from home. Indeed, until October 1862, Richmond paid its volunteers to clothe themselves.[8] During this period, Southern soldiers sent home countless letters requesting shoes, boots, blankets, and garments. Domestic supply lines connected families to their soldiers. Southern men knew that a loved one or a community member helped make the uniforms that they wore. These material linkages dissipated over time as state and central government depots assumed the responsibility of outfitting armies in the field. By midwar, government-issued clothing separated the Confederate veteran from the early war volunteer and demonstrated a new dependence on government. Soldiers' morale ebbed and flowed with the issuance of goods, and when deficiencies arose, they directed their vitriol at Richmond.

Military encampments, like uniforms, promoted a corporate identity but also allowed soldiers to carve out a personalized space. Regimental designations, military drill, and tented cities forged bonds among men. Historians have argued that small-group cohesion created a sustaining esprit de corps among enlisted men, even if they still clashed with authority.[9] Scholars have less frequently observed how group dynamics also shaped soldiers' emotional expression and psychological dispositions. As the last chapter demonstrated, Southern men possessed a complex range of emotions, even if the mode of expression was limited. Successfully navigating army life required both martial and restrained masculinities, as men had to act the aggressive warrior but also the intimate associate. Soldiers spent the vast majority of their military careers in camp among large groups of men with whom they lived in close proximity for prolonged periods. Through military service, many soldiers came to believe that they had shared a unique life that would forever bind them to other veterans. North Carolina infantry officer Thomas Ruffin Jr., son of North Carolina jurist Thomas Ruffin, maintained, "Being in the army makes us wonderfully selfish & utterly indifferent to every body except our own immediate comrades: with them we would share our very last cent, while we do not care what becomes of any & everybody outside of that circle."[10]

Confederates' military companions formed a closed and sacred circle; and their conceptions of self and their ideas of manhood became inseparable from wartime soldier communities. Uniformed men acted in concert on the drill fields and on the battlefields to execute complex military maneuvers. In camp they ate together and bedded with each other on a daily basis. Yet army life also created contradictions in men's military experience because they lived together for long periods under great duress. These tensions tested the limits of soldiers' bonds; therefore, rather than adhering to a rigid type of masculinity, many Confederate soldiers depended on flexible models of masculinity grounded in the antebellum era that encouraged mutual dependence among men while maintaining elements of antebellum independence.[11]

Outfitting an Army

Each year, the Confederacy's *Regulations for the Army* prescribed the same idealized uniform to be worn by men serving in Southern forces.[12] Commissioned officers were expected to wear a frock coat of gray fabric with a skirt extending halfway between the hip and the knee. The double-breasted coat included specific buttons, button arrangements, and insignia to designate men of different ranks. Enlisted men, too, sported a long, double-breasted frock coat of gray cloth. Trousers were sky blue, and the headpiece was modeled after the style of the French kepi.[13] The Confederate government constructed an elaborate vision of uniformity that encompassed how its enlisted men and their officers should appear in field and in battle. Uniforms suggested expertise, courage, and obedience.[14] Expectations, though, rarely reflected reality. Despite the Confederate government's unaltered prescriptions each year, a considerable discrepancy existed between the clothing designated and the garments worn.[15] Initially, the Confederate government could not marshal the resources to outfit the vast numbers of mobilized men; later, design could not meet demand. Thus emerged a motley assortment of uniform types and materials that little resembled the standards established in the *Regulations for the Army*.

White Southerners' often-naive ideas about the potential magnitude of civil war were reflected by their appearance. Many sons of the South came to war overburdened with baggage. The volunteers of 1861, Carlton McCarthy wrote in only partially exaggerated tone, sported heavy boots; wore large, bulky, double-breasted coats; carried pistols and knives; wore large, heavy knapsacks; and lugged around an almost endless assortment of other items. "All seemed to think it was impossible to have on too many or too heavy clothes, or to have too many conveniences, and each had an idea that to be a good soldier he must be provided against every possible emergency."[16] The novice soldier's overabundance of baggage and unfamiliar equipment created physical strains. Raw North Carolina recruit George Battle related to his mother that his company departed camp "with [their] knapsacks on [their] backs, and everything necessary to soldiers." Having marched four miles (a very short distance compared to his later service), George complained, "We were nearly worn out . . . the knapsack straps hurt our shoulders, besides the weight."[17] The summertime soldier's overburdened appearance reflected his civilian persona, according to Randolph A. Shotwell of the Eighth Virginia Infantry. He argued that the model of the well-clad, well-equipped soldier allowed men to maintain their individuality as *"citizen*-soldiers." Having not yet experienced deprivations, new recruits styled themselves as *"citizens* and *gentlemen."*[18] Over time, necessity forced adjustments, changing the Confederate's outlook, even character. While many men had militia experience, musters, parades, and tactical demonstrations hardly prepared them for prolonged campaigns and military combat. Extended service prompted change. McCarthy dedicated an entire chapter in his postwar memoir to the things that defined the Confederate soldier—chiefly, the evolution of military dress, an adjustment to the hardships of campaigning, and an understanding of what was necessary to perform the tasks of a soldier.

As soldiers grappled with unfamiliar equipment and uniform parts, the Confederate government struggled to supply the armies. Provisions were quickly established to mobilize civilian populations on the armies' behalf. Historian Harold S. Wilson explains that in the Confederate system, "the initial responsibility for securing soldiers' clothing fell upon company commanders, who were obliged by regulation to expend, twice a year, the commutation funds by making requisitions upon the Quartermaster Department or other sources, such as state authorities."[19] The government, in turn, allotted soldiers twenty-five dollars for six months' service; the ad hoc solution became known as the Commutation System.[20] Ideally, "each soldier in the first year of service was due one blanket and great coat; two caps and field jackets; three shirts, drawers, and pairs of trousers; four pairs of shoes and stockings; and other items in proportion."[21] The system ensured that the government did not have to build elaborate facilities for the production of cloth and clothing in case of a short war.[22] Civilian populations, moreover, had already sent most men off to war in the spring and summer of 1861 in garments made at home. Yet, as early as August 1861, "it was clear that this system was not adequate," explains historian Keith S. Bohannon, and legislation called for the secretary of war to clothe all Confederate forces.[23] The Commutation System itself officially ended on October 8, 1862, and most soldiers in the main armies regularly received government clothing by 1863.[24]

Confederate volunteers' early reliance on clothing from home not only ensured comfort but also triggered emotional responses. Homespun garments carried personal meaning because the men knew by whom they were made and what hands had touched the fabric. Confederate material culture reinforces historians' contentions about the linkages between the front line and the home front. Confederate officer Thomas Ruffin Jr. sought to resupply his men after their excess baggage was destroyed during the Peninsula Campaign in 1862. After Ruffin was frustrated by attempts to purchase materials from a North Carolina mill, the weaver suggested that he and his men look to Richmond or Raleigh for help. This would not do, however; according to Ruffin, "[The men begged] that we shall try to get the materials, & have the clothing made at home: They say, & say truly, that they have been better, & more cheaply clad than any other company in the service, & they do not wish, unless forced to do so, to change their system: & . . . they say that they can fight better in clothes made at home."[25] The garment's symbolic meaning for the soldiers carried over for those at home spinning or sewing. Ruffin's father wanted his son to know that he and the entire community felt "the utmost interest in & sympathy for [its] brave boys." He stated, "All were so alert to supply their wants that if we cant procure the cloth *every body* was ready to go to work & complete the job with very little delay." He continued, "Let your men know, that *this supply* is the *voluntary* offering of their fellow citizens, male & female," evidence of their "noble patience, endurance, & heroism of our men. They will therefore have not to account for these things to either Government."[26] These sentiments, likely conveyed to the soldiers suffering in the field, surely buttressed their flagging spirits and made them, if only for a moment, closer to home.

Within the war's first year, Southerners experienced cloth shortages or expressed fears over future shortfalls. As early as December 1861, William Joyner told his wife, Julia, to "look ahead and get whatever family necessaries" she would need. Cloth, in particular, he warned, was "becoming scarce and dear" in eastern North Carolina.[27] These conditions encouraged some Southerners to take up spinning and weaving.[28] The *Southern Field and Fire-*

side of Augusta, Georgia, for instance, recorded the attendance of a "homespun party." "Patriotic" ladies, prompted to inaugurate a system of "self-dependence," directed the event. "More than a hundred ladies and gentlemen, belonging to the most respected families in the city, were present, all of whom were attired in part or in whole in garments made of Virginia fabrics, woven in Virginia looms. It was strictly a Virginia cloth party."[29] Farther north in North Carolina, the female members of the Lenoir family and other women from their local community busied themselves sewing during the war's first years. Julia Lenoir, in writing to her grandmother, described the scope of their work. They had been working hard throughout the fall of 1861, surpassing their requests and asking for more. By November, members of the family were knitting socks and gloves, sewing overcoats for the upcoming winter, and making "jean shirts" to ensure the men's warmth. Beyond those items sent for military service, women also began the home production of cloth. In the same letter, Julia described some "very pretty homespun" woven that fall, though it was, in her words, "the most uncommon looking I ever saw."[30]

Public figures such as Confederate president Jefferson Davis encouraged textile production because this work demonstrated dedication to the cause across the sexes and engendered widespread support.[31] This homespun revolution received the praise of civilians and soldiers alike. In 1863, for example, Georgia soldier Hill Fitzpatrick congratulated his wife on her weaving efforts. The Fitzpatricks, though, were of yeoman stock. As such, both men and women engaged in hard domestic labor. Wealthy whites, reliant on slave labor for spinning and weaving, had considerable reservations about the potential decline in women's health and status when engaged in such work.[32] Further, postwar accounts heralding women's home production exaggerated the extent of their activities. Instead, historian Drew Gilpin Faust writes, "Southern households did not become factories; women were more likely to sacrifice, to live with deprivation and shortage, and to hope for a swift end to the war."[33] Piecemeal efforts and improvisations demonstrated women's resolve but also the extent of their deprivations.

Although not all Southern homes became factories, families were quite adept at helping support family members in the field. The transfer of parcels and handwritten requests for specific items formed the threads of correspondence and exchange that brought together otherwise separated loves ones. Hill and Amanda Fitzpatrick maintained an unusually extensive record of clothing requests and sewing accomplishments. What stands out in this correspondence is the importance of these material items as symbols of affection and remembrance. In one letter, Hill described his wife as "a true and heroic Southern woman" for her sewing efforts on his behalf. He continued, "I shall appreciate them the more when I get them because you worked and made them for me, but really I did not intend to burden you with that task, but you say and I know it is so that it is a pleasure to you to fix my clothes for me."[34] Julia Joyner maintained the family plantation in Franklin County, North Carolina, while her husband and four sons served in the Confederate military. In 1862 alone, Julia fulfilled shoe requests, made shirts, searched for sought-after garments stashed away at home to be sent to the front, and assisted one son in fulfilling his request for an officer's uniform.[35] Fellow North Carolinian W. J. O'Daniel created a veritable grocery list of requests from fellow soldiers who were encamped in Fredericksburg in December 1862. One soldier wanted "a pair of shoes, 4 pair socks," a pair of pants, and a coat; another requested "shoes & socks." O'Daniel needed shoes and "a pair of Jains pants," no matter the cost.[36]

The Commutation System resulted in considerable clothing shortfalls, creating real material want, especially during the fall and winter of 1862. Items such as shoes—likely purchased and used in the antebellum era without much thought—became fixations, as men depended on serviceable footwear for the long marches they had to endure. Hill Fitzpatrick, like many, was often inadequately shod. Though he states in one letter that his battered feet had mended, his shoes were nearly worn out. "I would wear out any thing," he wrote, "the way we had to march and the kind of roads we had to go over. A great many are entirely barefooted."[37] Tally Simpson, a soldier in the Third South Carolina Infantry, also complained of shoe problems: "My boots are giving way, and there are no prospects for another pair."[38] Soldiers' hardships could influence morale, as vividly illuminated in the correspondence of brothers John and William Cocke. After the Battle of Antietam, John and William found themselves in Winchester, Virginia, at a camp for barefooted soldiers waiting to be resupplied.[39] For John the situation had become intolerable. After the physical trials of the Maryland Campaign and a recent brush with death, he felt depleted and disillusioned. He asked his parents to tell "John Ashton & Geo Maupin they may thank their stars they were too young to join the Army, for theur will never realize what hardships are." He continued, "I never would have come away from home could I have seen this far ahead."[40] While his brother William remained more sanguine, even joking to his parents that John's last spark of patriotism "must have died out with his shoes," he had to admit, "We are having a hard time" of it.[41] These complaints were not anomalous, as scores of soldiers suffered from similar shortfalls throughout the war.[42] Yet, despite such harsh circumstances, soldiers in the Army of Northern Virginia exhibited remarkable resilience.[43] John Cocke, for example, despite his grumblings, continued serving until captured and imprisoned at Point Lookout, Maryland.

A soldier's outward appearance explicitly marked his station, thereby separating him from civilian populations. But in the war's first two years especially, Confederate clothing had familial imprints. Garments sent from home, and made by family, connected military men to the distant hearths they dearly missed. Further, the Commutation System reflected the Confederate volunteer's early war status as a citizen-soldier, with an emphasis on the former station. His self-identity and emotional life remained tied to the home front. Locally made material culture bolstered men's emotional relationships with wives, mothers, sisters, and sweethearts and demonstrated their dependence on women for necessary clothing.

Government Issued

By midwar, troops in the eastern theater were likely clad in government-issued uniforms and reliant on either a state government or authorities in Richmond for future resupply. While this shift was certainly not wholesale—officers by necessity and the wealthy by preference continued to send requests home—the majority of soldiers experienced a marked material break from the civilian world as they abandoned the physical trappings of the early war volunteer.[44] Accordingly, as the war continued, fewer requests were sent home as families' supplies dwindled and the quartermaster became more reliable.[45] As Ruffin Thomson told his folks at home in the late summer of 1863, "If I can not get along on what other soldiers do on, I am not fit to be one. Our rations are sufficient & Clothing abundant[.] So you see there is no need for me to absorb funds which I know is necessary for your Comfort."[46] Whereas soldiers fared increasingly better in the field, war had made their families poorer as they struggled with shortages and deprivations.[47] In April 1863 George M. Waddy assured his aunt that the government provided as much clothing as he wanted, as well as an allowance, but he worried about her state of affairs.[48] Leonidas Torrence assured his sister, "You neede not sent me any cloths I can draw any thing that I neede."[49] Fitzpatrick, writing to his wife, Amanda, related, "The reason I did not write for bedclothes is that I feared you would have none to spare . . . and we are to be clothed by the government and not draw any more computation money."⁵⁰ In another letter Hill sympathized with Amanda, who was unable to acquire footwear.⁵¹

Reduced to the minimum, the summertime soldier had become a seasoned veteran. The Southern soldier's outward appearance signaled his adaptations to outdoor living, environmental conditions, and inadequate supplies.⁵² A soft felt hat replaced the cap, a short jacket served in the stead of a cumbersome frock coat, knapsacks were often discarded for blanket rolls, and unnecessary items were discarded.⁵³ A soldier's spartan appearance reflected knowledge gained with difficulty. A hardened Fitzpatrick related to his wife, "I tell you the less a soldier is burdened with the better he can get along."⁵⁴ North Carolinian James A. Graham agreed. After arduous service, Graham learned never to "carry anything more" with him than he absolutely needed and could "carry on [his] back in case of necessity."⁵⁵ William Joyner, though working in North Carolina's Commissary Department, wanted his wife, Julia, to ensure that their sons were not overburdened with baggage as they prepared for active service.⁵⁶ Additional equipment and clothes offered luxury but were heavy and ultimately unnecessary for survival. Once the campaign season started, any excess items that had been collected were packed up and sent to Richmond for storage.⁵⁷

Although the campaign season wore clothing out, Confederate troops seldom appeared as the "ragged rebel" so prevalent in Lost Cause mythology. Museum professional Leslie D. Jensen, through an examination of extant clothing, photographs, and quartermaster records, locates the "ragged rebel" mythology among postwar apologists. He instead finds men well supplied, suffering only from the rigors of field service.⁵⁸ Indeed, W. W. Blackford's postwar account notes, "In books written since the war it seems to be considered the thing to represent the Confederate soldier as in a chronic state of starvation and nakedness. During the last year of the war this was partially true, but previous to that time it was not any more than falls to the lot of all soldiers in an active campaign."⁵⁹

Uniformed soldiers became an important point of pride and an outward signal that commanded the respect of white Southerners. Cut differently from civilian garb, a military uniform projected a man's investment in the Confederacy. While in Winchester, Virginia, for example, Richard W. Waldrop expressed his suspicions about the population's loyalties. Too many men, he related, wore "citizen's clothes," which provoked an "intense desire to run against some of them & knock them into the gutter."⁶⁰ As a uniformed soldier, Waldrop set himself and his comrades apart from and even above those retaining the "cowardly" garb of the civilian world. With a husband and

This image of Confederate prisoners, taken in July 1863, illustrates soldiers' appearance in the field during the campaign season. *Gettysburg, Pa. Three Confederate Prisoners*, one negative (two plates): glass, stereograph, and wet collodion. Image courtesy Library of Congress, Washington, D.C.

four sons in the Confederate army, Julia Joyner, too, was chagrined to see men out of uniform. After New Bern, North Carolina, had fallen, she noted many refugees in Franklinton, including "several stout well looking men . . . that ought to be in the army."[61] The soldier's military garb, or conversely the clothing of a civilian, conveyed a specific social message to observers.[62] Uniformed men were an important visual signal of the Confederate cause and reinforced white Southerners' hope, which, by the midpoint in the war, rested with Robert E. Lee and the Army of Northern Virginia.[63]

Although Confederate soldiers were mostly well clothed, uneven production, diverse suppliers, and sporadic distribution created a distinctly motley appearance among them in the field. So much so that Southerners' individualism and independence became, in a sense, part of their military attire. English observer Arthur Lyon Fremantle detected the correlation between man and material. In his famous account, *Three Months in the Southern States*, he observed, "Now, the Confederate has no ambition to imitate the regular soldier at all, he looks the genuine rebel; but in spite of his bare feet, his ragged clothes, his old rug, and tooth-brush stuck like a rose in his button-hole, he has a sort of devil-may-care, reckless, self-confident look, which is decidedly taking."[64] Southerners' appearance reflected their continued embrace of independence. But it also demonstrated a real problem, for by "the spring of 1863, the lack of cloth for uniforms became a serious concern for the Quartermaster's Department and, particularly, the Richmond Depot."[65]

Fremantle's comments uphold an orthodox view of Johnny Reb but miss the Southern soldier's new dependence on the government and, ironically, Great Britain. The varied appearance that caught Fremantle's eye reflected inadequate manufacturing. Southern mills simply could not keep up with the Quartermaster Department's demands. To address these shortfalls, Confederate agents looked abroad and purchased vital war materials from English and Irish companies. Many of the men that Fremantle inspected during his tour were armed with English weapons and warmed by English blankets; later, they would be clad in English and Irish cloth. As early as February 1863, Josiah Gorgas, chief of ordnance, recorded the impressive results of Confederate buyers who had secured 131,129 stands of arms; 129 cannon; 1,226 pieces of cavalry equipment; 34,731 sets of accouterments; 357,000 pounds of cannon powder; 74,006 pairs of boots; 62,025 blankets; 78,520 yards of cloth; 17,894 yards of flannel; and 170,724 pairs of socks.[66]

Gorgas's 1863 record marked the beginnings of the Confederacy's use of British and Irish companies to provide vital matériel. In some instances, Confederates were clothed in the uniforms of foreign firms. Peter Tait & Company of Limerick, Ireland, for example, was the largest firm of ready-made clothing in the world and supplied the Confederacy with hundreds of uniform sets at the war's end.[67] In other instances, massive bundles of cloth were shipped from Great Britain and eventually made their way into the hands of Southern seamstresses who made jackets and trousers. "During the last two years of the war," write Craig L. Barry and David C. Burt, "there were numerous reports of soldiers in the Army of Northern Virginia who appeared to be wearing blue-gray jackets produced of imported English broadcloth or woolen kersey."[68] Southern hands continued to put together men's clothing, but the cloth came from across the Atlantic Ocean, signaling the Civil War's international dimensions.

The Quartermaster Department's reliance on English and Irish cloth meant that by the war's last years, Confederate soldiers were incredibly uniform in appearance. The visual representation communicated the incredible esprit de corps guiding Lee's army but also signaled men's nearly total dependence on the quartermaster. Although wealthy soldiers were often able to supplement military items with goods from home or the army sutler, by 1863 soldiers of all classes wore government-issued garments and footwear. Every Confederate shared this experience, which rendered the objects of war as bonding agents among men. Without discounting the overriding importance of ideology, material conditions filtered soldiers' commitment to the Confederacy. Although not always pleased with the Confederate supplies, government clothing and equipment eased soldiers into the regime of army life by binding them together through shared dependence. The material of war ultimately helped enlisted men reconcile themselves to the new realities of military discipline.

Camp Culture

Within the confines of camp and away from home, soldiers struggled to create a semblance of community and stability. Although their efforts were not always successful, homelike camps bolstered men's emotional and psychological health.[69] Years after the conclusion of the American Civil War, former Confederate artillerist Carlton McCarthy fondly recalled "the cheerful, happy scenes of the camp-fire."[70] The military encampment, he continued, served as the soldier's "home, his place of rest, where he met with good companionship."[71] These vignettes of soldier life formed the substance of McCarthy's 1882 work, *Detailed Minutiae of Soldier Life in the Army of Northern Virginia, 1861-1865*. It is tempting to dismiss such claims as postwar propaganda or a reified memory. His portrait of camp life offers scant mention of the monotony and dangers experienced by soldiers. Moreover, his book often reads like a Lost Cause editorial deifying Confederate soldiers and vilifying African Americans.[72] Yet McCarthy's description of fraternity deserves further scrutiny, for it undermines a prevailing notion of white Southerners' manly, fierce independence and also reflects a common, albeit neglected thread woven throughout Confederate soldiers' wartime correspondence and diaries.

As the hardened veteran replaced the summertime soldier, he confronted the unavoidable truth that, for the war's duration, other soldiers were his closest, most immediate associates. Although reactions varied from man to man, many Confederates created transitional and temporary emotional communities tied directly to their wartime comrades.[73] Home and family remained paramount in soldiers' minds and hearts, but these same men came to see the military camp as their substitute home and their comrades as an ad hoc family.[74] Soldiers' potential to form bonds with other men in military camps should not be altogether surprising. A prominent line of scholarship contends that the majority of Confederates, especially those who served in the Army of Northern Virginia, expressed a nearly fanatical devotion to their comrades and commanders.[75] Still, were soldiers' reactions grounded more in distant respect than in deep devotion? An earlier generation of scholars characterized antebellum Southern white men as individualistic and self-determined. Males defined their public personae through an aggressive defense of reputation, or shaped their personal identities through the subordination of those deemed "dependents."[76] As Confederate soldiers, individuals who were independent and competitive felt little kinship toward their fellows. Indeed, even one historian's sensitive portrait of Southern manhood nonetheless contends that Confederates "kept each other at a distance; that was the point."[77] Alone and strong willed, the Confederate soldier truly embodied the image of the rebel. Such characterizations become even more striking if Johnny Reb is juxtaposed to Billy Yank. Historian David Blight observes that during the war, Union soldiers, like generations of men, found "love and respect for each other more readily in warlike activities than in civilian pursuits." Transformed by the routines of army life and embedded in a temporary community of men, these soldiers developed their own rituals and domestic relations.[78] Thus, the social spaces created by military encampments fostered the construction of a unique soldiers' culture born of the interplay between the individual and his material circumstances.[79]

Southern civilians began their military careers in camp; however, the transition into this unfamiliar sphere was anything but easy. "Anywhere the Army of Northern Virginia bivouacked," historian Robert K. Krick writes, "became instantaneously a community larger than any prewar Virginia city."[80] The encampment's congested atmosphere, historian Drew Gilpin Faust charges, juxtaposed "classes and cultures in what was to many a new and alarming propinquity." Clashes among soldiers arose inevitably as the privileged and less privileged lived together in the confines of an enclosed space.[81] Further, the camp's raucous atmosphere exposed men to an array of temptations and vices, leading many to become dissipated.[82] North Carolina soldier E. B. Mendenhall complained to his cousin Mary on New Year's Day

1862, "Camp is any thing but a place to improve a man's moral & religious feelings. It seems as if most men soon forget in camp that they have to be accountable for their words at least & a great many for their actions. There [are] all kinds of characters to be found in a regiment of 900 or 1,000 men."[83]

Most recruits had been born and raised in the same state; many continued to live and work in a very confined geographic area.[84] The sights, smells, and sounds of encampments proved disconcerting to the neophyte.[85] Confederate soldier John Dooley described his first encounter with a camp as strange and unfamiliar. Surrounded by foreign "faces and forms, the near and distant sounds of an army of men talking, shouting, singing, and all upon different subjects," created an unparalleled atmosphere.[86] Furthermore, as Randolph A. Shotwell contended, not all soldiers were equally matched to the challenges of outdoor living and protracted military service. Comparing an unattached, wild young man fond of outdoor living and male companionship to a man with a wife and children, Shotwell concluded that both "may have been patriotic, but surely not equal in self-sacrifice."[87] Still, however unfamiliar the environment and uncertain the future, many recruits readily embraced the exhilaration of camp, for it was something new and different. Ruffin Thomson, who had recently left the University of North Carolina for the army, told his father that it was "not like being at College for the stir of camp life & the excitement of being so near the enemy fills up all that time which at College is so very tedious."[88] Confusion commingled with excitement for newly minted soldiers in the early days of military service as they learned the duties and the routines of army life.

Soldiers' corporate identity evolved slowly over the weeks and months spent together. Military encampments provided the physical setting and environment that were integral to this process. As most recruits came to realize, these spaces were transitional, shifting with the vicissitudes of war. Size, permanence, and proximity to population centers directed the shape and scale of encampments. Semipermanent camps, which were typical during the campaign season, assumed an informal character. One Confederate complained during the Peninsula Campaign, for instance, of having to bivouac in the woods late at night after hard marching and fighting during the day.[89] In such arrangements, exhausted soldiers likely slept near the roadway on which they had just marched. Similarly, during campaign season, troops sometimes had to bed down in line of battle, often with scant protection from the elements. Sergeant Joseph D. Joyner of the Seventh North Carolina Infantry complained to his mother, Julia, that after being called out around eleven o'clock at night, he and the men of his regiment were "ordered to stack arms and sleep near them, with [their] accouterments so, so that [they] could get them at a moments warning."⁹⁰

Nothing signaled male dependency more clearly than winter quarters, which soldiers constructed and occupied together. Unlike during the campaign season, when bivouacs were possible, during cold weather, military maneuvers were generally halted, allowing the armies to create more permanent encampments that promoted healthful conditions and helped men endure harsh winters. Neatly arranged rows of small wooden huts, ranging in size from eight to twelve feet in length and width, composed the winter encampment.⁹¹ The huts' construction required group work. As Private John H. Stevens of the Fifth Texas Regiment explained, messes of "four to six men" divided up the task. Continuing, he noted, "We select a tree about ten or twelve inches in diameter" and "cut it up into cuts seven to ten feet long." The men proceeded to build up walls, close cracks, and make bedding.⁹² According to North Carolina soldier Leonidas Torrence, his winter quarter was "a verry fine House made of Pine, Cedar and Poplar poles it is covered with Pine and Cedar limbs and plastered with Dirt and has a verry nice Brick Cminey built with . . . sticks and mud."⁹³ Ordnance Sergeant James W. Albright took great solace in his warm winter home, which consisted of a tent stretched over "a form of poles and a neat little fire place & chimney," while Richard Waldrop proudly related to his mother that his mess was "comfortably fixed" in a tent-covered wooden pen.⁹⁴ The communal housing of winter quarters bonded men, and for many, deep affinity between soldiers developed accordingly. Writing from Fredericksburg, Virginia, in the winter of 1863, Thomson related to his father the comforts of winter quarters. He and his comrades enjoyed their "splendid" accommodations because "of the hardships" to which they had "become accustomed." "Men who have not slept inside a tent for *ten months* are apt to understand the blessing on houses & feel duly thankful for the uncounted comforts of a tight roof and a plank floor."⁹⁵ The members of Thomson's mess felt a mutual affection grounded in the shared conditions of military life.

Although winter encampments encouraged male dependency, they also reflected antebellum class hierarchies, as seen in an example of Confederate winter quarters at Orange, Virginia. Wartime privation, a lack of tools, and military hierarchy influenced the form and content of Confederate winter huts more explicitly than seen in their Union counterparts. An archaeological excavation revealed that architectural features were ephemeral and artifacts sparse. Spartan conditions, though, were witnessed only in those huts used by Confederate enlisted men and noncommissioned officers. The same class hierarchies that guided the antebellum South were also reflected in wartime material culture. Huts probably occupied by Confederate officers yielded significant quantities of plateware, dishes, and glass fragments, as well as inkwells and ink bottles.[96] The archaeological record thus demonstrates markedly different material circumstances between enlisted men and officers, predicated on distinctions in class and rank. Overall, though, the artifacts found at the Confederate camp paled in comparison to those found in "contemporary Union camps across the Rapidan River," where "hundreds of bottles, ceramic vessels, and military equipage and paraphernalia" were excavated.[97]

Just as Confederate camps reflected antebellum social hierarchies, so too did they demonstrate Southerners' continued dependence on slave labor. After the Virginia campaigns in the late spring of 1862, Ruffin Thomson wrote his father requesting help. He asked him to spare a family slave, Preston, or hire him "a Boy," for it would alleviate a good deal of suffering. Thomson wanted the enslaved laborer to do his cooking and washing, as well as help carry his load. He continued, "Whenever any of the boys who have servts get sick of course his servt goes with him. . . . And on this march the man with a boy fared best, by far."[98] Preston eventually arrived and bore a heavy burden, carrying extra baggage on marches, preparing meals, and catering to Thomson's needs. Thomson continued to use slave labor. By the late winter of 1864, now in the service of the Confederate marine corps and stationed at Drewry's Bluff, Virginia, he was supplied with "plenty of wood & plenty of servants." He required nothing more unless he could get a "good" slave, not "out of the fields" but one "who was accustomed to the duties of body srvt."[99] Others used intermittent slave labor—hired or borrowed—to wash underclothes or to cook meals.[100] These actions reflected a broader worldview that equated whiteness to privilege and blackness to slavery. And even while serving in the military and often reeling from its subordinating effects, many Confederates continued to define their independence through the dehumanization of African Americans.

So inured to racism, Confederate soldiers did not recognize that slaves, too, experienced the same hardships in camp that they themselves often complained of in letters home. Waldrop, for example, opined in his diary, "If our 'dear mamas' could look in on us now, our deplorable condition would" bring "big tears to their eyes." Days later he wrote, "I wish I were an *army nigger* until 'this cruel war is over[.]' They are the happiest dogs I ever saw— Don't know what trouble is."[101] Distasteful to modern readers, Waldrop's words epitomize whites' stark racism. In another instance of emotional detachment, upon the death of Thomson's first camp slave, Preston, he could only conclude, "Press was a good boy & I feel his loss . . . very much . . . but such is the world, and there is no use in opining."[102] Wrapped in a blanket, Preston, who had succumbed to illness and died in a camp near Fredericksburg in December 1862, was buried in a musket box far from home.

Enslaved African Americans were excluded from Confederates' tight-knit communities, which ultimately reflected and reinforced racial hierarchies. Dooley related that Ned, their "servant," "lies out side the shelter, and wrapped in his blanket rolls close to the fire, with his feet in the ashes and often missing but by little of burning his toes."[103] Ned's physical separation from the comforts within the tent served as a physical reminder that race afforded privilege in the South, and Confederate soldiers derived power and self-identity through the dominance of African Americans. Whites violently resisted black equality and consciously reconstructed social hierarchies in their camps to ensure their own superiority.[104] In this particular sense, military encampments reproduced a system of mastery created during the antebellum era.[105]

Messmates

The private's immediate sphere consisted of his messmates; a squad of four to eight men with whom he cooked, ate, slept, lived, and fought. According to the 1863 Confederate army regulations, "Messes will be prepared by privates of squads . . . each taking his tour."[106] For the military this system provided a means of cooking food and maintaining cooking utensils, but for the soldier the mess forged comradeship and created a rapport between men that was cemented in combat and reified in camp.[107] Thomson, writing from Fredericksburg in the winter of 1863, described a typical arrangement. He, Wesley Lewis, "Mumford & Stewart of Dry Grove Constitute[d] the mess, a convenient number for sleeping and small enough to be pleasant."[108] The military tested men's mettle but also served as a binding agent. Although it pushed Southerners' physical endurance and psychological health, messmates helped each other endure.

The small groups of men that composed a mess were integral to soldiers' tightly knit communities. Tally Simpson told his sister Anna that a soldier's happiness largely depended on the composition of his company. As he considered the prospect for reenlistment in the winter of 1862, Simpson feared the reorganization of his regiment and the accompanying loss of familiar faces—such fears were rightly founded, as many men declined to reenlist.

By that fall the loss of his original mess saddened Simpson greatly.[109] Confederates became devoted to their company and the men therein. As James A. Graham contemplated his future assignment—he was away from his company, serving as an adjutant—he told his father, "I would rather be with my old company than any company I know of; for it is the best drilled company I ever saw and one of the best companies I ever saw in every particular."[110] After returning from a prolonged illness, an elated Hill Fitzpatrick told his wife that his "heart throb[bed]" by the prospect of rejoining his comrades-in-arms, while John Charles Gaines told a friend, "[I] shall be apt to stay in this Regt till I die am shot out or the war ends."[111] Such reactions demonstrate the deep emotional bonds formed among Confederate soldiers. These men realized quickly that the war would be anything but short, and their comfort and safety demanded mutual dependence.

The camp's largely homosocial community meant that soldiers performed tasks that they had deemed women's duties in the antebellum era. Thomson and his messmates, for example, were delighted by the biscuits they made, describing the finished product as "light and nice."[112] They found their improved abilities in such areas pleasant: "When we first began the life of a soldier our biscuits would have given a mule the dispepsia—now *rolls* light & luscious grace our table."[113] The most thoughtful men came to appreciate more the considerable contributions made by their wives, sisters, and mothers at home. Fitzpatrick started sewing to repair worn garments and fill time in camp. He became so adept at patching his garments and modifying his clothing that he even started sewing for fellow soldiers. Before the war, he knew little about such "woman's work" and perhaps thought even less about the time and skills involved in the construction or modification of garments. Now, forced to take up the needle for repairs and other work, Fitzpatrick approvingly wrote to his wife, "Many a soldier can now realize the value of woman's work that thought but little or nothing about it before the war commenced."[114] Fitzpatrick's compliment represented a sentiment echoed throughout the South since the war's beginning as Confederate men praised women's work and sacrifices.[115] So too, though, did men look increasingly inward, positing the importance of their military family.

The strikingly domestic descriptions of men's comrade-in-arms should come as no surprise; for, historians have demonstrated that men went to war to protect their families and often used domestic imagery to make sense of war's abstractions.[116] Confederates entwined the personal and political, and white Southerners directly expressed their worldview by the defense of home and family.[117] A soldier's messmates formed the center of an extended military family from which men drew strength by replicating their distant homes in military camps. Waldrop related to his father the communal atmosphere that pervaded his mess: "Whenever one of us gets any thing from home he throws it into the general fund of his mess & in that way we manage to live very well."[118] Leonidas Torrence described a similar spirit among his messmates. After they were moved from their winter quarters, a spring snow made conditions uncomfortable outside Fredericksburg, Virginia. "It was verry cold," he wrote, so his mess "made a tent" with their blankets and were comfortably fixed.[119] Waldrop, Torrence, and other Confederates learned to rely on and share with their messmates to mitigate the harsh conditions of army life. In an important sense, the ersatz family of a soldier's mess or regimental company became as sustaining as the homefolks he sought to defend. And army mates, unlike distant family, were always present to boost morale and provide reminders of the necessity of continued service.

Messmates together endured the hardships of outdoor living, sharing resources when necessary. Tightly quartered in tents or huddled together near fires, soldiers strengthened their relationships by physical contact.[120] Often, inadequate clothing, thin blankets, and exposure drew men together at night, especially during the cold months, even when encamped in winter quarters. Although modern sensibilities may eroticize bed sharing, nineteenth-century men commonly bedded together out of necessity and for comfort.[121] Dick Simpson of the Third South Carolina Infantry, for instance, related without embarrassment to his cousin Caroline his sleeping arrangements: "We suffered very much with cold, but by crowding together and keeping close we managed to keep tolerable warm."[122] Graham told his mother that, after arriving at Fort Macon, North Carolina, he slept with Tom Whitted.[123] And Thomson wrote his father that after tiring of one bedmate, he "joined blankets" with another soldier in the company.[124] These arrangements ensured warmth. Dooley explained the process fully, including its accompanying benefits and pitfalls. He and his comrades had but four blankets among them, forcing them to "manage economically." He explained, "The way we adopt is for all three to sleep together, lying on one blanket and covering with the other three." If each man slept in the same position, the arrangement was ideal. But if someone moved, the blankets shifted and one man would go uncovered. Thus, the men positioned themselves closely together, each lying in the same direction. When someone required a "change of base," he announced his intention and the men shifted accordingly.[125]

Forced to endure night after night exposed to the elements, sometimes covered by tenting but often not during the campaign season, Confederate soldiers relied on their fellows to ensure even a modicum of comfort. The physical benefits of such arrangements are obvious. But such continued intimate contact and coordinated actions promoted deep relationships, thus forging strong emotional connections between men. In a moving letter to the parents of deceased Confederate James Hay Knighton, who died of disease, John Doyle described the terms of their friendship: "A long period as a messmate aforded me ample means to know him as he *was*."[126] Similarly, W. J. O'Daniel tenderly wrote to the mother of Torrence, who had been killed at Gettysburg. The two men had gone into the fight together and "promised each other if one go hurt to doo all [they] could for him."[127] Doyle's and O'Daniel's words demonstrate an intimacy soldiers acquired in each other's company. Long hours spent by the fireside fostered personal knowledge, revealing a more authentic inner self otherwise missed by others. Carlton McCarthy wrote years after the war, in a exaggerated and sentimentalized language that still conveyed an important truth, "In winter quarters every man had his 'chum' or bunk-mate, with whom he slept, walked, talked, and divided hardship or comfort as they came along; and the affectionate regard of each for the other was often beautiful to see."[128] Such a description recalls the words of Herman Melville: "There is no place like a bed for confidential disclosures between friends."[129]

For all the intimacy and familiarity that prevailed among soldiers' messes, exceptions existed. The mercurial Randolph A. Shotwell recalled with some bitterness that he was often avoided during the war and not invited to join a mess. "Indeed, throughout the war I had but little companionship," he wrote, "eating and sleeping by myself, not from pride or misanthropy, but because my quiet, queer, shrinking, reserved nature rendered familiar intercourse with the rough, uncouth, uneducated countrymen of the rank and file, utterly repugnant to my feelings."[130] Such stinging exclusion gave rise to feelings of isolation and estrangement for, as Shotwell knew, his fellow soldiers served as an important outlet for sustained friendship during military service. Shotwell's experiences also point to the fact that some men simply did not get along. His self-imposed isolation, although longer and more extreme than otherwise expected, was a necessary reprieve from the at times claustrophobic conditions of camp.

The same physical and emotional ties that fostered intimacy and a sense of comradeship also promoted social divisions in camps. Discounting those Confederates with prior military experience, little in most men's antebellum lives prepared them for the demanding and demeaning facets of military living. Soldiers' friendships faltered, and some men simply needed space. Contrasting views on religion, temperance, and vice created tensions as large groups of men, bounded by confined areas, had to interact with each other daily. Kentuckian John S. Jackman complained of a sleepless night, for instance, after his sleeping mate returned from a "bender"; throughout the night, he pulled Jackman's blankets and bothered him generally.[131] Camps were also confining and monotonous. James Albright recorded a diary entry on November 23, 1862, noting, "Sunday is a very dull day in camp—no friends to visit—no preaching—the same faces always around you and the same boring details of a soldier's life. I am a little blue."[132] An otherwise cheerful and social Tally Simpson eschewed his comrades one fall afternoon, feeling isolated and dispirited. "The soldiers are grouped around laughing and conversing gaily," Simpson wrote. "I however am differently inclined this afternoon and feel a short confab with the darling ones at home sweet home will afford me ten thousand times more pleasure than the participation in any little scenes enacted in camp."[133] Writing to his mother on a day of leisure, Thomson struck a similar tone. In low spirits and feeling sick, Thomson felt despondent, "with scarcely a gleam of sunshine to lighten [his] every way—weary only because of [his] present condition."[134] Both Simpson and Thomson found solace in writing home and receiving letters from their loved ones. Thomson related to his mother that her image was seldom out of mind, while Simpson maintained that a soldier's life was one of idleness until the "transcendently sweet" moment in which he received "a precious letter from home."[135] These words demonstrate that even men's cherished friendships could not substitute for home fully.

Antebellum Southern society rewarded men's independence, which contributed to aggressive, self-interested behavior. Military service demanded subordination to rank and regulations and the sacrifice of the individual for the collective. Unquestionably, as historians have persuasively noted, religion acted as a key force in easing Southerners' transition into the constrained sphere of military service, moderating conduct and easing tensions.[136] Emotional communities fostered by army life also facilitated behavioral shifts. Men resisted this process but also came to recognize, even embrace, its benefits, for as a unit they together endured the hardships of campaigns and camp. Tensions among soldiers and fits of homesickness reveal men's struggles to understand and function under the demands of Confederate military service. Disagreements and flare-ups were the naturally occurring by-products of living in crowded spaces, whereas distance from home and the death of friends or loved ones created despondency. Men grappled to control or resolve their emotions, and successes or failures illustrate the shifting terrain of gender relationships altered by war. The rigors of soldiering, the terrors of combat, and the mutual dependency required by communal camp living served as profound catalysts connecting men to one another, which often fostered indissoluble bonds. Although antebellum whites forged meaningful friendships—especially through churches, colleges, militias, and fraternal organizations—the circumstances of civil war created a constellation of situations that compelled men together. Yet the very conditions that drew men together also forced them apart. The tedium of camp, the stress of military discipline, and constant company engendered feelings of isolation and depression. These reactions only reinforce scholars' contention that home and family remained paramount to men's happiness.

Imagined Communities

If intimate messes anchored men, large, sprawling military camps reinforced the scale of war and the army's military might, which bolstered the bonds among men, boosted morale, and fostered the creation of imagined communities.[137] A Kentucky soldier related how a quiet August encampment in 1862 became suddenly alive with activity when orders came down to cook rations and prepare for movement. "Soon hundreds of camp-fires blazed . . . and cheer upon cheer, rose from the noisy thousands."[138] The scene proved inspiring and the men talked until morning. In the hundreds of burning fires, the chorus of excited voices, and the movement of countless silhouetted figures, the individual soldier witnessed and became a physical extension of the broader Confederate military project. Artillerist Edward Porter Alexander captured a similar scene of excitement and scale in Richmond, Virginia, during the early months of war as soldiers were mustered into service and organized into camps. Troops from across the South arrived daily and formed camps of instruction. Raw troops "were drilled, loose companies organised into regts. & regiments into brigades, field & staff officers were appointed & assigned, arms & equipments were issued."[139] Early recruits learned the duties of soldiering and the routine of military life while encamped. Louisiana governor Thomas O. Moore described a sight replicated across the Southern states in 1861 and 1862. Called on to raise eight thousand twelve-month volunteers by May 1861, the state of Louisiana housed four thousand men in camps of instruction and had started dispatching trained regiments to seats of war.[140]

Despite the awe camps sometimes inspired, for white Southern men who defined themselves more by independence than submission, the unrelenting pace of soldier life and discipline proved daunting. Most significantly, the military routine learned and repeated in camps tempered raw recruits. Although they possessed a deep sense of duty, Southerners' sense of honor insisted on self-determination, liberty, and manliness. Surrendering oneself to the army created turmoil.[141] One soldier, in the first year of the conflict, described the tension between individualistic men and army discipline. He told his sister that some of the "men go to the City and get drunk and come back and when the officers go to take them to the gard house they will curse them and then they get bucked and a bayonet tied in their mouth and stay double the length of time."[142] Military service forced men to relinquish self-interest for the collective. Tempering raw recruits contributed in no small part to a regiment's performance in battle.[143] A unit's fighting effectiveness—its very survival—could be decided by whether fear governed its soldiers' actions. Fear, anxiety, and apprehension were natural reactions to the experience of combat.[144] Such feelings could never be wholly alleviated, but taming their effects was crucial. Encamped soldiers drilled daily; formed for parades, inspections, and roll calls; and spent considerable time on guard or picket duty. By stripping away the volunteer's individualism and governing his life by routine and limitations, the military instilled discipline and created unit cohesion while never completely stifling individualism and self-esteem.[145] The repetition of drill and the creation of unit identity aimed at regimenting soldiers' behavior while under fire— responses were to be automatic and troops had to maintain composure in battle. Effective fighters could not surrender themselves to feelings of nervousness and the impulse to run and hide. The forging process could be tiresome, however. An exasperated Tally Simpson complained of a routine familiar to all troops North and South: "Drill, drill, drill; work, work, work; and guard, guard, guard. Eat, e-a-t. Alas!"[146]

A majority of Confederates entered their first fight only after spending prolonged periods with their comrades in arms training at encampments under the guidance of officers. For the citizen-soldier, the bonds forged between men helped shift the "burden of fear from the individual to the group," as Joseph T. Glatthaar explains.[147] These informal support networks significantly underpinned why men chose to stay and fight, or fled from the field. Men knew all too well that the eyes of their comrades and community were constantly watching. Their behavior and displays of bravado were not only emblematic of larger social ideals but also gave credence to prewar social hierarchies.[148] Second-echelon officers served as critical links between enlisted men and Confederate leadership and facilitated the creation of consensus across class lines.[149] Volunteer officers, as historian Andrew S. Bledsoe has argued, were especially critical in reconciling "antebellum democratic values" with an army culture that demanded obedience.[150]

In spite of markedly different backgrounds and class divisions, Confederate troops embraced a remarkable degree of cohesion, according to historians of Robert E. Lee's army.[151] In the Army of Northern Virginia, soldiers' ideas about war aims, honor, religion, race, and the home front developed "a shared outlook, generating a strong solidarity among themselves that supported their commitment to the war," according to Elisabeth Lauterbach Laskin.[152] Important elements for this sense of solidarity were formed in camp. The homosocial world of soldiers' bivouacs and the ersatz family of the soldier's regiment could never replace home and kin. But the emergency of war and the unbending structure of the army melded men into a collective whole that many embraced, even cherished. Men came to see their fellow soldiers as family whom they relied on and shared with to mitigate the dehumanizing conditions that many feared came with the military and curtailed freedom.[153] Joseph D. Joyner, for example, enlisted later than his father and brother and thus found himself in a regiment of strangers. The family worked tirelessly for his transfer. By the fall of 1862, however, he felt contented. "I had almost concluded not to trouble myself about a transfer," he wrote his mother, "having become very well satisfied with the company that I now belong to. . . . They are very anxious that I should remain with them, but seem willing to my transfer if I desire it."[154] Private James Thomas Thompson happily noted in a letter to his mother and sisters, "Wee love each other like a band of brothers."[155] Confederate soldiers came to rely greatly on their fellows to secure comfort, thereby promoting intimacy and creating group identity.

A series of images by Conrad Wise Chapman focuses on the domestic elements he and other soldiers valued. Indeed, in forest and field, many men found enduring friendships. Chapman, an artist by training who enlisted in the Third Kentucky Infantry in 1861, made numerous sketches of soldier life that provide a vivid illustration of what form many semipermanent camps assumed. One print, *Third Kentucky Confederate Infantry—at Corinth—May 11, 1862*, became one of the most famous published images of a Confederate camp.[156] After transferring theaters of war and eventually joining the Fifty-Ninth Virginia Regiment, Chapman produced more drawings. His father, John Gadsby Chapman, turned one into an etching titled *The*

Soldier-artist Conrad Wise Chapman offers a romanticized vision of Confederate camp life that still accurately captures soldiers' mutual dependence and material realities. *Confederate Camp during the Late American War*, chromolithograph (London: Louis Zimmer, 1871). Image courtesy Library of Congress, Washington, D.C.

Fifty-Ninth Virginia Infantry — Wise's Brigade/Diascund Brigade — May 1863. Both scenes, analyzed by Mark E. Neely Jr., Harold Holzer, and Gabor S. Boritt, convey the atmosphere of typical Confederate encampments, even if elements within each image were changed over time to advance the Lost Cause's vision of the Confederacy. African Americans are present in both scenes, for example, but rather than depicting the realities of forced labor, the etchings portray the slaves as lazy Sambos — departures from the original sketches.[157] The image of indolent slaves is especially striking when compared to contemporary photographs of Confederate soldiers and enslaved labor. Often the soldiers are playing cards or posing for the camera, while African American slaves steadily work over a fire or prepare food. Nonetheless, both prints' central elements stay true to the artist's sketches, revealing a great deal about the atmosphere of camp. A paucity of photographic evidence capturing similar impromptu scenes renders these images invaluable.

An array of tents and shelters demonstrates the appearance of Confederates' semipermanent camps. *The Fifty-Ninth Virginia Infantry—Wise's Brigade* by Conrad Wise Chapman (probably 1867, oil on canvas, 20 1/8 × 33 7/8 inches [51.1 × 85.9 cm]). Image courtesy Amon Carter Museum of American Art, Fort Worth, Texas.

Irregularly arranged tents and open-air arbors are nestled amid trees and forest in Chapman's print. The wooded, asymmetrical Confederate camps contrast to the "postcard lithographs" of Union encampments, which are depicted as more regimented and orderly.[158] John S. Jackman demonstrated such contrasts with his happy description of pitched tents "in beautiful dell, under wide-spreading liveoaks."[159] Ideally, encampments were convenient to wood and water, ensured the health and comfort of the troops, and facilitated communications.[160] These dictates, as outlined in the *Regulations for the Army of the Confederate States*, were intended more to answer soldiers' demands than shape physical appearance; thus, transitional bivouacs often stood in contrast to the creation of orderly "streets" bordered by regularly spaced tents in more permanent arrangements.[161]

The soldiers in both of Chapman's scenes are loosely attired, many stripped down to shirtsleeves, demonstrating a degree of familiarity. Such informality is especially striking when compared to the typically tight concealment of Victorian-era men's and women's bodies in public. Instead, the scene conveys intimacy and feelings of kinship, as groups of soldiers

Soldiers 57

are gathered together playing cards, cooking, or talking. Fires billow smoke into the air as laundry flaps in the breeze. The scenes are domestic, recalling genre paintings of the early nineteenth century, and powerfully illustrate how encampments became men's homelike sphere. The countless hours spent under these circumstances contributed in innumerable ways to the family-like character military companies and regiments assumed for their members.

Chapman's work invokes the pastoralism so popular in nineteenth-century art, thereby creating an ideal that overlooks the dangers and monotony of camp living. Remarkably, Confederate private John J. Omenhauser rendered a more informal watercolor of camp life, titled *Wise Brigade*, circa 1863, which offers a separate view of the same brigade around the same time period. Omenhauser depicts an intimate scene of messmates—members of Company A, Forty-Sixth Virginia Infantry—preparing a meal around a fire. Rather than embracing their domestic chores, however, the men complain of camp duties and military food with cutting remarks. Corporal William Snead, cutting a ham hock, wryly notes, "I feel as if I had Hog bristles growing all over me." Private Robert C. Carter bemoans chopping wood, which has elevated his heart rate to 240 beats per minute. He maintains that he might have to "see the doctor for a discharge." Finally, Private Charles H. Epps, who is lugging around a bucket of water for cooking, threatens to break the head of the first man who washes himself with it.[162] Omenhauser's scene is one of frustration with a dull diet, inconsiderate comrades, and laborious tasks. Confederate camps spurred conflict over the competition for resources and battles over controlling labor.

Omenhauser's satirical portrait of army life demonstrates the frustrations that came with soldiering. Although men bonded over the experience of communal living, they also bristled at its restrictions. With few opportunities to openly criticize command structure or military routine, Omenhauser's watercolor is a statement of dissent. The artist includes a scathing, if subtle, indictment of the officer class. Although the viewer is immediately drawn to the messmates, a careful inspection reveals three men in an open tent. One man kneels while another sits. The two soldiers are playing cards, perhaps gambling. An officer, clad in a jaunty cap and a double-breasted frock coat with braided sleeves, stands above the men, not condemning but seemingly condoning their behavior. *Wise Brigade* is an image of authority gone awry, army life at its worst.

A wartime watercolor humorously critiques the confining atmosphere of the encampment and soldiers' seemingly endless chores. *Wise Brigade* by John J. Omenhauser, probably 1863. Watercolor. Image courtesy of the American Civil War Museum.

Toward Veterans

Confederates' materials of war and military comportment signaled their status as veterans. The seasoned soldiers of 1862 and beyond became adept at ensuring physical comfort, which some men came to see as their break from the civilian world. Southerners who had enjoyed wealth and prosperity in the antebellum South were struck at how well they survived with the bare minimum. Encamped near Fredericksburg, Virginia, in the winter of 1862, a seasoned Thomson described to his mother the soldier's priorities. Army life had stripped away many of the luxuries Ruffin had once enjoyed, and his priorities centered now on physical well-being and comfort. First, he ensured protection from the elements. Thomson described a large protective fly that covered their heads and a bed of straw below. He next turned to food. "Rations consist of flour & beef—never any thing more—but you would be astonished to see how well we get on with these two articles." Finally, he described his clothing. A change of shirts, drawers, and shirts were essential.[163] Reduced to the minimum, Thomson reveled in privations that became sources of pride. Maintaining that it was only habit that had rendered extraneous items necessary, he felt a heightened sense of awareness and was unimpaired by the trappings of "Civilization," as he later contended.[164] Thomson further maintained that war had elevated his senses, bringing him closer to an imagined primordial, unfettered state of being. Long marches and field experience had indeed produced a streamlined soldier who carried what he needed and discarded the rest. Such experiences altered the soldier's material circumstances, fostering both real and imagined divisions between the spheres of civilian and military life.

Hardened veterans who endured depredation demonstrated a willingness to elevate cause over self. Martial men projected an outward persona that rested on bravado either to relieve the minds of worried relatives or to simply revel in their triumph over adversity. T. W. Harriss's letter to his uncle contained a bit of both. In late January 1862, after several difficult months of service, he was "doing better than [he] ever hoped to do." His regiment had "walked over 1200 miles, & at the late skirmish at Bath," he proudly touted, they "lay out in the open air without either blankets or any thing to eat with the snow about 6 inches deep."[165] James Thomas Thompson compared his plight to that of the "Great" George Washington, proclaiming that he gloried "in the honor and pride of a solgers life."[166] Harriss and Thompson met adversity with gusto, listing their travails as a series of accomplishments that had changed them into better men. Their sense of personal honor demanded that they meet and overcome the challenges of soldiering. Accordingly, as Laskin observes, for some men in the Army of Northern Virginia, soldiering became "an important part of a man's personal development," and its "exposure to hardship and sacrifice could also teach one's place in and duty of society."[167]

The Confederate soldier greeted 1863 as a seasoned veteran, but great challenges still awaited him. Clad in military attire, the Southerner's dress connected him to his comrades-in-arms and outwardly eclipsed class distinctions. Having survived the disease, discipline, and deprivation that governed camp, he increasingly viewed fellow soldiers as family. The emotional shift soldiering required marked a notable change for antebellum whites who had thrived on personal independence. Soldiers now had to succumb to military command structures and depend on their fellows for comfort, if not survival. Many Confederates came to see the men of their messes and regimental companies as intimate, enduring companions with whom they shared a common misery of cold nights and fatigue from long marches.[168] Having met the challenges of camp, the Confederate soldier still had to survive the ordeal of battle.

CHAPTER THREE

Battle

The men of the First Virginia Infantry, part of Confederate general James Kemper's brigade, were positioned in a hollow. To their far front ran Cemetery Ridge, the center of the Union army's line at Gettysburg. A host of Confederate cannon flanked them on either side. Some of the men, growing bored, sought amusement by tossing green apples at each other. "So frivolous men can be," observed Captain John E. Dooley of the First Virginia, "even in the hour of death." Firing soon commenced. Earth and sky seemed to "open and darken the air with smoke and death dealing missiles."[1] Amusement turned to anxiety as the men waited, concussed by the cannon's roar, for the inevitable orders to begin their march toward Cemetery Ridge. The firing quickened. A major from the First amiably conversed with a friend amid the Union bombardment. Straining to hear his companion's words, the officer turned to the man to ask what he had said, only to find him dead.[2] Anticipation gave way to action as the men were ordered up and forward. Dooley described some men *"fainting* from the heat and dread" as others desperately prayed for safe passage over the deadly Pennsylvania fields.[3] The climatic charge ended in overwhelming defeat. Cheers from excited Union soldiers rent the air as despair filled the hearts of their vanquished foe. "Oh," wrote Dooley, "if there is anything capable of crushing and wringing the soldier's heart it was this day's tragic act and all in vain!"[4]

Soldiers' competing emotions rendered the fields and forests of south central Pennsylvania fractured landscapes. In the hours before Pickett's Charge, the war's killing field transformed, albeit briefly, into a playground; a deadly projectile silenced an intimate conversation; praying soldiers made a profane space sacred; and the studious observer Dooley, a graduate of Georgetown College and later novitiate of the Jesuit Order, tried to make sense of the spectacle of battle. On the Gettysburg battlefield soldiers' emotions ran the gamut from exhilaration to anxiety, joy to sadness, thus reflecting both the heightened senses and the palpable uncertainty that came with war.[5] Despite the range of expressions, these experiences united soldiers. Many of the participants in Pickett's Charge had already seen battle, and the fighting, however horrific, "had become routine," as historian Carol Reardon notes.[6] The American Civil War had thrust white

Southern men together, tested their mettle, and asked them to endure. Amid the destruction, Confederate soldiers relied on the emotional communities forged in camp to endure the uncertainty of military campaigns and maintain a shared commitment to their comrades-in-arms that was critical in battle.[7] Indeed, the Army of Northern Virginia's continued military integrity and fighting capacity—even after the defeat at Gettysburg—reflect the importance of the bonds among veterans and the relationships between officers and the rank and file.[8]

Southern soldiers struggled in their letters home to convey the scale and carnage of Civil War battles. The process of explaining proved transformative, however, as men's disclosures undermined the tightly guarded public displays and attempts at emotional control so critical to their antebellum self-identities. Although battle certainly broke some men, the war's destructive powers more commonly shook Southerners' self-assuredness because, as historian Peter S. Carmichael explains, "soldier fatalities seemed so random, so purposeless, and so inexplicable, leaving men on both sides in a state of metaphysical bewilderment."[9] Carmichael's assertion points to the overt intellectual shift the conflict prompted, an observation that may be amplified by connecting men's intellectual lives to their emotional expressions. Despite the military's drive, bolstered by the dictates of Southern culture to regulate feelings such as fear, Confederates came to express and release a range of feelings on the battlefield rooted both in their varied responses to war and in their embrace of divergent masculinities.[10] Confederates' responses to campaigning reflect their measure of manhood and reveal their varied emotional expressions. Martial men portrayed themselves as ready for a fight and exhibited excitement in anticipation of battle. Marching broke up the monotony of camp life, while military action fostered a meaningful sense of purpose. Circumspect soldiers were more likely to exhibit anxiety before battle, expressing concerns about the continued distance from home or the potential for high casualties. Men's varied reactions reveal different responses to the chaos of battle and the uncertainty of military life. Feelings of depression, anxiety, and uncertainty intermixed with duty, honor, and ideology in explaining soldiers' experiences.

Historians have long assessed soldiers' reactions to battle by examining behavior. Measuring troop performance, examining displays of bravery, and trying to understand motives have been familiar approaches.[11] Yet, more attention must be given to the external expression of emotion, not the resultant behavior that has so preoccupied the scholarship. A focus on behavior alone misses an opportunity to examine intimate expressions of thought and feeling that reveal Confederates' often hidden inner experiences. Civil war heightened, if not awakened, white Southerners' awareness of life's fragility. For combatants, battle and the conflict's associated sufferings provoked meditation and deliberation but also metaphysical confusion, challenging antebellum self-perceptions and self-conceptions.[12] Battle particularly tried the most resolute, leaving many profoundly altered but, ironically, also unable to describe adequately the forces precipitating such shifts. North Carolina soldier Walter Clark related to his mother, "No one can imagine anything like" a battle "unless he has been in one."[13] The frenetic pace, the massive troop movements, and the brutal killing created surreal landscapes. Trying to make sense of the carnage and destruction altered many men's perceptions and identities. Ultimately, uncertainty shattered prewar certitude.

Unfamiliar Ground

Confederate soldiers greeted 1863 with increased trepidation. On New Year's Day, Sergeant Robert Wallace Shand of the Second South Carolina Infantry took stock and offered his musings in a small diary, realizing all too clearly that that year might be his last. The book had been a present from his friend John R. Osment as a "relic" from the Battle of Fredericksburg—the volume still included the former owner's name, an artilleryman from Pennsylvania. Shand soon expected peace, but he was also sorrowfully reminded of the "precious souls" now gone. The men he knew "in childhood & in youth, at school & at college," had "shed their life blood in the field of battle," and he hoped that this would remind him "of the uncertainty of human life."[14] The Civil War's combat had called into question the certainty and control that guided Confederate soldiers such as Shand because life on campaign had become fleeting and unpredictable. For the meditative, this proved troubling as antebellum friends fell by the droves and hopes for peace became increasingly urgent. Shand's dreams of a Confederate victory would never come, nor would his hopes for the war's quick end be realized. Instead, the conflict elevated to new heights, resulting in the further loss of life on an unprecedented scale. Shand's New Year's Day reflections capture a mood of uncertainty that prevailed among Confederates, but what prompted such reactions?

The Civil War paradoxically thrust men into worlds of confusion but also affirmed core beliefs. For some, these tensions caused mental consternation and emotional duress; others, nonplused, continued to affirm antebellum belief systems that provided a bulwark against the conflict. And many, such as

Shand, attempted to strike a balance. Religion, as scholars have amply documented, served as a key mechanism for personal solace.[15] Soldiers repeatedly affirmed their beliefs. Providence controlled destiny and determined how and when the war concluded. "May God in His mercy," Shand wrote, "visit our land with peace before its close."[16] This type of religious commitment allowed Shand to let go of earthly concerns to trust in a higher power. North Carolina private E. B. Mendenhall echoed these sentiments when he concluded that the future "is only known to the ruler of heaven & earth."[17] And Georgian James Thomas Thompson contentedly noted, "Trust in God and alls Well."[18] An omnipotent God determined the course of life, and by trusting in the divine, soldiers were able to endure the earthly. Ultimately, as historian Mark S. Schantz writes, "antebellum Americans could face death with resignation and even joy because they carried in their hearts and heads a comforting and compelling vision of eternal life."[19]

Although religious commitment may have propelled many Confederates forward at the height of battle, the circumstances prompting the validation of their beliefs were entirely new. The antebellum faithful were raised in a culture that demanded constant preparation for and fostered the graceful acceptance of death, but more often than not, convictions were affirmed rather than tested. Southern whites were now constantly exposed to deadly disease through communal camp living, and the threat of battle cast a pall across soldiers' lives; families agonized at an unanswered missive, fearing their loved one's fate. Historian Drew Gilpin Faust powerfully explains the disconnect between Americans' antebellum and wartime experiences by explaining how soldiers "worked to construct Good Deaths for themselves and their comrades amid the conditions that made dying—and living—so terrible."[20]

As young men confronted their own mortality, they wrote letters affirming their religious beliefs but also recognizing, if implicitly, the new and trying circumstances they had to endure. Such tensions played out in the letters Thompson wrote to his mother and sisters in the war's first year. "Soalgers runn the risk of their lives a 1000 times," he related, thus conveying the uneasy truth that came with armed conflict: killing and potentially being killed. He had resigned himself to this station. "It is said that the soalgers life is an unhappy one," he continued, "but with me it is a happy one, for i hav maid peac with my God."[21] But war's uncertainty had snared Thompson and he felt, perhaps for the first time in his youthful existence, life's ephemeral nature. As he wrote, "Wee no not the minute wee may be killed."[22] Certainly Thompson found succor through his belief in God, and undoubtedly religion provided genuine relief. Yet as Thompson knew, both the Confederacy and military service pushed him into an unknown realm filled with sorrow and suffering. For young men such as Thompson, this was the first great experience of their lives but also, for the unfortunate—Thompson included, for he, like so many, died from camp disease—their last.

Soldiers' pronouncements of complete trust in a higher power belie deeper fears. Without undermining the validity of men's core spiritual beliefs, it is also important to remember that religion offered soldiers a form of psychological comfort.[23] This need for solace reflects the emotional and mental strains that came with the rigors of combat and campaign. Southern men who had defined their antebellum relationships through firm control now confronted the randomness of the battlefield and the war's destructive power, which loosened their understanding of reality, even life itself. War created metaphysical confusion and control became chimerical. North Carolinian George Battle's 1861 letter to his mother from the Manassas battlefield demonstrates how men started to grapple with the unpredictability of military service. Blackened bodies and rotting horses dotted the fields and greeted him as a most "horrible" and unexpected sight. The fate of two Federal soldiers, though, prompted the day's most unsettling scene. One man had "only a little dust thrown over him," and his darkened hand stuck out of the grave. Battle then saw another grave with an exposed head; the "worms were eating the skin off his face," Battle gruesomely wrote. He contemplated the man and thought, "It made me shudder to think that perhaps I may be buried that way."[24] Dread, anxiety, and fear, although never overriding themes in soldiers' letters, made their way into correspondence as peace became but a distant dream and war's continued cruelty the only consistent reality.

Military routines strictly governed a soldier's day, but the campaign season paced time differently. As the last chapter demonstrated, the long months spent in winter encampments stretched time out to the point of being unbearable as men spent weeks cooped up in winter huts. Conversely, time sped up between the spring and fall as armies jockeyed for position. Soldiers wrote home worried letters that might contain last words. In one missive, T. W. Harriss of the First Tennessee Infantry assured his uncle that he remained "in the land of the liveing."[25] Similarly, Henry W. Smart took his pen in hand to write a few lines to his sister "before the Yankees [got him]."[26] Such simple sentiments served as important updates for anxious relatives, but they also shed light on the incomprehensible face of war. Although fully prepared for death, men endured the heightened tensions of not knowing when their end would come. In Confederate service the specter of death came in many forms and loomed in the background constantly. Time had become a precious commodity governed by an unknowable hand.

War's randomness and uncertainty prompted a vulnerability that jarred Southern white men who had in prewar life defined themselves by independence. Although antebellum diarists struggled with the vicissitudes of life, as illustrated in the first chapter, gender and class granted them considerable control over themselves and society. Military service demanded the relinquishment of such influence. The unrelenting pace of soldiering and the strain of combat proved daunting, as men realized that they could not control an exploding artillery shell or a well-aimed minié ball. As historian Megan Kate Nelson writes, "Men were horrified to find both friends and strangers mangled" and wrote vivid letters and diaries "about bullets 'tearing' and 'shattering' men's arms, legs, and heads."[27] Men's revelations of fear partly displaced the martial manhood so proudly conveyed in early war letters overladen with bravado. North Carolina soldier, and future Gettysburg casualty, Leonidas Torrence maintained regular correspondence with his parents over the course of his military service. As he struggled to both comprehend and convey the face of battle, his letters became more revealing. Torrence's regiment, the Twenty-Third North Carolina Infantry, saw their first combat during the 1862 Peninsula Campaign. In 1861, like countless green recruits, he had eagerly wished "to get in to a battle"; he and his comrades refused to "go home satisfied with out a fite."[28] Now, in June 1862, he penned a letter to his mother during a lull in the fighting that revealed the campaign's strain and emotional duress. He informed her that he had come out of the fight safely, though a bullet had passed through his coat. He continued by writing, "The balls were falling around us as thick as hale all the time it did not look like there was any chance for a man to go through them without being hit."[29] Relentless enemy fire during battles and the continued presence in combat zones during early June 1862 prompted feelings of insecurity, even defenselessness. Perhaps reeling from the effects or simply wanting to embrace the present, Confederates such as Torrence jotted off notes to their kin as a means of controlling the present. By writing letters, soldiers were affirming life during periods when they fearfully wondered who was ultimately in control.

Whereas Torrence maintained control over the tone and content of his 1862 letters, his feelings ran freer in 1863. Battles beggared description but only rendered confusion. In one letter to his mother on May 7, 1863, Torrence expressed his dazed horror after the fighting at Chancellorsville. The letter's vivid descriptions warrant quoting at length:

Mother I thought I had saw as distressing sights on Battle Fields as I ever could see to look at the men Killed and Wounded but where we Faught last Sunday the Burns set the woods a fire and to look at Killed and Wounded men burning was the worst looking sight I ever saw or heard of. . . . I cant give you any idea what a sight it was to walk over the Battle Field and see the men lying with their cloths burnt off their hair burnt [?] close to their Head their arms and legs all drawed up with the fire I never saw such a distressing sight before and hope I may never see such another.[30]

Surely Torrence must have wondered what meaning could be gleaned from the burnt bodies and bloodied landscape. His outpouring is remarkable. Distressed, he desperately tried to communicate to his mother a battlescape that had left him overwrought and reaching for words. The sight of dead men was far from foreign. As he himself noted, "I thought I had saw as distressing sights on Battle Fields as I ever could see to look at the men Killed and Wounded." And as a combatant he had participated both in the killing and in the destruction; however, his soldier identity had not canceled out his compassion. Instead of reaching for familiar concepts anchored in nationalism or commitment to cause—ideas perhaps more comforting to family members—Torrence rooted his words in raw emotions and visceral reactions.[31] Victorian culture could hardly account for scenes that Confederates witnessed. Southerners confronted a failure of language and used feelings as the best means for expression; soldiers were part of an extended community of sufferers.[32]

Arguing more powerfully than perhaps any other scholar of the Civil War era, Gerald F. Linderman contended that the Civil War's scale of destruction forced minds to grope for an understanding of "why courage had failed to secure victory." Soldiers shifted their thoughts and language as they attempted to make sense of the carnage.[33] Linderman's emphasis on courage fits squarely within the primary concerns of Civil War soldiers. Building on these conclusions, it is useful to also consider the broader confusion rendered by the war's destructive power, which prompted levels of emotionality that were once thought to be only possessed by women.[34] Southern men expressed these feelings in letters home as a means to convey war's suffering and confusion, thereby demonstrating resilience in the midst of hardship. Confederates were able to adapt to the trials of military service because they continued to practice a flexible masculinity. Thus, as the Gettysburg Campaign approached, the majority of Robert E. Lee's army continued to navigate successfully the difficulties of campaign by giving voice to their frustrations and fears but also demonstrating a willingness to continue fighting and following their leadership.

The March North

By the spring of 1863, Confederate fortunes ran high but the mood was anything but easy. The death of famed Confederate general Stonewall Jackson had cast a pall over the Army of Northern Virginia's resounding victory at Chancellorsville; the situation in Vicksburg, Mississippi, looked increasingly dire. And in early June the Battle of Brandy Station "had shattered the aura of invincibility that Confederate cavalry had earned."[35] Spirits nonetheless remained high among both civilians and soldiers, who continued to demonstrate unwavering faith in Lee and his execution of the war in the East.[36] Recalling the sentiment among many soldiers, artillerist Edward Porter Alexander noted, "We looked forward to victory under him as confidently as to successive sunrises."[37] In an audacious move, Lee hoped to capitalize on this confidence and strike north into Maryland and Pennsylvania to instill fear among Northern populations, use Northern grain and livestock to feed his army, and relieve pressure on Vicksburg.[38]

The Northern invasion and anticipated battles elicited mixed reactions.[39] Circumspect veterans expressed misgivings, knowing well the dear cost of past fights. Charles A. Wills, for example, wrote his wife, Mary, "I think they ar going to try to take us to . . . Meroland I dont intend to go if I can help it and I think I can dont be oneasy about me I will wright to you if I think they ar about to get me there."[40] The grim mood was not lost on civilian observers, who knew Lee was playing for mighty stakes. William H. Thomson, writing to his son Ruffin, related that white Southerners looked on the advance into Maryland and Pennsylvania with "intense anxiety." The results of the contest, he continued, were of the "most important character to our cause & of the deepest interest to those of us whose sons are on that march."[41] Even the Marble Man himself seemed to be suffering. "Old age & sorrow is wearing me away & constant anxiety & labour day & night leaves me but little repose," Lee wrote while preparing for the spring campaigns.[42] But uneasiness mixed with enthusiasm as many soldiers eagerly awaited the chance to bring the war north again. Tally Simpson reported that, despite hard marching, the army was happy to be on invasion in the hopes of forcing peace. The men, he continued, seemed to be "in fine spirits" and had "the most implicit confidence in Genl Lee."[43]

Although soldiers knew vaguely that they were part of a Northern invasion, uncertainty clouded the vision of many, for ultimately the army's leadership directed the rank and file. As Virginia artilleryman William Beverley Pettit explained to his wife, Arabella, "It is said we will move further down this evening. I still think we are going into Pennsylvania. The question is involved, in doubt, and uncertain—to all except General Lee, and perhaps even to him."[44] Earlier that month, seasoned troops had sensed a movement. Randolph A. Shotwell of the Eighth Virginia Infantry explained, "During the fortnight past almost any old army veteran might have detected signs and symptoms on the horizon of camp life that betokened a stir of some sort, and by the entire army."[45] Yet the army's destination remained unknown.

It is tempting to suggest that soldiers' highly regimented lives might have dispelled their anxiety or confusion. Order and repetitious action governed their days.[46] Men were largely unable to decide on the direction or course of their actions because they were under the control of commanding officers and guided by strict daily schedules. Most immediately, this loss of independence created tensions between enlisted men and officers. Confederate soldiers were "most often . . . rural youth[s] who had every expectation of becoming . . . independent landholding farmer[s]" and therefore had trouble with discipline, notes historian Drew Gilpin Faust.[47] Soldiering meant succumbing to the demands of others, and duty bound whites to act. With that said, few were left paralyzed completely, and many men inevitably resisted this order. Some enlisted men struck out at officers who asserted too much authority, others engaged in acts of small-scale violence, and droves of men deserted the army entirely.[48] But focusing solely on acts of aggression misses the very real emotional suffering that many soldiers quietly endured. Although military formalities could be relaxed, especially during prolonged encampments, the unrelenting pace of the campaign into Pennsylvania allowed for no such latitude.

The long and demanding march through Virginia, Maryland, and Pennsylvania exhausted Lee's army. In mid-June Shotwell questioned whether the army was "dead or alive." He continued, "I am sure I hardly know which! If not dead we soon shall be, if there is not a change of some sort. Flesh and blood cannot sustain such heat and fatigue as we have undergone this day."[49] Torrence was also part of the invading force. By the late spring of 1863, the once youthful and enthusiastic Torrence had become a hardened veteran who had survived many of the Army of Northern Virginia's largest fights. Writing to his mother on June 17 near Williamsport, Maryland, he complained of "verry sore feet."[50] Despite physical discomfort, Torrence maintained a brief diary of the Northern invasion. Typical entries described the day's hard marches and the endless miles covered.[51] On the same day Torrence wrote to his mother, another member of the invading force, Lieutenant Joseph J. Hoyle of North Carolina, told his wife, Sarah, that they were "beginning to see hard times." But he was "very willing to endure them," for he and his fellow officers were "no better than the poor soldiers who ha[d] to endure such hardships."[52] Hoyle universalized the soldier's experience, expressing empathy for and understanding of the strains of hard marching. This "spirit of compassion," historian Peter S. Carmichael contends in his reading of the phrase "poor soldier" within the letters of a New York soldier, reflects how men both controlled and perceived their worlds "even during moments of horrible violence and rampant despair."[53] It was this empathy that connected Lee's "poor soldiers" on the long march north and reminded them of the powerful emotional bond forged by the hand of war.

Caught in the drudgery of the military routine, some Confederates were overcome by feelings of powerlessness. Hoyle asked his wife to pray fervently for peace and looked hopefully to the "happy time" when they could live together once more.[54] Thoughts of home likewise preoccupied Pettit on the march north. He told his wife, "My thoughts are on you and our dear ones. You are constantly thought of by day, and are the object of my sweetest dreams at night."[55] But these prospects were distant hopes and abstract longings, for neither could control the war's outcome or determine its end. Instead, the men simply marched onward. Toward the end of June near Chambersburg, Pennsylvania, Simpson related his frustration: "We are still on the march northward, and there is no telling where we will stop—nor am I able to say to what point we are destined."[56] Farther northeast, in Harrisburg, North Carolina soldier Private John Futch of the Third North Carolina Infantry told his wife that they had "bin 23 dayes on this March." The Federal army was now ahead of them, he thought, as the Confederate invaders probed enemy country.[57] For Simpson, Futch, and other members of Lee's army, now spread across a huge front in south central Pennsylvania, their long march to an unknown destination only heightened feelings of personal surrender and uncertainty. Rumors traveled up and down the ranks as to where they were heading and why, but ultimately the soldier's life was unpredictable.

Long marches, outdoor living, and inadequate food reshaped men's bodies and created a lean, sinewy silhouette. The soldier's physique outwardly demonstrated his service to the Confederate cause, and his physical bearing adhered to socially prescribed gender roles for men in war.[58] Confederates came to recognize how physical transformations and hard living changed them as men and connected them both to each other and to the Confederacy. A report from Confederate major general Robert E. Rodes reveals how Southern leadership perceived the foot soldier's difficulties. In describing a rapid movement from Culpeper, Virginia, to Williamsport, Maryland, Rodes stated, "Very many of these gallant fellows were still marching in ranks, with feet bruised, bleeding, and swollen, and withal so cheerfully as to entitle them to be called the heroes of the Pennsylvania campaign."[59] The soldiers' cheerful suffering may have reflected their acceptance of a broader Victorian ethos that asked for submission to cause, no matter the personal cost; or men exhibited sangfroid out of a need for survival.[60]

Military culture was intended to diminish soldiers' resignation while they performed arduous service. Although men complained about the long march north, the majority of Lee's command continued moving and maintained discipline. Yet, as historian Kathryn Shively Meier observes, veterans also practiced "self-care," such as by straggling in order to preserve their health and spirits. These acts of individualism defied the regimentation of military life that "compelled soldiers to complete the mundane and unpalatable duties necessary to maintaining an army."[61] Shotwell recalled in late June that the roads of Pennsylvania were "full of stragglers" as "hundreds of men" fell out of the ranks.[62] Veterans' decisions to fall out of the ranks for water or rest demonstrate how men could maintain a degree of autonomy even within the folds of the military.

A soldier's physical break from his home was perhaps never more deeply felt than when on campaign. In the case of the Gettysburg Campaign, Lee's men were out of their native homeland entirely and moving through enemy territory. Simpson, for instance, related that Pennsylvanians looked "grim and sullen and treat[ed] the southern soldiers very coldly."[63] Further, correspondence with families became harder. Hoyle warned his wife as they crossed into Maryland, "My letters will necessarily be irregular now."[64] In both a literal and symbolic sense, the farther Lee's army traveled into Pennsylvania, the deeper they became immersed in the soldier's world. Covered in dirt and grime, material conditions, however horrible, fused disparate bodies into a dirt-caked collective. John Dooley described a typical scene from the march north: "Terrible had been that march along the scorched and blazing plains of Virginia. . . . Choking, blinding were the clouds of dust that rose from beneath the army's unsteady tread; parching was that unquenchable thirst which dried the tongue to its very roots."[65] Consumed by filth, soldiers surrendered their personal comfort and cleanliness while on campaign. The material conditions produced by the Northern invasion were by no means unusual.[66] Veterans were well versed in deprivation. Earlier in the war, for example, Dick Simpson related in a letter to his sister, "Dirt is all the go, in fact we live in dirt."[67] Similarly, Hill Fitzpatrick told his wife, Amanda, "I am having my undershirt washed today for the first time in five weeks, only dabbled out in cold water and no soap once."[68] Both James A. Graham and William McLean used a familiar analogy in commenting on their filth, as both described themselves as being dirty as a hog.[69] Large swarms of men in close and constant proximity to one another bred disease and spread vermin. Soldiers' clothes during prolonged campaigns could be covered with lice, making life unbearable.[70] One soldier told his father that when not drilling, soldiers spent their time killing body lice.[71]

The accumulated effects of material deprivations and filth startled soldiers, especially when contemplating their eventual return to the civilian world, which demonstrates the difficult balance between soldier and citizen that Confederates had to maintain. Although Southerners often lightheartedly referenced their dilapidated appearance in letters home, their great distance from family and the comforts of domesticity engendered fears over the real and imagined alienation from civilian life. Southerners recognized both explicitly and unconsciously that women helped set the standard for what it meant to be a man.[72] Long periods of absence from the company of women concerned many of Lee's men. In the midst of his march through Pennsylvania, Tally Simpson kept up an extended correspondence with family, including an exchange with his aunt Caroline about his courting prospects with a young South Carolina woman. "If she be as pretty as you represent," he wrote, "I am sure to fall in love with her when I see her."[73] Simpson was grasping for something familiar, dreaming of a future life without war and personal suffering. But his South Carolina home must have seemed like worlds away. Two days before he penned his letter to his aunt, he wrote his sister complaining about the brutal conditions he endured while camped in the mountains. He and several men were on picket duty with "wet clothes and not a spark of fire."[74] Acting the invader in a foreign country and without a firm destination, Simpson wanted more than anything to be at home among family and toasting the health of his new romantic interest.[75] The contrast between civilian and army life also struck Shotwell while on the Gettysburg Campaign. He received a letter from home and wished he had not received it because of the "strange . . . contrast between the simple home affairs in the backwoods of North Carolina . . . and the stirring, exciting situation" in which it found him.[76] J. D. Joyner simply reminded his parents,

"Tomorrow, as you are aware, is my birth day. . . . I do hope to be able to spend my next at home, in peace + quiet."[77] While on the campaign, Simpson, Shotwell, and Joyner felt increased estrangement and detachment from the civilian world they so yearned to rejoin.

Similar to colonial Americans who feared that the wilderness would transform them into "savages," Confederates worried that they were so altered by military service as to become unrecognizable or, even worse, unwelcomed in civil society. Families provided soldiers a bulwark against the trials of war and the results of military service, and in their correspondence home, many men searched for consistency and familiarity. Soldiers drew comfort from domestic scenes around table and hearth, and hoped that their place would remain unfilled.[78] Men obliquely expressed their worst fears. Remarks about changed personal appearance marked one manifestation of inner worries. Fitzpatrick told his wife, "I doubt whether you would know me or not hardly if you were to see me now," while Tally Simpson wagered his sister that she would not recognize him at ten steps. "I am very ugly," he wrote, "my beard is shaggy, teeth black, clothes dirty and worn, finger nails long and black, nose little inclined to drip."[79] Ruffin Thomson, after being invited to a social event, declined the invitation, stating, "[I do not] care to mingle in that gay assembly of Beauty &c&c without I could do so with perfect care to myself, which is impossible in the present condition of my wardrobe—You see my little spell at 'soldiering' has not destroyed my old pride of personal appearance."[80] All three used hyperbole to describe their situations as absurd, but each expressed a concerning reality: soldiering had transformed them in fundamental ways that proved disconcerting. They worried about their acceptance in an outside world in which they once were welcomed.

The political and military implications of Gettysburg are clear, but the designs of leaders did not necessarily frame the ways in which soldiers perceived and ordered their daily existence.[81] Shotwell revealed this contrast, writing, "How few of those who read the newspaper accounts of army operations ever realize the cost of brilliant *manoeuvers* in flesh and muscle, pain, hunger, toil and wretchedness *to the men!*"[82] The increased urgency with which men greeted the Northern invasion was rooted as much in nationalistic goals as personal needs. Men such as Simpson and Hoyle went into the campaign hoping for a decisive victory to advance the Confederate cause and promote peace. These men also wanted their personal trials and sufferings to end. Plagued by uncertainty, exhausted by arduous marching, and fearful that the warrior had subsumed the civilian, many of Lee's army viewed the campaign through a lens filtered by fluctuating emotions and an unfocused worldview. Military life had joined them and created an unfamiliar environment to which many grew accustomed, but subtle doubts continued to surface, prompting some to question how much longer they could endure the army.

Battle Joined

Confederates struggled to convey the enormity of a fight, the scale of destruction, and the number of deaths. As historian Elisabeth Lauterbach Laskin notes, soldiers "believed themselves unable to provide an accurate depiction of what they had been through" when they tried to describe battles.[83] Southerners' writings are nevertheless revealing. Their values, beliefs, and perceptions shaped content and shaded events, thereby providing historians a treasure trove of materials on how men portrayed and remembered a fight.[84] Language often failed men because of their attempts to retain emotional control; thus, they experimented with the best ways to communicate their experiences. Two accounts of the Battle of Gettysburg will serve as a guide, supplemented by other sources, to demonstrate how Confederates struggled to record their perceptions and understandings of the transformative event. John Warwick Daniel, an educated and articulate Lynchburg, Virginia, native, proved himself a trenchant observer of the battlefield and offers the perspective of a Confederate officer. Daniel quickly rose through the ranks of the Confederate army, and by the time of Gettysburg he served as a major with Major General Jubal A. Early. Some time after the Confederates' defeat, Daniel wrote an extended but rather eccentric "account" of the action.[85] Daniel's vivid description relates the military actions he both witnessed and experienced but also conveys the competing landscapes that came with war. John Futch gives a view from the ground.[86] Having enlisted in the winter of 1862, the recently married Futch served with his brother, Charles, who was killed during the battle. Futch's letters home—written by different people with varying degrees of education, as reflected in grammatical mistakes and phonetic spelling—variously portray, interpret, and understand Charley's death, thus demonstrating how white Southerners quite distinctly and differently responded to death.

On July 1, Daniel, along with the other members of Early's division, marched from Heidlersburg to Gettysburg. On the approach to town, the men heard with greater clarity the distinct boom of artillery. Despite overcast skies with "murky clouds," nothing could "dampen the ardor of the troops who were," according to Daniel, "in the highest degree cheerful—even enthusiastic."[87] Lee's men had reason to shine after the first day's action concluded. By day's end, the Confederate forces had pressed the Union army's First and Eleventh Corps through Gettysburg and onto the heights beyond town. Excited troops declared the fight an overwhelming victory. Capturing the high spirits among the Confederate army, Daniel wrote, "While the fortunes of the enemy seemed so dark, ours were full of light. . . . They were enthused with success" and "they had the fullest confidence in their leaders."[88] Instead of pressing forward, though, the army halted, leaving the day's survivors to survey the carnage.

Daniel's use of the imagery of darkness and light conveys a tidy battle that resulted in victorious and vanquished parties. These representations hew closely to a Victorian view of an orderly universe.[89] Enthusiasm and depression rightfully denoted the respective feelings of Confederate and Union soldiers. But, importantly, Daniel wrote this piece in hindsight, knowing well that the Confederates' victory on the first day was chimerical. He subsequently blurs these clear emotional boundaries, reflecting broader ambiguities. While we cannot recapture an essential emotional experience, Daniel's expressions convey his representations of the battle, lending insight into how combat continued to undercut the core beliefs of an antebellum worldview.[90] Daniel, it will be recalled, had offered a speech to the students of Lynchburg College in 1859. In clear terms, he outlined men's duty to country and called for fond remembrance of the "illustrious dead." Although firmly committed to the Confederate cause, Daniel had now seen battle. His enthusiasm for martial valor had dimmed as he found himself, like so many Americans, "in a new and different moral universe, one in which unimaginable destruction had become daily experience."[91]

Scenes of death and dying triggered incomprehension, terror, and revulsion, thereby signaling the soldier's difficulties in processing his immediate reality. Although feelings ran high among the day's victors, Daniel carefully viewed the destruction, which elicited a range of observations and emotions. The conflicted feelings he recorded echoed the competing landscapes: "While the front in Gettysburg had been so illustrative of the joys, & animation of war, the rear has been equally exemplary of its woes." A hardened Daniel was well aware of the day's costs and sought an account by traveling the battlefield. He juxtaposed the Confederates' front lines, overwhelmed by "beaming faces, elastic steps, gay voices, stirring music, [and] waving banners," to the ghastly fields behind, which were replete with groaning bodies, figures heaped in the dirt, and the grotesque "all white eye turned back within its socket." Both compelled and repulsed, Daniel assumed the role of narrator and tour guide—"Let us look over the field"—taking his reader across the terrain. Viewing the killing fields, his party "came suddenly upon a long line of dead mingled with the dying, or the suffering survivors of their wounds." Union soldiers "were scattered in every direction—some on their faces, some on their backs—some with countenances arrested with agony, either with a smile still wreathing their lips as is in gentle sleep. The wounded writhing in pain, & imploring aid."[92]

Daniel attempted to assume the role of detached observer but was drawn to the destruction, though unsteady in his response. Abandoned guns, knapsacks, blankets, and other detritus littered the ground. Amid this chaos, he fixated on one scene. The "noble appearance" of a dead Union artillerist who had fallen by his gun struck him. The man lay just below the cannon's mouth, "his arms composed on his breast, & the rammer lying across his body." In moving terms, Daniel continued, "His countenance expressed no pain—but was serene & beautiful. No blood stained his clothes. The bullet had done its work, but had left but little trace. I could but sigh as I passed by, but it was no time for lamentation particularly for a foe, and I went on to mingle with the joyful & forget the dead."[93] The scene at the Union cannon affected Daniel, who carefully surveyed the body, acknowledged the man's bravery, and detailed his countenance but then attempted to casually dismiss the defeated foe in order to join the celebrations. Internally conflicted, he produced an ambivalent response. Daniel could not help but be moved. The dead gunner exemplified the type of battlefield heroics Victorian culture expected, for the man had gracefully died at his post. And the dead soldier even appeared to embody some of the prerequisites of the "Good Death" and showed no signs of traumatic wounds, only exhibiting a "serene & beautiful" expression.[94] Yet Daniel quickly recoiled from the sympathy elicited by the honorable death. He sighed and moved on, without giving time for the lamentation of a foe, in order to join the celebrations instead. By so doing, Daniel attempted to master his varied sympathy for and disgust at the dead in order to act the good soldier. His fluctuating responses demonstrated a convention for managing ambivalence.[95] He was ultimately unsure as to what he should feel and how he should convey it, which reflected, however subtly, the confusion rendered by war.

For John and Charley Futch, July 1 marked the conclusion of a "very long and tiresome march," according to a history of the Third North Carolina Infantry.[96] Deployed in line of battle by the evening, the regiment waited throughout most of July 2 until seeing action in the late afternoon and early evening on the slopes of Culp's Hill, just outside the town of Gettysburg. The men of the Third were under heavy artillery and musket fire before their assault. As they advanced across Rock Creek and toward the slopes of Culp's Hill, the fortunate took refuge behind trees and small rocks strewn across the landscape.[97] Charley and John were exposed, pinned down by unrelenting fire. Charley, lying prone, was in the process of loading when a bullet hit his head. Unable to speak, he seemed anxious to talk to his beloved brother.[98] John waited with Charley—whose condition worsened—throughout the evening of July 2 and into July 3.

The Third North Carolina's failed assault on Culp's Hill echoed down the line as Confederate troops came near to but never fully penetrated the Army of the Potomac's position throughout the afternoon and evening of July 2. The day's inconclusive results darkened Confederates' once bright spirits. Daniel could only reflect, "The night before we had been elated with joy. Not so now. The enemy were shouting on the hill above us—it was our turn to morn."[99] Daniel's descriptions reinforced his initial black-and-white portrait of the contest's results, albeit with an elevated purpose. By controlling his response and creating firm, understandable categories, Daniel directed his circumstances in a moment of defeat.[100] Though he was displeased with the results, the conflict could be understood, as witnessed in his representation of contrasting feelings among Confederate and Union soldiers. This measured response proved fleeting as the battle progressed.

The inconclusive results of July 1 and 2 forced Lee's hand and resulted in George Pickett's famous charge. John Dooley—part of General Pickett's division, which would not see action until the third day—described a "solemn feeling" that pervaded the ranks as men of the First Virginia approached Gettysburg, entering "the very jaws of destruction and death."[101] Although his observations were rooted in his reaction to Confederates' military failures, for Dooley wrote after the fact, he goes on to describe his general anxiety when battle approached. "For myself," Dooley thoughtfully wrote, "I must confess that the terrors of the battlefield grew not less as we advanced in the war. . . . For, in every battle they see so many new forms of death, see so many frightful and novel kinds of mutilation, see such varying fortunes in the tide of strife, and appreciate so highly their deliverance from destruction" that the dread seemed unending.[102] Each death and every mutilated man represented a new horror for Dooley. His mental orientation toward the conflict's meaning was deeply personal, rooted as much in emotional responses as in ideology and nationalism.[103] Furthermore, Dooley's repulsion is echoed, if subtly, in Daniel's ambivalence. Even by mid-1863, most Confederates "had not lost their sense of revulsion over the violence of war."[104]

The sight of Federal forces, the artillery's relentless fire, and the volleys of hot lead had severely tested men's mettle at Gettysburg. Shot and shell eviscerated regiments, creating gaping holes where men once stood. Before Pickett's Charge, Confederates endured intense shelling. Joseph Hoyle was part of the attacking force that, after the cannonading tapered off, rose up with thousands of other raggedly clad men looking to their front over the open fields through which they would advance. "We moved forward, exposed to a hot fire of grape shot and shells, yet we moved on. When we came in range of their small arms their fire became destructive in the extreme."[105] Down the line, men of the First Virginia started falling, creating holes in the line. "Close up!" shouted the regiment's officers. "Close up the ranks when a friend falls, while his life blood bespatters your cheek or throws a film over your eyes," Dooley explained in gruesome, painful detail.[106] Dooley gave faces to the otherwise abstract casualties, making sure his reader knew these men were messmates, husbands, and brothers. The lines surged forward until the most advanced elements were "within about 100 yards of their line," when the regiment's ranks "were so thinned that [they] could proceed no further." "So," as Hoyle explained, "our line broke in confusion and every man got out the best he could."[107] Confederates' supreme faith in victory was shattered. Rendered wordless by the contest, Dooley recorded, "I will not attempt to describe."[108] Once again, battle had made the Southern soldier speechless.

As the United States celebrated its independence on the Fourth of July, rains fell on Gettysburg. Daniel described the day as miserable, "and was passed with no manner of comfort. The soldiers huddled around bivouac fires seeking some protection from the rain, and preparing their scanty food. Some slept on the wet ground with the water trikling over their faces." The stormy weather echoed Confederates' moods. Reflecting on the battle, Daniel wrote, "Never is ever in the history of the army of No. Va, had the troops drunk so deeply of the gall and worm wood of disappointment." He gloomed, "From the height of enjoyment, and anticipation they had suddenly been plunged into the depths of pain, & disappointment. The castles upon which they had feasted their eyes, has suddenly proved an illusion, and had vanished like a dream." Utterly devastated by the battle's results, Daniel tended toward nihilism, unable to comprehend the battle's meaning and fearful of the war's continuation. "Every ingredient that could add to the poignancy of their grief was mingled in the cup—the hopes of their friends at home which had been so highly elated were denied gratification, and all the hard marching they had performed, all the hardships they had Endured, all the battles they had fought, were to be done over again." What meaning could Daniel extract from Gettysburg? How could he make sense of the destruction? Daniel created a bleak landscape populated by a vanquished army. Their elation of July 1 had turned into extreme dejection by July 4. In reaching for words such as "grief," "pain," and "disappointment," Daniel had cast the battle's results in familiar terms grounded in Victorian culture. He pushed the issue further, though, making note of the hard marching and difficult fighting that were performed without, he is horrified to note, purpose. And worse, they must be repeated. Here Daniel's orientation appears to become unmoored, as his words reflect a palpable sense of uncertainty about the future and demonstrate an overt ontological shift prompted by conflict and defeat.

Whereas the Battle of Gettysburg had devastated Daniel, other Confederates remained confident in the aftermath. Writing to his mother in early August, Joseph D. Joyner looked to the lessons of history for inspiration and perspective: "From what I can learn a great many people are disposed to be somewhat despondent on account of late reverses, which I think is without any foundation, if they will only but read the history of the revolution, where the British had possession of the National Capital and all other cities of importance, and how Washingtons little army . . . suffered, and at last came out victorious." He concluded, "As for my part I am just as sanguine of success as I ever was, and am willing to continue this struggle to the bitter end or achieve our independence."[109] William Beverley Pettit scolded his wife for being "too severe on General Lee and President Davis" after Gettysburg, for "they are without their peers."[110] Joyner, Pettit, and other Confederates remained confident in Lee and left Pennsylvania with their faith in the cause relatively unshaken. Gettysburg "was merely a setback on the road to independence," writes Joseph T. Glatthaar, "nothing more."[111]

Although many Confederates remained steady in their assessment of military matters after battle, the deaths of friends and family proved affecting. Charles Futch died on July 3 from a wound sustained during the fight on Culp's Hill the previous day. John Futch wrote six missives about his brother's death that deserve sustained attention not only because of the content but also because of the hands by which they were written. John, either semiliterate or illiterate, employed different men—presumably from his regimental company—to either entirely write or help him compose letters to his wife.[112] Each letter, therefore, demonstrates the thoughts, perceptions, and biases of not one but at least two individuals. And, even more revealing, Charley's death is portrayed differently in the respective letters.

The first letter, sent from Martinsburg, West Virginia, on July 12, contains a few grammatical errors and occasionally employs phonetic spelling but generally reflects someone familiar with the English language and aware of mid-nineteenth-century writing decorum. After offering a brief explanation of the fight, the writer related, "My brother was mortaly wounded and died the 3rd about 2 oclock PM." The letter continues, "He was wounded in the head by a minney ball he suffered grately before dying but since he is Ded I beleav he is happy and no doubt far better off then eny of us."[113] Charley's death is described, transporting family members to the battlefield. Further, the writer followed form by carefully noting, "He is happy and no doubt far better off then eny of us." By looking to the afterlife and embracing Charley's death, the missive reflects a Victorian ethos that accepted a "robust vision of a glorious life beyond death."[114] John's letter ultimately served as a notification and documentation of Charley's death and aligned with Victorian principles.

In the subsequent days and weeks, more letters were sent home. The repetition of news reflected John's awareness of haphazard mail service, as well as the great importance of personally notifying his family of Charley's death. In letters from July 19 and 31, John first disclosed how deeply the loss had affected him. Although the letters are by different hands, both open formulaically, demonstrating an awareness of writing procedures. The writer of the first letter leaned heavily on phonetic spelling, while the one from July 31 has few spelling errors. Significantly, though, both had troubling disclosures. Charley's death was detailed but the afterlife no longer mentioned. The July 19 letter related, "I dont want nothing to eat hardly for I am all most sick all the time and half crazy I never wantid to come home so bad in my life but it is so that I cant come at this time but if we came down south I will try to come eny how."[115] In a similar, if more refined, vein, the letter from July 31 contended, "I want to be there [his home] so Bad I can taste it. . . . I am at very great loss since the Death of charley I am so lonesome I do not know what to do."[116] Vague talk of desertion and deep personal anguish replaced the metaphysics of death, as the sights of the battlefield and the war's catastrophic scale had shaken John to his core. Less concerned with social protocol, these letters approach an unvarnished reflection of John's deteriorating psychological health. Significantly, John disclosed these feelings not only to his wife, Martha, but also to the letter writer—likely a messmate or member of his company. Strong personal relationships developed among soldiers, as explored in the previous chapter, fostered by the intimacy of military encampments and the trauma of combat.[117]

Of the letters, two missives from August 2 and 20 demonstrate some striking similarities, thereby fully revealing John's deep emotional pain. The literary production was sparing; the hand appears nearly identical, as seen in word construction and penmanship; the same phonetic spelling is used; the content is not controlled but instead intimate and conversational. He could only relate to Martha, "I havent sean no plesher sence charley got kild . . . I am all Most crasey."[118] John's concerns drifted away from the Confederate cause as he looked instead to home with increased anxiety. Deeply distressed, psychologically pained, and physically exhausted, he could only find succor and comfort in Martha.[119] He worried about losing his perspective, perhaps even his sanity. By way of conclusion, John recounted Charley's burial and the confusion rendered by war: "I codent get a cofen to bearey him but I dreased him the best I cod it was somthing that I never expected to haft to do but we dont know waot we will do tel he gets in the [situation]."[120]

Futch's revelations are remarkable, for he had been raised in an antebellum culture that demanded the maintenance of both public face and personal self-control. As Confederate soldiers, men such as Futch embraced a masculine courage that was "equated with fearlessness; acknowledging fear to one's self or another amounted to cowardice."[121] The solid veneer, though, had a soft interior. As historian Stephen W. Berry has shown, antebellum men's hearts were opened to women only.[122] If we follow Berry's argument, the August 2 and 20 missives are the most intimate, authentic items of the letter collection because only to Martha could he fully reveal himself. The other letters are more guarded and offer fewer personal disclosures. In the early and late August letters, John admits that he has not seen any pleasure since Charley's death, longs for his wife, talks of desertion, and feels "all Most crasey." It is both a personal expression and a desperate plea from someone undone by the war's random killing.

The Civil War changed its participants' emotional dispositions and expressions in entirely unexpected ways, joining soldiers in a "community of suffering," which "remapped the cultural and intellectual contours of the region."[123] Charting this new terrain was neither quick nor easy; thus, soldiers' varied responses to death and combat created tensions between social prescriptions and the tortured reactions to the grim reality of seeing death in its most grotesque forms. Interpreting death through social conventions remained important for many white Southerners, and despite John's profound sadness and mental anguish, clearly documented in the aforementioned letters, a missive from August 6 directly embraced a Victorian understanding of Charley's death. The hand is clear, the spelling nearly flawless, and the content controlled. The letter relates a careful narrative of events: "[After charging] the enemies entrenchments on the heights near Gettysburg PA on the night of July the 2d, he was wounded on or near the top of his head—it did not pass through the brain—but I think it must have bruised them—as he did not speak after he was hit." The nature of the wound was vital to the writer's narrative, for Charley could not utter the last words so essential to the Good Death.[124] Unable to provide this comfort, the writer instead turned to the ultimate solace, life everlasting and personal salvation through faith. The writer continued, "Only God Knows the bitter anguish this sad bereavement sent thrilling through my sad heart—It seems hard to part forever from those our heart treasures—But the Lord's will be done—Let us put our trust in Him He alone can comfort the grief stricken soul, and bind up the broken heart."[125]

The "fallen had solved the riddle of death," historian Drew Gilpin Faust writes, "leaving to survivors the work of understanding and explaining what this great change had meant."[126] The work of understanding and explaining is borne out in the contrasting letters about Charley's death. The August 6 missive fully accepted, or at least publicly affirmed, an orthodox view of death and suffering. Religious faith and language frame death, dying, and bereavement. Moreover, the writer embraced a divinely ordered universe in which providence ultimately controlled destiny and determined how and when the war concluded. The individual is largely rendered powerless when religion provides personal solace.[127] Yet such certainty is entirely lacking in the August 2 letter, which, of course, appeared before the letter of August 6. This not only reflects the obvious difference in writers but also suggests the transitional nature of emotional communication and disclosure being enacted by war.

Filtered language conveyed the deeply unsettling death of a loved one, as reflected in the August 6 missive. Stunned by Charley's death, John could only manage expression by looking to an emotional center—the heart—to convey bitter anguish. His "sad heart" fits squarely into the lexicon with which nineteenth-century Americans were familiar. Doctors diagnosed Civil War veterans "with 'Soldier's Heart' for the postwar anxiety and associated heart palpitations many soldiers experienced."[128] Despite this revelation, formalized rules still controlled the letter's content. Importantly, though, those letters divorced from epistolary etiquette have unfiltered sentiments. John looked not to his heart to explain his suffering but instead to his mind: "I am all Most crasey."[129] The divinely ordered universe—so clearly conveyed in the letter of August 6—collapsed as John struggled to maintain his sanity and control his deep anguish. Letters such as this one (and those from late July) capture emotional expression rooted not in Victorian sensibilities but instead in profound personal loss. Combat and death had annihilated antebellum self-assuredness, pushing some, such as John Futch, into metaphysical bewilderment.[130] Stretched to their capacity of understanding, soldiers responded with confusion but also tried to assert control over the uncontrollable. For Futch this meant desertion, which led to his execution in early September.[131] John Warwick Daniel, on the other hand, continued to serve under Early and played an invaluable role as an officer and a leader. He suffered a devastating leg injury at the Battle of the Wilderness that necessitated the use of a crutch for the remainder of his life. Nonetheless, Daniel went on to have a distinguished political career in postwar Virginia.

Aftermath and Accounting

For many men, such as Futch, attempts to convey the battle's enormity and its personal consequences fell flat as they grasped for words to describe the incomprehensible. Emotions once again served as a means for communication, even if the feelings themselves could not always be described. In his letter home, for example, Virginian John Cocke noted that a Major Carter had been "very low spirited since the last fight, his son (a capt in the 8th Va Reg) was wounded & left on the field, and he can hear nothing from him."[132] For the men who composed regimental companies, formed messes together, and came to rely on one another, postaction reports were deeply troubling. The absent soldier and missing face altered men, throwing them into emotional turmoil. "You cannot imagine my feelings," wrote C. W. Avery to the father of Johnny Caldwell when his friend did not return with the regiment, having been killed on the fields of Pennsylvania.[133] Some men tried to order the battle through an accounting of the dead and wounded. In a letter written to his parents, John Cocke related "how much [their] Division suffered in the fight [at Gettysburg]" and the "death of the different persons" known to the family.[134] Similarly, Joseph Hoyle methodically maintained for his wife a list of those killed, wounded, and missing in his company.[135] These records exposed the physical cost of combat and began to penetrate the human face of war. But these letters could hardly communicate the prolonged suffering these men now endured and would continue to endure.

Soldiers' letters to friends and families recounted loved ones' last moments and conveyed the emotional weight of the recent death. W. J. O'Daniel tenderly wrote to the mother of Leonidas Torrence (quoted earlier for his extended account of the march north), who had been killed at Gettysburg. On July 1 a ball had entered his head and another hit his thigh. He came to his senses, but his health faded quickly until he finally succumbed to his wounds. "When I went to tell him goodby he told me that I would never se him again. He said he was a going to die. He also said that he was willing to die. When he was shot he was lying in a hollow in a verry mudey place. All that ware badly wounded and killed was shot in this same hollow." The two men had gone into the fight together and "promised each other if one go hurt to doo all [they] could for him." O'Daniel painfully concluded, "You do not have any idea how bad that I hated to leav Lon."[136] These two men, tested by continued combat, looked to each other for support. Torrence retained his faith and willfully died the warrior, but far from home in a "verry mudey place." And after his death, O'Daniel could only convey his pain.

In the numbers of dead and wounded, Southern men were forced, however unconsciously, to confront the impact of their national project and to see the results of their decision to secede. Here men surely began to doubt themselves and question the certainty with which they had lived for so long. Gerald F. Linderman has argued that, as time wore on, men reacted by becoming immune to the dying, hardened in their senses. Such distancing, cynicism, and disillusionment allowed soldiers to cope with the war's incomprehensible face and, for some, to continue fighting when quitting seemed justifiable; yet it is easy to exaggerate these sentiments.[137] A hardened veteran often remained a feeling man, and individuals' reactions varied. Moreover, it is important not to underestimate the eventual emotional toll of combat. Eric T. Dean reminds us, "The bluster and apparent ruggedness of the veteran should not always be taken at face value, however; when one carefully examines accounts of men professing to be unconcerned about the dangers and terrors of war, one often discovers that these stoic declarations of indifference hid a deeper fear and horror, held at bay for the time being, but lurking within nonetheless."[138]

Southerners ultimately conveyed an array of feelings after the Pennsylvania Campaign, which reveal contradictory reactions to the culminating fight. Soldiers celebrated personal survival or searched for greater purpose, which gave rise to select memories of the fighting.[139] Accordingly, the assessments of historians have varied. Gary W. Gallagher contends, "A canvass of Confederate sentiment in the summer of 1863 suggests that many southerners did not view the battle of Gettysburg as a catastrophic defeat." Continuing, he writes, "R. E. Lee's soldiers typically saw it as a temporary setback with few long-term consequences for their army."[140] Conversely, Elisabeth Lauterbach Laskin charges, "While a few perpetually optimistic, or perhaps just misinformed, souls referred to Gettysburg as a great victory, many ANV [Army of Northern Virginia] soldiers recognized the severity of the blow their army received in Pennsylvania that summer. Despondency over the loss was compounded by the hard retreat back through Maryland and into Virginia."[141] A solution to these seemingly intractable contradictions is found by distinguishing men's commitment to the cause from their comprehension of battle. Scores of Confederates continued to affirm their allegiance to the Confederacy and maintained faith in Lee's execution of the war, thereby indicating that their morale, however shaken, remained unbroken. Once in Virginia, removed from the campaign's rigors, men recovered and readied themselves for the next offensive. Although still committed to the Confederacy, Southern men had difficulty in conveying the experience of battle and processing the scale of carnage. Soldiers could only respond with an ambiguity that demonstrated both their awareness of the higher cause and also sorrow over the loss of life. As Hoyle wrote to his wife, "We also damaged the yankees a great deal, but I cannot say who was hurt the worst."[142]

CHAPTER FOUR

Demobilization

For many Americans, then and now, the surrender at Appomattox Court House marked the end of the Civil War.[1] On the carpeted floors of Wilmer McLean's refined parlor, separately seated and accompanied by staff, Union general Ulysses S. Grant met with and accepted the surrender of Confederate general Robert E. Lee on April 9, 1865. A stream of popular prints and paintings immortalized the moment. "The Appomattox prints," writes one group of scholars, "intentionally or not, helped elevate Lee to a status not shared by any other figure of the Confederacy—that of a living symbol of reconciliation."[2] The work of war had ended and the process of reconciliation had begun. An emergent narrative, bolstered by men from both sides, emphasized how Lee's surrender and Grant's actions helped initiate a spirit of brotherhood that facilitated Reconstruction. Confederate artillerist Edward Porter Alexander nostalgically maintained in his postwar memoir, for example, that Grant had promoted a "spirit of kindness" with his surrender terms.[3] The victorious Union general did nothing to diminish the image. In his *Memoirs*, Grant recalled how he had ordered Federal soldiers to halt the celebrations upon news of the surrender. He and his men, Grant wrote, should not exult over the Confederates' downfall.[4]

The American Civil War did not conclude on April 9, 1865. Indeed, as historian Gregory P. Downs argues, "surrender marked a turning point, not an end point, for the state of war."[5] President Andrew Johnson did not officially declare the war's end until August 20, 1866, and war powers were exercised in the South until 1871.[6] Rather than an ending, Appomattox marked the beginning of the Confederacy's collapse and initiated the long process of military demobilization. Extending narratives past April 1865 demonstrates a range of postwar political, social, and military challenges that might otherwise be missed and illuminates how Confederate soldiers became civilians.[7] With the successive wave of surrenders—most prominently, Joseph E. Johnston's Army of Tennessee, after prolonged negotiations, surrendered on April 26; the Department of the Trans-Mississippi entered a "military convention" on May 26; and Confederate brigadier Stand Watie surrendered in the Indian Territory on June 23—tens of thousands of veterans were released from the army feeling both loss and liberation.[8] Paroled

Confederates flooded into Southern population centers and by so doing taxed resources, sparked conflict, and fomented disorder. Military demobilization proved a catalytic event.

Nineteenth-century Americans evoked the Greek and Roman citizen-soldier as an ideal to be followed. American military officers as far back as George Washington had exhorted their men to maintain a balance between the citizen and the soldier.[9] Confederate leadership faced this timeless problem in the spring and summer of 1865 as they confronted two particularly difficult questions: On what terms would the Civil War end, and how would their veterans become citizens? Southerners considered the possibilities of continued fighting, military surrender, or guerrilla warfare, realizing that each option carried long-term social and political consequences. After Lee and Johnston chose surrender, they urged their men to embrace moderation. Lee called for his troops to return home with the "satisfaction that proceeds from the consciousness of duty faithfully performed," while Johnston asked his men to follow the "obligations of good and peaceful citizens" as commendably as they had "performed the duties of thorough soldiers in the field."[10] Veterans from the Armies of Northern Virginia and Tennessee could return home assured that they had faithfully performed their duty and maintained their honor.[11]

Other Confederates could not so easily separate the soldier from the citizen because the sacrifices of war and the outpouring of blood were impossible to forget. Southern veterans who feared Northern retribution or were unable to give up the dream of independence forsook the tranquility of the hearth and remained in the field past official surrender. Confederate general Edmund Kirby-Smith, commander of the Trans-Mississippi Department, charged, "A conciliatory policy, dictated by wisdom and administered with patient moderation will ensure peace and restore quiet." Yet he feared an "opposite course [would] rekindle the flames of civil war with a fierceness and intensity unknown even in this sad and unfortunate struggle."[12] Kirby-Smith decided to flee the United States because his "honor" would not be sacrificed for the purchase of "a certain degree of immunity."[13] Different conceptions of an honorable peace directed on what terms Confederate high command ended their wars.

Journeys Home and Abroad

The Confederacy's collapse set in motion soldiers, politicians, and freed slaves who, as historian Yael A. Sternhell writes, "crowded the pathways of the war-torn region, their movements eroding the social and political order of the land."[14] On these roadways Confederate soldiers made critical decisions about whether they would return home peacefully, continue fighting in other theaters, or leave the South entirely. In the spring and summer of 1865, Confederates were on middle ground, "neither soldiers nor citizens," in the words of one veteran.[15] The rapid movements, scarce supplies, and unreliable mail service at the Civil War's end created a gap in the historical record, as few Confederates had the means or ability to write about their experiences.[16] Despite the paucity of evidence, several accounts from this period remain that shed light not only on veterans' journeys home after they mustered out of military service but also on the travels of members of the Confederate high command who fled the country, fearing legal prosecution.

Although military surrender marked a formal capitulation of arms, the war continued to shape its participants. White Southerners' emotional reactions to military news in the spring of 1865 reflect the Civil War's difficult close. Shifting between deep depression and nearly maniacal joy, Confederates confronted disheartening news of military setbacks and hopeful rumors of foreign intervention, unwilling to believe the war was at an end.[17] One Confederate observed from Danville, Virginia, for instance, that the city was "in a perfect fever of excitement and the highest officials [were] clutching eagerly at the . . . most improbable rumors."[18] In the last days of Lee's army, Sergeant J. E. Whitehorne of the Twelfth Virginia Infantry noted that "rumors [were] everywhere" as Confederates desperately sought news about military affairs.[19] But even the wildest dreams could not stop the pressing realities of defeat, which evoked emotional outpourings. Northern journalist Whitelaw Reid observed veterans' shifting expressions at the war's end: "The first feelings were those of baffled rage. Men who had fought four years for an idea, smarted with actual anguish under the stroke which showed their utter failure. Then followed a sense of bewilderment and helplessness."[20] Reid's words capture the unfamiliar ground veterans traveled as they transitioned back into civilian life.

Demobilization had an emotional dimension not easily contained as men balanced the sadness of defeat with the excitement of returning home. For some, surrender compared to physical pain because defeat at first could not be understood, only felt. Overwhelmed, Confederates struggled for words. One week after Appomattox, Whitehorne described the memory of Lee's surrender as stinging "like an open wound."[21] Farther south, near Greensboro, North Carolina, Confederate officer Joseph Frederick Waring could only relate after Johnston's capitulation that his "heart was too sad to enjoy anything."²² Whitehorne and Waring give voice to those Confederates who felt disbelief and humiliation after the painful experience of defeat. Yet veterans also expressed relief at having served the Confederacy and pride at having endured until the end while others had shirked.²³ William Alexander Hoke, stranded in Texas after the war and yearning for his North Carolina home, conveyed soldiers' contradictory sentiments. Writing to his mother after a lapse in correspondence, he related, "I could not write . . . in fact could not for some time open my mouth to any one [as I] felt so badly about our national affairs[.] The result of the hard contest left such a heavy weight upon my heart." But, he continued, "I'm just as anxious now to work and work hard and *profitably* as I was two months ago to continue this unprofitable war."²⁴ Musician Julius A. Lineback of the Twenty-Sixth North Carolina Regiment, captured on April 5, 1865, realized that "each step" he and his comrades "were forced to take was away from home, and all that [they] held most dear." After his arrival at home in July, Lineback expressed the great emotions he and his mother felt upon their reunion. His mother "had been longing and praying that she might once more see her long absent boy; her Lord had graciously heard and answered her prayer."²⁵ Although saddened by defeat, concerns over work and family framed demobilization for soldiers such as Hoke and Lineback.

Military surrender elicited a range of reactions as men tried to comprehend that their four-year contest had ended and that they could once again enjoy the comfort of home and the embrace of family. According to Atlanta's *Intelligencer*, many of the veterans from the Army of Northern Virginia who had passed through the city in early May walked with "buoyant steps and exulting smiles at the thought of soon again meeting with 'loved ones at home,' from whom they had been separated for years." So, too, did many men express "anxiety and despondency."²⁶ Just as Confederate soldiers had had difficulty in articulating the experience of battle, so too did they struggle to comprehend reentry into the civilian world. Many had been soldiers since 1861 or 1862 and could not comprehend a world without war. Indeed, as Whitehorne wrote, "Lord! The war has been going on so long I can't realize what a man would do now it's over. All I know is to drill, and march, and fight."²⁷ Poised at the edge of war and peace, Confederate veterans performed actions and expressed emotions that shaped on what terms the Civil War closed while also carrying within themselves the remnants of war.

Hordes of men, footsore and threadbare, choked the dirt roads leading from Appomattox Court House shortly after Lee's surrender on April 9.²⁸ Even if their hearts were not quelled, thousands were content to go home.²⁹

Desirous of reunion or pressed by the necessity of want, the majority of Confederates peacefully returned home, started working, and attempted to restore order. Richard W. Waldrop of the Twenty-First Virginia Regiment maintained that the further "effusion of blood would have been useless," and therefore embraced surrender. Starting out on April 12, he had arrived home by April 18 and was "doing nothing."[30] Whitehorne similarly started home immediately after surrender. His party soon encountered a woman who offered the men bread and water. "She made me feel," Whitehorne wrote, "that the world had not really come to an end," although "I know tonight that Appomattox . . . will always mean the same thing to me."[31] As Whitehorne was a resident of Greensville County, Virginia, his journey was quick. Exhausted by war and wanting to lessen the pain of surrender, he took solace in his family and looked forward to putting in a crop. Still, war had changed him in subtle ways. The familiar domestic sphere now melded into his former military life. In his diary's final entries for April 1865, he longingly wished that Lee had ordered his brigade "to burst through the invaders back in Appomattox." Clearly, Whitehorne's inner war had not ended, and he noted hopefully that many of the local "boys" wanted to start a "Confederate Veterans Organization."[32]

Whitehorne's thoughts about the war, his conflicted feelings about surrender, and his desire to start a veterans' group suggest the Virginian's transitional status at the war's close. At home, he would presumably attempt to reassert control of his household as the male head, though one fundamentally altered by the war's destruction of slavery.[33] But his personal requirements had changed. As Whitehorne settled into old patterns of domestic life, he also looked to his wartime comrades as his postwar friends, with eyes filtered by the fallen Confederacy. Most prominently, then, family and fellow veterans would now partially underpin former soldiers' emotional support.

The experiences of Second Lieutenant Kena King Chapman echo those of Whitehorne and Waldrop. After Appomattox, he and a small group of men quickly started out for home. The party first arrived in Richmond, Virginia, in the late morning hours of April 18, 1865. They were exhausted, their uniforms soiled and frayed by rain, mud, and hard marching. Having traveled over a hundred miles of dirt roads and countryside in one week's time, the men were "foot sore and almost broken down."[34] An emotional collapse subsumed the men's physical exhaustion as they gazed over the blackened cityscape. By April 20, Chapman and his men had exchanged the darkened streets of Richmond for the blue waters of the James River. The steamer

Red Jacket plodded down the meandering river toward Smithfield, Virginia. The journey must have been hard, a painful close to a difficult war. While resigned, Chapman was not defeated. With an almost naive optimism, he recorded, "It galls me to think of it but I must submit *for the present* hoping always that the tide will again turn in our favor."[35] Three days later Chapman was home, physically at least. Mentally, he was still fighting the war and "marching with [his] old brigade."[36]

Whereas moderation marked the actions of thousands of veterans such as Chapman, Whitehorne, and Waldrop, other Confederates confronted the prospects of defeat with defiant stands. In late May 1865, Confederate general Kirby-Smith angrily stood by as the surviving remnants of his trans-Mississippi army were formally surrendered.[37] The cause, he realized, was all but lost. Earlier that month, Kirby-Smith had asked one of Shreveport, Louisiana's leading private citizens, Robert Rose, to convey his regards to the emperor of Mexico and to make certain that the emperor understood that the services of Confederate troops "would be of inestimable value to him."[38] Whatever preparations were made for this plan collapsed in mid- to late May as the armies of the trans-Mississippi evaporated and Kirby-Smith became a commanding general in name only. Unable to secure "terms honorable alike to . . . soldiers & citizens," Kirby-Smith did not participate in the formal surrender and pledged instead to "struggle to the last." He admonished his men's actions in a public proclamation: "Soldiers! I am left a command without an army—a General without troops. You have made yr. choice. It was unwise & unpatriotic. But it is final. I pray you may not live" to regret it.[39] The speech's strident tone suggested a man in total control of his own destiny and determined in his resolve. By late June, Kirby-Smith had traveled through Texas and crossed into Mexico.

On June 26, 1865, the beleaguered band of Confederate soldiers buried their frayed battle flags under the sands of the Río Grande's north bank, forded the river's warm, murky waters, and then crossed into Mexico. Kirby-Smith led the party. The once dashing leader was now in shirtsleeves with a silk handkerchief around his neck, a revolver at his side, and a shotgun across his lap. Traveling by mule, he fled the South, having left behind everything except, he later explained to his wife, "a clear conscience and a sense of having done [his] duty."[40] Though he was assured of his personal honor, Kirby-Smith's future remained unclear. But even the "darkness and uncertainty" that awaited him could not "entirely check the feeling of lightness and joy experienced" when he felt himself to be "plain Kirby-Smith," relieved from all cares and accountable only for his own actions.[41] Unburdened by the responsibilities of command, he seized his newly gained freedom as essential in his quest to close his civil war—ephemeral feelings he would realize only later.

Once in Mexico, Kirby-Smith cast his fortunes elsewhere and traveled to Cuba, compelled by prudence and duty to escape the "excited feelings" of the Northern people and the federal government.[42] In truth, his bold public posture betrayed a deeper reality of personal conflict that formed his inner experiences and outer persona.[43] His otherwise strong facade quickly dissolved as he penned loving words to his wife, sentiments deeply burdened by his troubles. Once settled in Cuba in the late summer of 1865, he anxiously related to his wife, Cassie, "I do not know rightly how to determine upon my future course, whether I shall adopt a new country, see a new home . . . or return to my own people, share their fate and recommence the battle of life amongst those we have long known and loved and who will sympathize with and cheer us in our trials and difficulties."[44] Conflicted, he continued his public stand against the federal government, though in his private correspondence this decision weighed heavily. Kirby-Smith wanted to both return to his wife and maintain his public honor. His place as a prominent Confederate veteran demanded resolve and defiance, but his role as a husband required love and a commitment to home.

Throughout the late summer of 1865, Edmund and Cassie exchanged letters that attempted to resolve the tangled web of his exile: a resolution that could bring them together while maintaining honor. "I cannot nor, *will not*, live much longer," Cassie pleaded while separated from him, and she pledged to do "anything *in honor*" to have him with her.[45] Edmund preferred to return to the United States if it could be done "without degradation and humiliation." He refused to sacrifice his personal respect or his monetary interests and did not want to lose face. To Cassie, though, he also admitted defeat: "The war is over & our cause irretrievably lost." He questioned his earlier actions as perhaps unwise but refused to ever acknowledge his course as wrong.[46]

Kirby-Smith's words both reveal and obscure. Self-doubt and internal turmoil wend through his letters, but a strong external demeanor and a determined course of action counterbalanced those sentiments. By late summer the couple determined a strategy. Cassie would petition President Johnson, in person, for her husband's return, while Edmund would write Grant, his friend from the Mexican-American War, about his status.[47] Once assured that he could return to the United States without penalty or imprisonment, Kirby-Smith set sail.[48] Now, steeled by his family and assured of his honor, Kirby-Smith cast his lot with the Southern people within the borders of his native land. He wrote, "Our people should not leave, instead of seeking asylums abroad, their own destines and the triumph of the principles for which they fought are in their own hands, let them seek by every possible means the reestablishment of the state government in the natural course of events the military must then give way to the civil rule."[49] Kirby-Smith thus resurrected his earlier stand against the federal government, perhaps more vested in the South after his experiences abroad and more assured of his manliness by rejoining his family.

Scores of soldiers from the Confederacy's eastern and western armies eventually joined Mexico's fight for independence from French control, while others established the short-lived Confederate colony of Carlota.[50] Even those Southerners who had traveled beyond the South's borders, however, never let home drift far from their minds but instead incorporated these experiences into their Southern self-identification.[51] Thomas Caute Reynolds, Missouri's former governor, wrote to diehard Confederate general and Virginian Jubal A. Early that he still considered himself "a citizen and resident of Missouri" while in Mexico. He hoped to return there one day and wished "success to all efforts to restore the South to equality and *power*." But he would stay abroad, where the president and his armies were "powerless to hurt a hair" on his head.[52] Perhaps unknown to Reynolds and other exiles, the presence of Confederate troops on the Texas border and Mexico's volatile government was enough for Grant to dispatch Philip Sheridan and an entire army corps to the Rio Grande to patrol the border. Sheridan's command eventually numbered fifty-two thousand men.[53] Defiant under defeat but still desperately yearning for home while exiled, these Southerners maintained a position precariously balanced between two lands.

Between the years 1865 and 1867 especially, Mexico, the Caribbean, Canada, and Central and South America appealed to diehard rebels as last refuges from Northern rule. Ultimately, some eight to ten thousand Southerners fled the United States rather than face defeat and emancipation, though exponentially more dreamed of leaving.[54] Many historians have rightly portrayed the exodus of white Southerners in the immediate postwar period as the bold stand of so-called unreconstructed rebels. While the motivations behind flight were mixed, many remained "angry, unforgiving enthusiasts of human bondage," in the pointed description of historian Matthew Pratt Guterl.[55] It is important not to diminish this image, but the public posturing of exiled Southerners belies a deeper reality. Exposed by the war's uncertain conclusion and concerned over their future standing as U.S. citizens, many white Southerners fled the country out of fear. Confederate naval officer John Taylor Wood, for instance, noted that, once in Cuba, he was anxious to reach Canada as soon as possible but was loath "to run any more risk, for they [the Federal authorities] [were] as liable as ever to capture." The news from the United States, he continued, was anything but pleasant.[56] Exiled soldiers remained tenuously suspended between military and civilian masculinities—not yet residing fully in either station. Southerners abroad embodied several vying personas: Confederate soldier, exiled citizen, and, in many cases, devoted husband and father. Southern whites had to move this cultural material from one order of significance to another to carve out a new position.[57] Negotiating these private landscapes, veterans tried to comprehend what the Civil War meant and how it changed them as men.

As Confederate veterans entered the postwar South, depression intermixed with defiance, and defeat gave birth to regeneration. Military service and the Confederate cause had altered white Southerners' self-perceptions and redefined their understanding of civilian life. Those veterans who returned home made a decision for moderation that represented an impulse typical of Southern whites who supported the restoration of civic order and believed that defeat was providential.[58] By unifying martial and civil spheres within the domestic realm, Confederate veterans who returned home pronounced the importance of a restrained, if still volatile, manliness. Even if these men were relieved by the war's end, many maintained their allegiance to the Confederate cause, although in different forms, contributing to the rise of the Lost Cause. Other veterans greeted Confederate collapse by refusing to submit to "Yankee" rule. Confederate colonies in Mexico and asylum in Cuba, Canada, or Europe afforded white Southerners, albeit at others' expense, an opportunity to continue asserting independence from the United States. Many, as noted earlier, ultimately sought to return home because they missed their native land. For both groups, civilian life began on Southern roadways, and their ultimate destinations defined how they confronted defeat.

Civic Strife

The successive waves of Confederate military surrenders created discord and confusion as thousands of Confederate veterans reentered a Southern society that the collapse of wartime governments had destabilized. In the most spectacular instances, large crowds of paroled soldiers bent on plundering and violence overran cities and towns.[59] More commonly, the massive influx of men overtaxed communities by exhausting food supplies and creating overcrowded conditions. In both instances, large swarms of demobilized soldiers contributed to instability, and by "the late spring and early summer of 1865," the South "was a land without law."[60] The devastating effects of this violence reverberated through Southern culture deep into the postbellum era, and, importantly, Confederate veterans—irrevocably changed by war and defeat—were often agents of disorder.[61]

In part, Southern whites were predisposed to aggression, many having been raised in a culture of violence. Historians of the antebellum South have posited that codes of honor authorized and compelled men to patrol their social and ethical spheres. White men often violently responded to impudence, signs of rebellion, or perceived slights. Rooted in reputation and authority, brutality and bloodshed were socially condoned and legally sanctioned.[62] Many white Southerners charged that a vigilant citizenry ensured the maintenance of social order.[63] The collapse of the Confederacy marked an end to this order as whites confronted the consequences of emancipation and military defeat. The wave of postwar violence and militarization presaged the later, and widespread, creation of vigilante groups, as domination, resistance, and violence continued to shape postbellum Southern culture.[64] Postwar white militancy is critical in understanding Confederate veterans' transition into civilian life and men's emotional upheaval after the war. Ultimately, the disorder provoked by the Confederacy's collapse in central Virginia, North and South Carolina's Piedmont, and middle to upper Georgia was largely quelled by the late summer of 1865, mostly through the efforts of armed white Southerners and Federal soldiers. The Southern landscape remained unpredictable and dangerous, however, during the ensuing years. Even if time quieted the chaos of the Civil War's untidy conclusion, the consequences of military defeat held sway over the emotions and politics of Southern whites. From 1865 and beyond, white vigilantes vied with Federal authorities and African Americans for social and political control.[65]

The South erupted into a series of small conflicts as the main thoroughfares and southern railways stretching across Virginia, North Carolina, and Georgia became lightning rods of unrest, charged by throngs of homeward-bound soldiers beginning in early April and continuing well into the summer. Scores of Confederate soldiers fled the Virginia countryside once Lee's surrender appeared imminent. Men who had defined themselves in relation to the army collective were now liberated from the military's restrictions; yet many pledged to continue fighting.[66] The conflicting emotions propelled soldiers to take individual action to sustain the Confederate cause—responses that privileged the ideals of a militant masculinity. Virginian John "Ham" Chamberlayne, for instance, refused to participate in the "funeral at Appomattox" and instead slipped through Federal picket lines to travel south.[67] Lieutenant Colonel David G. McIntosh, joined by Chamberlayne, went into North Carolina. McIntosh found Confederate general Joseph E. Johnston and offered his services but was promptly refused. Johnston contended that he had "more artillery than he knew what to do with."[68] Similar to Chamberlayne and McIntosh, John Dooley, a recently paroled prisoner of war, heard of Richmond's fall in early April 1865 and vowed to join "the shattered Southern army and participate in some more fighting."[69] For officers especially, the Confederate cause burned deeply, and they were determined to prolong the fight. The *Milwaukee Daily Sentinel* remarked that while Confederate soldiers expressed "regret at the bitter necessity" of Lee's surrender, they accepted it as "unavoidable." The *Sentinel* went on to observe, "Among the officers, however, the sentiment of pertinacious resistance seems to be universal."[70] For these recalcitrant rebels, the Confederate cause died hard, and their martial lives and aggressive impulses held sway over the terms of surrender agreed on at Appomattox.

Rather than joining Confederate armies elsewhere, others demobilized at Appomattox considered radical alternatives. For many, vengeance and hatred of the North served as motivating forces that sustained their morale. Although exact numbers are unknown, it is likely that throughout the spring of 1865, hundreds of soldiers set out to fight in the hills and countryside of North Carolina, the trans-Mississippi, and beyond. In the hours and days before surrender, hushed discussions turned to the realm of alternatives for those who deemed capitulation unthinkable. Edward Porter Alexander—a trusted Confederate officer to both Confederate president Jefferson Davis and Lee—suggested continued resistance in correspondence with Lee, James Longstreet, and William Mahone on April 9. "If there is *any* hope for the Confederacy it is in *delay*," Alexander stated. The Army of Northern Virginia should join Johnston's command in North Carolina, Alexander urged, or take to the hills and become guerrilla fighters.[71] Lee rejected this course as dishonorable, and perhaps even disastrous; many Confederate officers agreed. Still others, such as Davis, offered support through word and deed.[72] Indeed, small pockets throughout the South became hotbeds of violence as desperate bands—composed of soldiers and civilians alike—harassed black and white Southerners.[73]

The majority of Confederate soldiers adhered to the terms of surrender, but the war's close also created a divisive atmosphere and internal conflict. Men such as Dooley, Chamberlayne, and McIntosh were suspended at the threshold; they were detached from the army but still wanted to serve as soldiers. These men followed an internal sense of duty that allowed them to disregard the terms of formal surrender. Moreover, their allegiance to the Confederate cause, broadly defined, demanded that they resist Federal armies until the bitter end. Historian Jason Phillips argues that such men were "diehard rebels" who subscribed to an ethos of Confederate invincibility that outlasted the Civil War.[74] Phillips's argument sheds light on the strength of Confederate sentiment even during the Confederacy's darkest days and explains why some soldiers refused to return home. Still grappling with the prospects of defeat, these men chased the dream of secession into the spring and summer of 1865.

In the end, efforts to continue fighting in other theaters of the war and proposals for guerrilla warfare proved untenable. Instead of the widespread destruction associated with a guerrilla struggle, the South erupted into a series of small conflicts initiated by men often driven not by ideological commitment but by raw emotion or physical needs. Hungry and tired veterans swelled the populations of dozens of Southern communities, which already had weakened infrastructures because of the strains of war. Contests over resources, displays of violence, and outright conflict ensued. For Confederate veterans, these quarrels were part of a broader struggle that tested the boundaries of their manhood. White Southerners negotiated this unfamiliar terrain as the station of citizen gradually subsumed the role of warrior.

As the Confederate government became increasingly ineffectual and still-active Southern armies faced numerous military setbacks, civil authority faltered in communities such as Danville, Virginia; Greensboro, North Carolina; and Augusta, Georgia. Such civil instability augmented social ferment as demobilized soldiers and civilian refugees were drawn to these major rail centers, which held supplies stores.[75] As Union chaplain Samuel H. Merrill explained, "When the military power of the rebellion fell the civil government, which had been carried on in the interest of the rebellion, fell with it. There was no law but the will of the strongest, and the weak were without protection."[76] Subsequently, black and white Southerners often had to fend for themselves as Federal authorities and local vigilante groups vied for supremacy.[77] For some, the Confederate cause no longer resonated, as their concerns centered on the necessities of life—food and clothing in particular. One defiant soldier told a newspaper, "I lived four years on goobers, parched corn and rotten meat, and I saw nothing wrong with taking blankets & such from the commissary."[78] Such reactions became widespread as soldiers grasped for meaning once their cause was lost.

Danville, Virginia, served as an immediate destination for many of Lee's men after their paroles were issued in mid-April. Arteries leading into the Virginia community swelled with straggling soldiers, overloaded wagons, and wandering civilians.[79] Admiral Raphael Semmes, who had burned most of the Confederate navy and outfitted his men as infantry in early April, took note of the scene and described a "stream of fugitives" from Lee's army, "which now came pressing into our lines."[80] The massive influx of people, coupled with Lee's men, created a deadly combination. "Large crowds of savage and blood thirsty looking stragglers" paraded the streets, wrote Dooley, and they were desperate from hunger and exhaustion, "awaiting an opportunity to do some ugly deed."[81] Without purpose or a destination, the crowds grew restless.[82] Veterans' aimlessness, unbounded with the collapse of authority, propelled violent acts against people and the destruction of Confederate property.

Danville's atmosphere was electric. Men "mingled in one promiscuous mass, every one asking [where to go] and but few answering."[83] Others, demoralized by the Confederacy's collapse and depleted from their personal travails, turned to the quartermaster's stores.[84] A South Carolina soldier described large groups of soldiers who wanted "meat, flour, and molasses." Plundering followed. The South Carolinian continued, "The man in charge wanted to give us corn meal and things such as that. But that didn't suit us, we made a rush and took such things as we wanted."[85] Dooley related further that "bales of cotton, wool, bundles of raw cotton, boxes of licorice," and sundry other items that could be moved quickly were either stolen from or dispensed by the warehouse's commissary.[86] Released from military service and internally conflicted, these veterans lashed out at the institutional features of the nation that they had once sought to defend. In the midst of the confusion, the sound of an explosion rocked the town and scattered the crowd. Confederate ordnance stored near the warehouses had ignited. Burning debris and pieces of shell rained from the sky, killing at least fourteen people, including a number of surrendered Confederate soldiers.[87] One soldier who witnessed the scene recalled seeing a white man "black and badly torn." The soldier mournfully continued, "He was the worst looking sight I ever saw in my life."[88]

Farther north in Lynchburg—a community that the war had severely taxed—paroled soldiers and white civilians looted Confederate supply stores that held shoes, clothing, and assorted valuables. Even though the government had generally adequately supplied Confederate soldiers, civilians often did without. It is unclear whether these groups were lashing out at the symbolic representations of the government that had deprived them for so long or whether they were simply taking for themselves that which they did not before have. Civil authorities quickly lost control and were forced to close businesses and suspend city services.[89] Fearful of riots and pressed by plundering, community leaders agreed that Federal troops must fill the vacuum in power. "Yankee rule," it seemed, proved an appealing alternative to civil strife. Union general John W. Turner, the ranking officer, turned over all remaining military supplies to Lynchburg's poor African American and white populations. On April 16, the Federal troops left, thereby initiating a period of uncertainty until the establishment of the Military District of Lynchburg on May 24, 1865, which solidified Federal control in Lynchburg and the surrounding counties.[90]

The Civil War's close provoked self-reflection, leaving some veterans to conclude that their cause had been pointless. The shock of surrender produced immediate rage, but these feelings abated and transformed into an emotional depletion.[91] One Confederate maintained that he had lost the best four years of his life in war. "Oceans of blood has been shed, thousands of lives sacrificed," he wrote, "all, all for nothing, accomplishing no end leaving the country embittered, distracted, ruined, & no prospect nothing but anarchy & tyranny."[92] The anonymous author exhibits both grief over the war and anger at the world it created. For those white Southerners who had fought for the maintenance of the antebellum South's racial order, the contest's results were indeed hard to swallow. Relief for some came through acts of racial violence in which perpetrators "invented and communicated a fantasy post–Civil War world wherein white men's power approximated that before the war, thereby erasing military defeat."[93] Surely these sentiments swirled in the minds of many after the Confederacy's defeat. Disillusionment with a cause lost, coupled with want, partially explains why demobilized soldiers attacked symbols of Confederate authority. Once the tired veterans from Lee's army traveled into North Carolina, their influence on still-active troops proved disastrous. As former members of Lee's army came through Johnston's command, they quickly spread news of their defeat. Disbelief and bewilderment seized the members of the Army of Tennessee, though they continued to function as a viable, if shaken, fighting force.[94] As if word of

Lee's defeat was not enough, members of the defunct army plundered the still-active Army of Tennessee. A stunned Johnston watched in dismay as groups of Lee's men stole horses, mules, and clothing.[95]

As with Danville, Virginia, the vast supply stores and rail lines of Greensboro, North Carolina, attracted demobilized troops. Soldiers came into the town "rapidly, broken down, hungry, ragged and careworn," noted a newspaper account from 1866 recalling events from the previous spring.[96] As the local home guard evaporated and anti-Confederate sentiment grew rampant, authority within the community faltered, igniting waves of violence. An unruly crowd composed of veterans from Lee's army and local civilians targeted the military warehouses located on East Market Street. According to the *Greensboro Patriot*, "The great houses of Commissary and Quarter Master stores were thrown open and the contents to the amount of millions of dollars worth were distributed." Anger and necessity drove many to take what they had been deprived of in war.[97] Confusion followed as active Confederate units were called to the scene, resulting in a terrible instance of carnage and commotion. Lieutenant Colonel A. C. McAlister's North Carolinians disbursed the crowds that were pillaging the warehouses. Shortly thereafter another crowd appeared—mostly Kentuckians and Tennesseans from Brigadier General George G. Dibrell's cavalry of Johnston's army, according to historian Mark L. Bradley.[98] McAlister ordered these men to disperse. Perhaps drunk from looted liquor, the soldiers continued to plunder, despite McAlister's orders. The Kentuckians and Tennesseans stood their ground and fired into McAlister's men. The Tar Heels fired a deadly volley in response. One man fell dead; three others were wounded.[99] Whatever bonds shared by these Southerners had clearly dissolved in the slow close to a costly struggle. These Confederates had seen the dream of secession fade, and now they fought each other in the disorderly streets of Greensboro.

In late April and early May, paroled soldiers and Confederate deserters flooded the North Carolina landscape, crowded towns, and precipitated lawlessness. Concerned citizens asked Union occupiers for protection from marauders.[100] Scarce resources provoked desperate struggles between civilians and Confederate soldiers. Union cavalry general Judson Kilpatrick observed squads of Johnston's men traveling through the countryside and committing numerous depredations. In Roxboro, North Carolina, Confederate veterans and white citizens held a meeting. Things went poorly for Roxboro's civilians, though, as the soldiers proceeded to take mules and horses belonging to a Confederate wagon train.[101] While this incident passed without violence, the victims in others were not so fortunate. Elizabeth

Collier, a refugee of war living near Hillsborough, North Carolina, recounted how a group of men burst into her home and commenced sacking it "until they had taken everything to eat the house contained."[102]

The atmosphere created by the collapse of Confederate armies frightened white Southerners. Prominent Chapel Hill, North Carolina, resident and Southern sympathizer Cornelia Phillips Spencer described April as a "most remarkable" period; yet her soul "sickened to see the marauders coming in day after day from every road—loaded with spoils. Much of what was so ruthlessly taken was wantonly wasted."[103] While Spencer's "marauders" remain anonymous—in fact, given the tone of her other writing, she may have been referring to Federal troops—the collapse of the Confederate government and the Army of Tennessee's surrender helped initiate this state of confusion. North Carolina's provisional governor Jonathan Worth complained in late April that the vast supplies "along the R. R. are destroyed, wasted and consumed and our troops supplied by foraging parties."[104] For the next several months, lawlessness and disorder defined the entire state.[105] Historian William McKee Evans succinctly captures these conditions: 1865, he writes, was a time "when governments disappeared, when institutions vanished, and when the loyalties of men were divided."[106]

Following the rail lines through South Carolina and into Georgia, Confederate veterans descended on Atlanta, Augusta, and Macon. One newspaper story reported that Atlanta—a city devastated in 1864—had "suffered severely from mob violence."[107] The attackers professed to be soldiers from the armies of Lee and Johnston, though their exact identities remained unknown. The distinction between paroled soldier and marauding deserter blurred. The list of abuses included the theft of supplies, horses, and mules from state and Confederate stores and private homes.[108] Other veterans passed through on their way home, desperate for temporary shelter and food, which Georgians provided for as efficiently as possible, given the circumstances. Chief of Confederate Ordnance Josiah Gorgas—who had fled south from Richmond, Virginia, in early April—described Augusta as being "ruled by a mob." Once all the public stores and many private ones had been raided, the crowds turned to "lay violent hands" on large stores of powder.[109]

The Confederate armies mustered out of service in 1865 only further fractured the shattered white South. Veterans, fresh from the battlefields of Virginia, North Carolina, and beyond, could both help promote a return to normalcy, as witnessed particularly in those who peacefully returned home, and create disruptions, as seen in the unruly crowds and marauding raiders. How these men affected Southern society is difficult to quantify.

Demoralized soldiers, discussions of military defeats, and attacks on symbols of Confederate authority promoted social upheaval, but only temporarily.[110] In the unsettled period between the spring and fall of 1865, white men continued publicly to shape the postwar South as they privately confronted the consequences of war.[111] The violent reactions of some veterans reflected a desperate attempt to gain control during a period of uncertainty. Although defeated in war, men's varied responses demonstrate how white Southern men attempted to reassert themselves as masters of their private and public worlds.

Authority Restored

Changes came rapidly in the spring of 1865, and nothing, by any measure, was inevitable. As the scenes from Danville, Greensboro, Atlanta, and Augusta demonstrate, the wave of military surrenders, coupled with the collapse of the governing authority, produced an ideological collapse among many white Southerners that manifested itself in feelings of animosity and hatred. For these men, the transition into civilian life proved halting and difficult. Once released from the war's killing fields, many veterans unleashed their aggression on the Confederacy's physical and material landscape and, in some cases, black and white civilian populations. For every act of violence committed, however, there were countless instances of restraint and even reconstruction. While violence continued throughout the rest of 1865, local patrols and Federal authorities gradually restored order in most communities to promote the broader good of rebuilding the South.[112] North Carolina leaders, for example, pointed to the regenerative value of industry. In the summer of 1866, North Carolina governor Zebulon Baird Vance invoked the language of destruction and reconstruction in a published speech: "Though the destruction is so wide-spread and thorough . . . it should be remembered that there is nothing which can exceed the recuperative powers of nature when aided by the industry of man."[113] Ironically, the same military training that may have heightened chaos in many areas also facilitated the restoration of order.

For Southern whites, the prospects of peace offered, for a time, the hopeful return of a familiar social order. Although defeated as soldiers, Confederate veterans could assert their manliness and authority within their respective communities by assuming positions of power. As in the antebellum era, men's authority rested on the subordination of others, especially African Americans. Newly freed blacks became targets of white anger. Armed bodies of men were particularly deadly because they had received military training and created powerful mechanisms for the restoration of a white social order. During the same period, through memorial associations and similar organizations, white Southern women became the public guardians of Confederate memory, which created a potent political dimension to burgeoning Lost Cause mythology.[114] Southerners masked their militancy through the prose of remembrance and celebration.

From the late spring and into the early summer of 1865, white men organized themselves into armed bodies. Most often, these groups were sanctioned by the then governing authority—be it Confederate or Federal. Lawlessness drew the ire of Vance, who issued a proclamation in late April exclaiming that bands of soldiers and citizens disposed to commit violence against people and property filled the countryside. Vance asked for restraint and pleaded for all North Carolina soldiers to return home after parole from Johnston's surrendered army.[115] Once entrenched in their communities, Southern veterans could "unite themselves together in sufficient numbers ... under the superintendence of the civil magistrates thereof" to restore order and "arrest or slay any bodies of lawless and unauthorized men who may be committing depredations upon the persons or property of peaceable citizens."[116] Vance's drastic orders had wartime precedent. An 1863 North Carolina law had stated, "The Governor shall have the power to use the guards for home defence for the purpose of arresting conscripts and deserters."[117] Ex-Confederates and Union forces used these acts to create provisional forces. As Assistant Adjutant General J. A. Campbell explained, North Carolina's "most responsible loyal citizens" were organized into a "local police force." After taking the oath of allegiance, the Southerners were armed, given ammunition, and authorized to begin patrolling the countryside.[118]

Federal authorities were quite willing to employ former Confederates in the peacekeeping mission. North Carolina lawyer and rebel sympathizer David Schenck complained of "armed mobs of Confederate soldiers, deserters, & c" that the citizens of Lincolnton put down through confrontation and arrests.[119] General John McAllister Schofield, commander of the Department of North Carolina, organized Confederate veterans and members of the Home Guard into county militia companies.[120] Veterans-turned-police under Federal military control battled with lawless groups of former Confederates to determine who controlled the countryside. Such bands of white soldiers, often commanded by their former officers, were found throughout the state. While they suppressed outbursts of violence, they also harassed former slaves.[121] These draconian measures, enacted over the course of late April and early May, proved successful in restoring white social order in central and eastern North Carolina.

To the north, in the Virginia countryside, scenes of unrest, which were reminiscent of the problems in North Carolina, provoked Confederate veterans to take action in the spring. In the seventh installment of George Cary Eggleston's *Atlantic Monthly* article "A Rebel's Recollections," the Virginian recalled the emotions and experiences of Confederate soldiers during the spring and summer of 1865. Nearly a decade after the fact, he still had great difficulty expressing and describing the great uncertainty of this period and its lasting impact on mind-sets and emotions. Southern men went to war in 1861 with steadfast confidence, he contended, but this conviction eroded into doubt, subtly changing men's perceptions of themselves. While he found it impossible to chart when confidence changed into "despondency," Eggleston remained painfully aware of its repercussions as former Confederates faced the bitter fruits of defeat. Though he ended military service at Appomattox Court House, Eggleston wrote, the real difficulties had not started until later, when the South became engulfed in disorder and its population was gripped by suffering.[122]

Lawlessness in the Virginia countryside provoked Confederate veterans to take action; even if defeated in war, Southern men refused to lose control of their communities. Eggleston arrived home only to find the landscape infested by "lawless bands of marauders" who harassed black and white Southerners because of the absence of constituted authority. Former Confederates, longing for the comforts of home and a return to stability, instead confronted a dangerous, unpredictable landscape. After the community's soldiers returned to their homes, Eggleston wrote to their district's Union commanding officer. According to Eggleston, "[He] granted us leave to organize ourselves into a military police, with officers acting under written authority from him." The ersatz police force patrolled the countryside, disarmed suspicious persons, and arrested individuals and dispatched them to the provost marshal. The soldiers-turned-police remained active until relieved by the establishment of a Union military post.[123] Historian Mark K. Greenough documents similar activities in Appomattox County. He describes an initial period of confusion following surrender that was replaced by greater tranquility during Federal military occupation.[124]

In some cases, Southern police groups quickly exceeded their authority and committed flagrant abuses that drew Federal ire. In Virginia, for instance, Appomattox County sheriff William D. Hix, originally granted authority by the chief quartermaster of the Union army's Twenty-Fourth Corps to distribute abandoned Confederate property to the destitute, began stealing. According to the report of a Federal officer, Hix, with an armed force of civilians and paroled Confederate soldiers, had taken horses from "common people" and turned them over to wealthy planters. The "common people," in turn, had organized and armed themselves for their mutual protection. Before the class-based civic strife exploded into civil conflict, Federal authorities stepped in to disarm Hix and his men.[125]

South Carolinians adhered to the routes pursued by Virginians and North Carolinians as the state's provisional governor, Benjamin Franklin Perry, "ordered the formation of Volunteer companies in every District" of the state "for the purpose of preserving order & keeping peace." These men were to augment the Federal military presence and received "their instructions from the commandants of the different posts." Perry reported that such measures had relieved the state's white population and helped to restore order. But the companies' linkages to white supremacy became clear as well, for these armed bodies "had a salutary influence in . . . keeping the negroes quiet, & relieving the apprehensions of the people."[126] Armed bodies remained intact throughout the summer of 1865 and well into the fall. In one community, a group of citizens wrote to Perry requesting the organization of local police forces—an extension of the ad hoc bodies formed in the war's immediate aftermath. "Our people are anxious to organize such a company to act *strictly* as a police force to preserve the peace and order & prevent the commission of crimes," they declared, "and act as constabulary force to summon parties before the Provost Court to be guard duty or any other service outside of the great object we have in view, the suppression of crime & the preservation of order."[127]

The patrolling bands of armed white Southern men who used force to uphold their conceptions of law and order connect directly to the later rise of the Ku Klux Klan, which gained widespread membership in South Carolina and North Carolina especially. Efforts to reconstitute law and order dovetailed with whites' desire to resurrect an antebellum racial order, as seen in the creation of black codes between 1865 and 1866. "Although the laws differed from state to state," writes historian Leon F. Litwack, "the underlying principles and the major provisions remained the same." A "freedman could be arrested as a common vagrant, jailed and fined; if unable to pay the fine, he would be hired out to an employer who in turn assumed the financial liability and deducted it from the laborer's wages."[128] In Goldsboro, North Carolina, for example, an 1866 law included provisions for the arrest of "all suspicious persons found upon the streets" and the arrest of "all idle or vagrant persons found within the limits of the town." So, too, did the ordinance prevent the concealment of firearms unless used by the military or police.[129]

Black codes, local police forces, and organized bands of armed veterans each contributed to the resurrection of the antebellum racial and social order that had been shaken by Civil War and emancipation. Confederate veterans played an active role in the resurrection of this order as they became Southern citizens once more and navigated a world changed by Civil War. Indeed, if the years of Congressional Reconstruction were marked by episodes of extreme violence in the South, the roots of this insurgency can be traced to the immediate postwar period. And Southerners, even if immersed in an antebellum culture of violence, assumed a cloak of increasingly aggressive manliness.[130] George C. Rable, Richard Zuczek, and James K. Hogue have each argued that Reconstruction-era violence demonstrates continuity with the Civil War, even if the means and intensity changed over time.[131] Crucial to white Southerners' campaigns of political and social control were locally sanctioned, armed bodies of men that attacked white Republicans, African Americans, and the socially marginalized without remorse. The organizational efforts of Confederate veterans in 1865 adumbrated these later campaigns of terror. Known variously as "police forces," "regulators," and "Home Guards," these groups represented, in essence, antebellum militias reconstituted—or the resurrection of slave patrols.[132] Zuczek goes so far as to argue that the antebellum system of slave patrols had fully reappeared in South Carolina by the late summer of 1865.[133] Confederate veterans actively sought to establish order and reform the South's torn social fabric, at least on their terms.

Toward an Uneasy Peace

Confederate soldiers traveled home or abroad in the uniforms that had become so central to their wartime identities. Some veterans, out of necessity or in a statement of defiance, continued to wear their military garb and insignia past the war's close. Federal authorities were troubled by the continued use of Confederate symbols; accordingly, they curtailed the further use of military buttons or rank. In North Carolina, for example, former Confederate officers were ordered to "remove all badges, military buttons, braid, cord, or other articles designating rank."[134] As North Carolinian Charlotte E. Grimes remembered, "The Yankees issued an order forbidding our soldiers to wear the Confederate uniform, they had nothing else, and no money to buy any clothes." She subsequently covered the buttons of her husband, General Bryan Grimes, "with black, in mourning for the Confederacy."[135] Carlton McCarthy remembered a similar experience in Virginia in which the provost compelled Confederate veterans to "cut the brass buttons off their jackets."[136] The conversion of Confederate material culture marked the soldier's entry into civilian life. Indeed, North Carolinian and former soldier Randolph A. Shotwell captured the symbolic importance of changing materials. He wrote, "The battered sword was steadily resolving itself into the husbandman's blade, where it had been rudely fashioned at the village smithy. The shattered spear readily became the crook of the pruning-hook. The blood-stained army ambulance relapsed into its olden service as a market-cart."[137]

While the chaos associated with military demobilization eventually ended, veterans' inner wars continued, shaping the trajectory of Reconstruction toward white reactionary politics of violence and fraud.[138] Southern men sought different paths toward reconstruction, and through these journeys they aimed to mend the wounds of war and reaffirm veterans' positions as Southern men and citizens. Rather than offering tidy conclusions, the stories of these men remained unsettled as they tried to reconnect with their families but also maintain the ties with other men fostered during military service. Confederates' transitions into civilian life proved halting.

Veterans' actions and experiences dictated the atmosphere and direction of postwar life in many Southern communities. Domestic reunions were integral to families' personal reconstructions. The spring and summer of 1865 set the stage for the longer process of social and familial reconstructions as Confederate veterans embraced contrasting models of masculinity. The vast majority of veterans never pursued guerrilla warfare and readily returned to their prewar occupations, thereby providing a model of men who practiced a restrained manliness and found redemption within the household. Federal armies had soundly beaten Southern forces, and Confederate soldiers accepted military surrender, if still expressing sadness, anger, and even confusion over defeat. Yet, significantly, instances of violence and efforts at local policing presaged Reconstruction-era violence. Ex-Confederates, if willing to acknowledge the war's end, refused to concede a new social order based on black equality. Veterans' contrasting patterns of behavior explain men's different responses to defeat while also highlighting the division of the white Southern mind, which surrender further fractured. The consequences of 1865 echoed for decades.[139]

CHAPTER FIVE

Reconstructions

While imprisoned at Fort Delaware, Confederate brigadier general Rufus Barringer maintained a small, leather-bound diary. On April 10, 1865, he heard of General Robert E. Lee's surrender, noting feelings of both "great depression" and "mournful relief." Fourteen days later he learned of Joseph E. Johnston's surrender and exclaimed "Grapes!" He then dashed off the words "Prisoners to be released."[1] Writing to his children in early June, Barringer noted that he had witnessed "many sad scenes" and much "suffering" but ultimately thanked "Our Heavenly Father" for protection. He promised that, once he was home, he would relate his experiences and share with his children small trinkets made while imprisoned.[2] Their father would come home a survivor, bringing artifacts from war and bearing witness to Confederates' extreme suffering. By early August, Barringer had been paroled and returned to his North Carolina home. He concluded his diary with a series of staccato notations: "At Home! How joyous the greeting! How sad. Oh! How sad the scenes, the changes, the remembrances of four years of war, now before me."[3] Elation clashed with dejection, and joy competed with sadness.

Barringer's mixed emotions communicate the transitional space between war and peace and capture Confederate soldiers' personal reactions to the experience of defeat and the prospects of reentering civil society. The diversity of responses should come as no surprise for, as historian Gaines Foster reminds us, "no one interpretation of the war dominated all of the South all of the time."[4] The Civil War had cast a long shadow over the white South. For some it was but a passing cloud and these former Confederates eagerly looked toward peace and the quietude of family life. They often concluded their wartime diaries once they had arrived home. Resuming the rhythms of life, the war had not significantly altered their ability to function. For others the darkness became impenetrable. Some of these men were unwilling to give up the Confederate cause, eschewing formal military surrender and desperately searching for ways to continue the war, whereas others, profoundly traumatized, were gripped by depression for years to come. For both groups, even when peace dawned, the Confederacy continued to shape their self-identifies and preoccupy their minds.

The bonds forged among Confederate soldiers during military service were only strengthened by the contest's outcome, as manifest in the shared experience of defeat.[5] The war had changed its participants; as Virginian John "Ham" Chamberlayne poignantly wrote, "The war and its objects, its causes, & causes of its failure" had been seared into his heart "as with a branding iron."[6] Southern men had been soldiers for several years, if that, but they would be "veterans for the rest of their lives." "And the process of becoming a veteran, of being a civilian again," charges historian James Marten, "lasted longer and was much harder for many of them than anyone would have expected."[7] Sharp divisions between war and peace do not accurately reflect the ambiguities of the immediate postwar period or the experiences of its participants. Veterans' different reactions to defeat exemplify the division of the white Southern mind, which surrender further fractured.[8]

At first the Confederacy's defeat left veterans dazed and disheartened. Uncertainty soon clouded the vision of many as they looked uneasily toward the future. Eventually former Confederates came to strive for self-control and emotional moderation in an attempt to suppress the unfettered feelings expressed at the war's end and to reassert a stronger public face. Southern men, moreover, "had to find new ways to frame white manhood without the mastery that slavery had offered or the honor that victory would have provided," as Craig Thompson Friend explains.[9] Men who struggled to reconstitute white manhood and prevail over personal pains lashed out at freedpeople in the postwar years, directing the course of the white South's "redemption." Reconstruction was an emotional experience, and men's feelings shed light on their public actions.[10] Writers' use of words such as *sadness* and *despair* reflects the palpable sense of uncertainty about the future and demonstrates an overt ontological shift prompted by conflict and defeat. Soldiering promoted a shift in attitudes and emotional dispositions among men. Veterans' expressions of or language about defeat and readjustment, though born from crisis, served as a path for social communication and the continuation of veteran communities.[11] This chapter examines how Confederates personally navigated the process of reconstruction, which dovetails with the last chapter's consideration of the war's public close. The surrenders at Appomattox or Bennett Place were but brief moments in a soldier's life, whereas their station as veterans shaped Southerners' self-identification for the remainder of men's lives.

Historians once maintained that Civil War soldiers quickly turned away from the war when they returned home, only to revive their interest in martial matters decades later.[12] More recent scholarship has called into question the strict dichotomy between hibernation and revival as too schematic and points to the fact that veterans began "sorting out" the war and "assembling meaning" for it immediately after its close.[13] In the years after 1865, the "southern spirit" thrived in the press, regimental histories, and survivors' associations, as historian Caroline E. Janney has recently observed.[14] Veterans also continued in their private writings to parse out the war's meaning; these personal records underpin the discussion that follows.

Civil War to Personal Peace

Although the process of military demobilization can be confined to months, even weeks—as discussed in the last chapter—Confederates' personal transition into postwar life is more difficult to quantify.[15] Southerners' responses to defeat and strides toward civilian life framed reconstruction in strikingly personal terms. That should not suggest that whites became apolitical or accepted black equality, for many actively resisted Republican governance and angrily denounced freedpeople, as will be explored in the next chapter. In letters home, though, men worried about finances, looked happily to family reunions, and struggled to comprehend the war's meaning. The traumas, triumphs, and setbacks of the Confederates examined herein, while certainly not universal, do shed light on how some Southerners made sense of the conflict at the war's end and beyond.[16] Uncertainty over the future became, for at least some Confederates, pragmatic realism as men found redemption in family and civilian pursuits. Indeed, as Louisianian James Burdge Walton of the Washington Artillery wrote in May 1865, "For myself I shall submit to the condition of things as I find them, having no reproaches for the past, no fear of the present, and abundant hope of the future."[17] Military service and civil war filtered the lens through which men viewed postwar life as they came to value the present and take comfort in the everyday.

Many Confederates first seriously considered life without war in the late winter and early spring of 1865. Two soldiers, Henry Brown Richardson and Walton, demonstrate contrasting reactions to the prospect of defeat, as the former pledged to continue the war by any means and the latter happily looked toward reunion with his family. Grievously wounded and captured at the Battle of Gettysburg, Richardson finished his war on Johnson's Island, Ohio. In late March 1865, he arrived in Richmond, Virginia, where he was granted a leave of absence for thirty days unless exchanged sooner. Still in his late twenties, Richardson remained in Virginia, recovering, until he could strike south and get to "any thing like a *Confederacy*."[18] Like countless other veterans, Richardson resided within a culture of invincibility that shaped both his commitment to the Confederacy and his reaction to its defeat.[19] Conversely, as an enfeebled Richardson recuperated in the Old Dominion, waiting for his chance to fight again, Walton anxiously looked to the war's end. A veteran of the Mexican-American War, Walton was Richardson's senior by over twenty years and had a wife and children waiting for him in Louisiana. Between the winter and spring of 1865, Walton's letters home expressed his fears and doubts about the Southern cause, starkly contrasting with the public hopes of those Confederates who continued to believe in their nation's survivability.[20] Walton's attachment to home and family were paramount in his mind and drove his wish to see the war's end, unlike his youthful counterpart, Richardson.

Ensconced in Richmond, Virginia, in February 1865, Walton projected a bleak view of the war. The two sides, he maintained, were "as wide apart, to day, as they were this day a year gone." The armies, entrenched in Virginia, were deadlocked, and it was as though all the bloodshed and fighting had resolved nothing. "The South," he wrote, "will have nothing Short of Independence & recognition, and the North demands unconditional submission & the ultimate abolition of Slavery." The fighting would thus continue until the South was exhausted and subjugated or the North was tired and bankrupt. Walton feared an interminable struggle; yet "fortitude" and "manhood" demanded his continued participation.[21] He feared the humiliation of defeat but also remained painfully aware of the war's tremendous costs. In the conflict's final months, many soldiers, such as Richardson, had lost touch with the bleak realities undermining the Confederate cause, instead projecting wildly optimistic prognostications for the future success of their cause.[22] Walton's vision of the war remained grounded, and he feared the South's course toward total destruction.

Enduring the conflict required him to maintain close connections to his family and friends in Louisiana. To them he expressed a range of sentiments, giving voice to his masculine ideals but also exposing fears. Maintaining an antebellum model of behavior, he projected a stoic exterior and continued to define himself as a provider for his family's wants and needs. It was the male's prerogative, as he and scores of his comrades maintained, to protect and defend family and home.[23] Though the cause was imperiled, war legitimated men's claims as heads of households. If his "dear friends were only comfortable," he noted, and "beyond want or care," he "could bear the long separation & exile from all" he held "most dear in this world."[24] Their continued comfort ensured his persistence in the army. But war had weakened men's reliance on postures and poses, and Walton also turned to his family to express his innermost fears. His emotional revelations, which expose vulnerabilities and doubts, modify interpretations of white men's protection of domesticity and authority at the expense of personal exposure. Instead, Walton willingly wrote home expressing his intense longings, which were severe and disarming. Such desperation made him "murmur & bewail [his] misfortunes." Only reflection relieved him, and again Walton felt "that Providence will direct all finally for our good."[25] In the divine he could find succor, and through reflection and writing he could ease his troubled mind. His revelation of personal feelings suggests the dynamic interpersonal relationships and deep levels of trust shared among members of his family. Such personal commitments and longing, however sustaining to Walton himself, increasingly eroded his faith in the war and the Confederacy.

By April, he had moved to Augusta, Georgia. Frustrated, he opined, "When Oh! When will the straining of the heart strings cease, when again shall we be united never more to be separated. How I long for . . . that day of supreme happiness which when it is realized will compensate for all the past privation & suffering. I am hopeful ever—and believe now there are long days of happiness in store for all of us. Keep up your courage. We are near the end."[26] Gripped by feelings of powerlessness, Walton continually returned to thoughts of hearth and home. Only in reunification with family could the war's trials have real meaning. Only in the hopes of domestic bliss could Walton dull his painful miseries, because only with family and at home could he make sense of the war he had experienced.

While Walton struggled with military service, Richardson's faith in the cause remained unshaken, though his long tenure in prison and youthful exuberance may have emboldened him to renew fighting. He left Virginia in April to seek a new theater of war. Federal soldiers took him prisoner in Tennessee, sometime around May 1865, thereby quickly ending his crusade. Imprisoned, the rebels were administered the oath of allegiance in groups of fifty or more men. Richardson and two other men refused. After a brief period of confinement and the realization that it was "no use for *one man* to try to be the Confederacy," he succumbed. In a bitter letter to his parents, he detailed the ordeal. Asserting that he had sold himself "for a very inferior 'mess of pottage,'" Richardson "worshipped the great golden image, and became a prostitute." Emasculated and pained, he felt frustration and anger. Yet, despite his extreme displeasure at the war's conclusions and his new prospects as a U.S. citizen, he endured. He needed to explain to his parents his new obligations. He intended to keep the oath faithfully while in the United States. No cause could justify breaking it, for his personal honor decided his external actions. But his sense of public honor did not govern his personal feelings. His fidelity to the United States could never "change the desires and emotions" of his heart.[27]

Public reputation directed feelings of self-worth, thereby suggesting men's continued need for outside validation. At the war's beginning, men such as Richardson understood their commitment to community and citizenship to be central to the rationale for enlistment. These same forces drove Richardson to dedicate himself to the Confederacy. Public actions do not always reveal private feelings, however. A rich constellation of emotions framed his thoughts, and the heart often moved him. He understood well the dictates of honor and loyalty but maintained an internal balance between what society asked of him and what he intensely felt. Even after he became a U.S. citizen again, he remained emotionally committed to the Confederacy and racked by the pains of defeat. These traumas shaped his bleak outlook for the remainder of 1865.

Richardson's mother, Eunice, sough to buoy her broken child by writing a heartfelt letter of cheer. Solace could be found, she contended, in his meritorious service. She could not comprehend what he had endured and survived, but honor could be found in these sacrifices. "You have *almost* laid down your life for the Confederacy," she observed, advising that "after all [he had] done, and suffered, now that the Confederacy had ceased to exist," he should spare himself any reproaches for taking the oath.[28] A mother's soothing words could not calm Richardson's aching heart. Drifting between the homes of friends in Louisiana, he lived an unsettled existence and found the inactivity tiresome. But he was without alternative. Not knowing what to do, he declared the country "ruined—dead" and asserted that it would "continue so till some labor system is fixed." He bemoaned African Americans' freedom and wished that some of "your anti-slavery people could see the condition of the negroes in this country now and compare it with what it was before the war. Talk about the 'sin of slavery'! If ever there was a sin it was in putting the negroes in their present condition. Who is responsible?" he wondered.[29] A nonslaveholder himself, Richardson struck out at Northerners, at abolitionists, at African Americans. Embittered, lonely, and despairing, he remained without purpose.

Reconstructions 113

Comprehending the trials they had just endured proved difficult for many veterans. In the spring of 1865, Josiah Gorgas—chief of Confederate ordnance—reflected on what had transpired: "The calamity which has fallen upon us in the total destruction of our government is of a character so overwhelming that I am as yet unable to comprehend it. I am as one walking in a dream, and expecting to awake. I cannot see its consequences."[30] George Anderson Mercer, too, expressed disbelief and wonderment. He recorded in his diary that he was unable to recover from "the stunning effect of mingled surprise and grief caused by the sudden prostration of our cause. The noble structure we had reared was leveled like a house of cards."[31] Engulfed by defeat, these men were forced, in the words of Bertram Wyatt-Brown, "to drink the bitter cup of psychological ruin."[32] The foundations that defined Southern men and manliness had been shaken by war, and white Southerners now had to refashion their culture, reconstruct their "civilization," and recover from a stunning shock; they had to confront the history they created.[33] But the ambiguities of the war's results did not create tidy conclusions—a fact placed in stark relief by veterans' varied responses to, and interpretations of, war and defeat.

Official military parole meant little in the hands of men such as Gorgas, Mercer, and Richardson who found no honor or place in the newly reformed country but instead uncomfortably resettled into postwar life, gradually adjusting to momentous changes. The inability to secure steady income and interactions with Federal soldiers, in particular, left Southern manliness embattled. Confused and deeply unsettled, Gorgas decided to travel to Alabama. Here, in his adopted state, he would wait before again coming under the authority of the U.S. government.[34] Though he remained silent on the subject, Gorgas was perhaps drawn to a familiar place to anchor him during a period of uncertainty. One of his first interactions with Federal soldiers produced a variety of personal reactions. Feeling amicable enough, he took tea with a group of Federal officers. A novel sensation, he wrote, but one to which he had to adjust, as white Southerners' "late enemies" were now their new "masters."[35] By using the word "master," specifically, Gorgas assumed a prostrate stance and relinquished control of full liberties to the war's victors—gestures that were unfathomable only weeks before as he, like many soldiers, pledged to continue the war at all costs. Occupying Federal soldiers made the specter of defeat a tangible reality. Gorgas recognized his ambiguous place in a social structure leveled by war. Federal soldiers and the results of emancipation dispossessed Southern whites of the mastery they wielded in the antebellum era. At least for a time, they were no longer masters of their destinies or agents of power.

Usurpations provoked depression, and though his military service was over, Gorgas's inner wars continued. Without an occupation and in Alabama, far away from his family in Virginia, depression consumed him.[36] "With no right to life, liberty or property," he renewed his interest in leaving the country, though this dream, too, proved fleeting.[37] Men such as Gorgas struggled in the postwar South, often unable, especially in 1865-66, to reach any real sense of settlement or finality. For these veterans the past and present mixed together as they grappled with self-definition. During this period of transition, they expressed feelings of compromise and recalcitrance. Mercer captured the stormy feelings of many when he wrote, "The southern people have in good faith given up their patriarchal system of African slavery as the result of the war; they are in good faith willing to maintain union under the Constitution; but they have not consented to surrender their freedom and manhood."[38] Freedom and manhood, while altered, became foundational to veterans' personal reconstructions during the postwar era and, once considered in conjunction with racism, help explain their reactionary stand against the forces of federal control and the advancement of African Americans.

In striking contrast to Gorgas and Richardson, Walton found calmness amid the calamity of the spring and summer of 1865. By May, U.S. soldiers garrisoned his temporary home of Augusta, Georgia, and the stars and stripes flew over prominent buildings. "For myself," he wrote, "I shall submit to the condition of things as I find them, having no reproaches for the past, no fear of the present, and abundant hope of the future."[39] We may question the sincerity of Walton's words, for such sentiments could very well have been intended to soothe a worried family. After all, they, not he, had fully felt the economic ruin and personal privations of civil war on the home front. He nonetheless seemed possessed by a very real presence of mind, thereby suggesting genuine sentiments. He had done his duty and felt glad to have neither brought on war nor fostered its disastrous close. With these ideas, especially, Walton joined a chorus of Southern whites who refused to acknowledge any wrongdoing in bringing about the conflict.[40] Now that the war was over, he wrote, "we must reconcile ourselves to the Will of God" and hopefully embrace the future.[41] More importantly, Walton gladly turned to his family, people for whom he felt great pride.[42]

Absolving himself of both the war's causes and its conclusions, Walton turned to higher powers to locate the conflict's ultimate meaning. Is it not "manifest in this result that Providence has never been with us?" he wondered. If God had desired to give the South victory, God would have spared

Generals Stonewall Jackson and J. E. B. Stuart, thought Walton. And "the carnage & flow of the dearest blood in the land would have been stayed." He continued, "I have always been a believer in the efficacy of prayer—this end makes me almost a skeptic."[43] With these powerful words Walton questioned the effectiveness of prayer, wondered about the meaning of God's actions, and doubted the righteous of the Confederate cause. The events of the spring and summer of 1865 provoked Walton to reflect deeply on the core foundations of Southern culture. Yet, importantly, the troubling questions had only shaken, not destroyed, his faith. Metaphysical pondering could not sustain a family's wants, however. Hoping to secure "happiness & comfort" for both himself and his loved ones "in the uncertain days" that were before them, Walton left Augusta for New York to negotiate the sale of cotton.[44] Walton once again balanced the two faces of his manhood. In the same letter that questioned the very foundation of the Christian tradition, he also expressed his great concern over his family's material well-being. Although the Civil War had provoked Walton to examine deep and sometimes troubling theological questions, he also emerged from the conflict clinging to a paternalist worldview that remained strikingly antebellum in nature.

The continued absence from family caused consternation for Walton and necessitated explanation. The experiences of the past war suggested the need for continued patience and demanded pragmatism. He wrote to his wife, Amelia, that he must "do what seems to be right," having learned in "these late long years of trial & privation, to submit to the dictates of fate."[45] With these material comforts he hoped to rebuild his family's fortunes and offered his wife optimistic promises for the future: "I begin to conclude I have a cheerful & hopeful spirit, for really I am not at all desponding and feel I shall be very happy. May I hope that your own, always brave heart, responds to this temper. We may have more to bear up against than we now discover—but I do not believe it—at all events, I am not going to give up. Be assured I am quite equal to the occasion."[46] His life spared and now having passed through the horrific trials of war, Walton hoped to be born anew, to become a changed man. His joyous outpouring to his wife reflected a man who hoped to embrace life with renewed vigor and filter his experiences through the lens of a newfound happiness.

Whether Walton and his family achieved and maintained the happiness they so desired remains unknown. As it did for scores of Confederate soldiers, the final return home concluded the Walton family's extended correspondence. Perhaps the very silence suggests success. Where Walton's pen fell silent, however, Richardson's wrote with renewed vigor.

Richardson slowly conquered the sadness that consumed him for months after the war. By the fall of 1865, he worked as an engineer, maintaining levees in Tensas Parish. The monetary reward and steady work paled in comparison to his newfound joy. In an excited letter to his mother, Richardson proclaimed, "I have been here for two days, passing the happiest Christmas of my whole life. And I want to tell you what makes me so happy. It is because I am with Miss Nannie Farrar, whom I love more than anybody in the world, and who, I hope, loves me."[47] In Anna "Nannie" Farrar, Richardson found a new life. Shattered by the death of the Confederacy, he thought "there was nothing left to live for, and as if [he] never could be happy again." But now, he wrote, "I have been a new man—happier, and I hope better than I ever was before. Indeed it seems to me almost as if I had never *lived* at all before, and as for the Confederacy, though my views and feelings as to the right and justice of the matter are unchanged, I can smile to think how small and insignificant a matter it was to set my heart on, when there is still left such a treasure as Miss Nannie."[48] Having once lived for the Confederacy, Richardson was ready now to die for Nannie. Deciphering this transformation is difficult. In the midst of an untamed bliss, Richardson's urge to separate himself from the Confederacy and from the pain of war is an understandable reaction. But to suggest that his happiness completely voided the war's meaning seems wrong. While he would forever remain a veteran of the conflict (and in later years often discuss his wartime service), his future role as a husband, perhaps even a father, took precedent. Marriage completed him as a man in a way that military service never could. Devotion to his wife and his job as an engineer had fulfilled him.

In a devoted relationship, Richardson found an array of new obligations and joys. He happily finished one letter for Nannie after she was called away. He playfully wrote to his parents, "Nannie says 'write' and finish her letter while she attends to sundry household matters; and like an obedient and dutiful husband I am writing."[49] Obedience to her wishes gave Richardson great pleasure. In her he could lose himself. Yet he also recognized his new position as a household head. He told his parents, partly in jest but also reflecting his new responsibilities, "The fact is that since I have become the head of a family, with authority and dominion over the other members thereof, I have delegated to her [Nannie]—she being a weaker vessel, a number of my former occupations and duties; among which are patching and darning, sewing on buttons and writing letters, and the general supervision, direction and care for and of the respectability and decency of the entire family."[50] Unable to control the Confederacy or refuse the oath of allegiance,

Richardson now found himself in charge of a household and delegated tasks to its members with glee. For within the household, among its members, he finally realized his role and place as a man.

Despite divergent paths, Richardson, Walton, and Mercer found personal redemption in the domestic realm, for family underpinned their personal reconstructions. Many Southern women, as historian LeeAnn Whites and other have argued, reassured weary veterans that the values underpinning antebellum Southern manliness—honor, virtue, and sacrifice—had been preserved.[51] These beliefs would now serve as the building blocks for the reconstruction of manhood and facilitate veterans' shift from soldier to civilian.[52] Confederates' embrace of the present demonstrates how they overcame, or at least reconciled themselves to, the shattering experience of defeat by focusing on the importance of everyday life. Still, though, men remained emotive, and dark moods could be consuming. The tension between melancholy feelings and moderating pragmatism is revealed in the immediate postwar correspondence of two youthful veterans who had been at college together before the war. James B. Mitchell, from Glenville, Alabama, returned to the University of North Carolina in 1866 after having discontinued his studies in 1861 to join the Confederate army. In a revealing letter to his friend Ruffin H. Thomson—also a student from North Carolina who left in 1861 for military service—Mitchell laid bare his raw emotions. He was much pained to see his friend "so much disposed to melancholy" but remained helpless, for he, too, found himself "in the same condition" and unable to offer consolation. This dark depression cast a long shadow over Mitchell's future. Not able to see "any light ahead," he lost all faith in a once promised bright future. During the war, he recalled, "old wiseacres" had cried out, "Never mind Boys, keep a good heart. You know the darkest hour is just before day." These sentiments now disgusted Mitchell, who believed that happiness could only be found in those who contented themselves with "the old aphorism that 'whatever is, is right' and endeavor to make the best of it."[53]

Steering between life's extremes, wary of fanatical doctrines, Mitchell embraced a few simple truths, especially the enjoyment of life's simple comforts. Deprived of basic necessities while in the army, Southern men enjoyed niceties but were now constantly reminded of just how fleeting such luxuries could be. By instilling deeper meaning into what was once meaningless, they found life more enjoyable. Mitchell composed his letter while comfortably seated by a warm fire. Outside, sleet and snow covered the ground. He could remember only a short time ago when it was different: "I had nought but the ground for a bed and rocks for a pillow, and in this I perceive a blessing." Taking Alexander Pope's words to heart—"One truth is clear, whatever is, is right"—Mitchell stopped here. For now, his "limited vision" was "incompetent to pierce the thick darkness further." He continued, "The future of the South is to me a mysterious horror and I decline to contemplate it. My imagination has not even yet shaped my own future but awaits the development of events."[54] In strikingly similar tone, another Confederate veteran recalled "campaign privations" and pledged to his mother never to pass another such winter.[55] Taking solace in the present but always reminded of the past, former Confederates navigated an unsure future as they confronted Reconstruction.

From the war's final months to the first years of the postbellum era, Confederate veterans pursued divergent paths to begin the processes of personal reconstructions. When Walton found himself ensconced in the trenches of Richmond, he feared an interminable conflict that would keep him away from family and home. His duties as a man demanded faithful service, but his feelings as a father, a friend, and a husband made his yearnings for the Civil War's end powerful. Perhaps in this period his loyalty to the Confederacy waned and he began questioning the conflict that had removed him from those he loved.[56] Feelings and longings, then, not patriotism, shaped Walton's understanding of the war's ultimate meaning. He felt sadness and loss at the Confederacy's death but also found pride in his family and excitement in what was to come. Ultimately, he distanced himself from the conflict, questioned the Confederacy, and concluded that the war's results reflected God's will. War now suggested nothing but pain and agony, whereas family could bring happiness and joy. He worried less about the future, for anything was better than what he had experienced. Richardson reached a strikingly similar conclusion, but only after a period of terrible mourning. Walton's junior and a veteran of one war, not two, Richardson had no family attachments in the state of Louisiana. These factors surely directed his unwavering devotion to the Confederate cause in the war's final months and partially explain the divergent reactions of these two Louisianians. And yet the public postures that initially defined Richardson's commitment to the Confederacy and defiance of his parents' wishes gave way to strong internal feelings. Like Walton, strong passions governed Richardson. At the war's close he maintained a nearly fanatical commitment to his fallen nation. Inactivity and the humiliation of taking an oath of allegiance drove him to despair. But during this darkest period, the promise of love uplifted him. As the pains of war dulled with time, he found unimaginable happiness with his wife and their burgeoning family.

Understanding how Confederates dealt with Reconstruction requires a consideration of their emotional lives in conjunction with material realities and family life because white Southerners viewed the postbellum era through these personalized lenses. Remarkably, despite different wartime experiences and contrasting reactions to defeat, each of the men examined here came to embrace reconciliation and political moderation, albeit on his own terms. Southerners' angry resignation gave rise to personal concerns, thereby marking a critical transition into civilian life.[57] Further, as scholars have ably documented, public redemption came through invention, as ex-Confederates turned their military tragedy into a historical triumph. Lost Cause mythology eclipsed pained reactions to the Confederacy's collapse in an effort to justify the unfathomable scale of loss and destruction.

Personal Transformations

The Lost Cause mythology that rose from the ashes of Confederate defeat shaped not only the Civil War's social remembrance but also characterizations of the Southern soldier. An April 1868 account from South Carolina's *Yorkville Enquirer* included a typical excerpt describing the Confederate soldier: "He was a curious compound," it noted, "a bundle of virtue, frailty and old clothes." Nine-tenths of his character "consisted of what may be called don't care-a-damn-ativeness. This was his marked individuality, and five years of discipline, hardship and danger did not tame the unruly spirit in the least."[58] These public narratives buried the psychological strains many endured. Privately, though, prewar certitude wavered, as witnessed in white Southerners' pained reactions to the terror of the battlefield and the shock of military defeat. Thus, Lost Cause mythology paradoxically elevated, if not deified, Confederate veterans while refusing to acknowledge their conflicted reactions to war.

Public accounts that emphasized the importance of rebuilding the South bolstered the view that the demons of war had been exorcised.[59] In the summer of 1866, for example, North Carolina's wartime governor Zebulon Baird Vance invoked the language of destruction and reconstruction in an 1866 published speech. "Though the destruction is so wide-spread and thorough," he noted, "it should be remembered that there is nothing which can exceed the recuperative powers of nature when aided by the industry of man. These gaping wounds in our country's bosom are to be healed, these enormous losses of our wealth are to be repaired, these wasted fields are to be restored to the glorious verdure of peaceful abundance."[60] Vance's language resonated among many Southerners who emphasized the importance of regrowth and maintained a strong public facade. It would not be accurate to contend that all or even most former soldiers suffered from depression in the years after the war. It is notable, however, that these feelings surface time and again in veterans' writings. It is notable and telling to whom veterans disclosed themselves. Although family served as a source of solace, many veterans turned to their former comrades-in-arms for support after the end of hostilities. Only other veterans, many held, understood the jaundiced vision produced by defeat, so eloquently captured by historian Elizabeth Fox-Genovese: "Their cause had been just, their defeat brutal. And with their defeat had come the destruction of all that was good and bold and gracious in a mindless, faceless, gray world."[61] Grappling with a series of profound changes, men responded in ways ranging from bewilderment to depression. The conflicting personal emotions of anger, pain, and confusion shaped the contours of civilian life just as much as any ideological commitment to either the Confederacy or the United States.

Former Confederates worked to create a new self-identity for themselves as Southerners who remained culturally distinct from Northern society.[62] Veterans' introspection revealed internal discomfort at the prospect of being defined as U.S. citizens, while their future status as Southern civilians remained unformed. Mercer reflected on his place as an American and a Southerner after having read an excerpt of William Makepeace Thackeray's *Vanity Fair* in which an English traveler to foreign lands rejoices after hearing "God Save the King." Mercer was moved to tears, stating, "[I] reflected that now there was no national song capable of producing similar emotions in me—that I could enjoy none of those grand public feelings that the citizens of a noble and free Government . . . so constantly experience. Alas, I must confess, all my national feeling is buried with the overthrown Confederacy, and there is nothing in the attitude of the U.S. . . . calculated to arouse similar emotions."[63] While attempting to parse out his feelings, Mercer maintained "an accurate diary of the workings and feelings of the mind."[64] His reflex echoed his rationale for keeping a diary when hunting as a child and attending college as a young man, periods crucial to his passage into manhood. Aided by this device, he tried to dissect his intellectual contours, reestablish his elevated prewar social position, and create a proper place in the postwar South. He sought, in a sense, to reconstruct himself as a man and as a Southern citizen.

Over time Mercer enjoyed financial success, though his mind remained "in a most restless discontented and unhappy state." Geographic place, in particular, provoked considerable reflection and consternation. As with other Confederate veterans, Mercer's self-conception remained deeply invested in a sense of place. Beginning in the fall of 1866, he renewed annual trips that he had taken before the war to New York City and Saratoga Springs. Once in these cities, his "excited temperament was carried away by the noise and busy life—the crowded streets—the gay equipage and handsome buildings—and the beauty of the women one sees in the moving throng." He continued, "After reaching home," however, "everything . . . seemed dull and listless."[65] Mercer justified his Northern excursions with his wartime experiences, reinforcing the proposition that both war and peace now formed equal parts of his self-identification.

During military service, he noted, he had "seen no gaiety and had necessarily submitted to many privations." Now he sought to embrace fully that which he had been deprived of in war. Moreover, he wanted to escape the "stern requirements" of his profession—wanderlust the excitement of war might have stirred.[66] Mercer's emotions ebbed and flowed cyclically after each visit north. Neither completely resigned to his new station in Savannah nor willing to resettle in the North, he constructed an uncomfortable middle ground during the Reconstruction era. He would never fully escape the South that he both loved and loathed or his former travails as a soldier, for these mixed emotions were foundational to his new sense of self. Whatever financial gain Mercer enjoyed proved unattainable to Gorgas, who drifted from job to job in Alabama, his destination in the spring of 1865. In the final months of 1866 and into the winter of 1867, Gorgas complained of severe depression caused, he perversely hoped, by poor health, though "mental anxiety" seemed the only real explanation.[67] On January 6, Gorgas entered a troubled passage into his diary. For the last four months he had lived "in a state of profound depression," which had made life a burden. He desperately wrote, "I am certain that for no imaginable recompense would I live this life over again. . . . Annihilation must be the only thing left. Nothing is so terrible as despair."[68] Nearly paralyzed by depression, Gorgas struggled in the years after the war to resettle and reestablish himself in an increasingly foreign South.

Returning Confederate veterans equated the South's collapse to that of a fallen republic from antiquity and their position to that of tormented victim. John Dooley wrote that if only amid the "universal desolation the cheering form of Liberty would emerge bright, glorious, and triumphant," what a reward the "haggard war-worn veteran" would meet. "But no! From this mournful wreck and frightful ruin the foul and unseemly head of despotism towers above its destined victims."[69] With Southern social systems unsettled and the hopes of an independent nation dispelled, white Southern men turned within, feeling wretched and hopeless. Failures both personal and political undermined Southern manhood. In responding to these trials, many succumbed to depression, for their prewar world was now lost and the foundations for their self-identities crumbled. Nowhere is this more apparent than among those who lost the most: members of the middle and upper classes.

William J. Clarke served with distinction in the two major conflicts of his generation, but war had hardened him. As a captain in the Mexican-American War, he had been severely wounded at the Battle of National Bridge and promoted to major for gallantry. A faithful soldier, Clarke gained the admiration of fellow Confederates while serving as colonel of the Twenty-Fourth North Carolina Regiment. In 1864, at the Battle of Drewry's Bluff, a shell fragment shattered his shoulder.[70] While convalescing, over ninety men signed a petition asking for Clarke's promotion.[71] Yet Clarke could be quarrelsome and often argued with his commander, General Robert Ransom. He never achieved further promotion. When he returned to service in January 1865, Federal troops captured him at Dinwiddie Courthouse, Virginia; he remained imprisoned at Fort Delaware for the duration of the conflict.

After the war Clarke could recount his admirable service record and boast of his regiment's reputation.[72] A proud, stolid veneer left the war's other legacies unacknowledged, however. Physically scarred and battered, Clarke felt great pain from his wounds. Bedridden from time to time, he struggled. Few sources denote what must have been his daily trials because of painful wounds.[73] Physical pains were matched by powerful memories, for Clarke recorded the anniversaries of the battles in Mexico and Virginia in which he was wounded.[74] He remained fortunate in that his profession, law, allowed him to continue working despite these disabilities.[75] But the physical scars of war left an indelible impression that affected his work and family.

Financial distress, physical pain, and an uncertain future left Clarke short tempered, depressed, peevish, and prone to excessive drinking. His wife,

Mary, in particular, bore a heavy burden from her husband's behavior. Confiding to their eldest son, Frank, she asserted that Clarke had not been himself since the war and imprisonment. She felt his mind "weakened," his temperament "very irritable." Together, Mary hoped, she and her son could hide Clarke's troubles from the "world and the other children as long as possible."[76] They walked a razor's edge. On the one hand, Mary wanted to hide from the outside world the family's very real hardships, in particular, Clarke's weakened body and irritable disposition. By so doing, she upheld an antebellum ideal. In a postwar South destabilized by emancipation and war, the household served as a central avenue to rebuild shaken social hierarchies.[77] Clarke's intemperance and inability to fulfill his roles as father and husband were unmanly. Exposing these failures to the outside world would undo him and his family. On the other hand, because of his condition, Mary continued to maintain control over the household and the family — power that war had initially afforded her.[78] In particular, she worried about Frank's future and suggested that he carefully heed his father's advice but seek other opportunities if available, even if they went against Clarke's wishes.[79] Mary's authority over the household and its members extended beyond the war and continued to shape her role as a woman and a wife.

Southerners' inability (forced or purposeful) to articulate their inner feelings only heightened their sense of isolation. Southern culture, controlled by public faces and masks, permitted little public disclosure of mental or emotional breakdowns. These trying conditions were perceived as signs of weakness, which affected the family's image.[80] Efforts to hide family hardships capture the contrast between Southern whites' public and private lives and demonstrate the great difficulties Southerners experienced in their strides toward reconstruction. The Clarkes illustrate the difficult workings of Southerners' new emotional expressions. Antebellum codes clashed with postwar chaos. The crisis of civil war certainly elicited unprecedented emotional disclosure, thus suggesting new forms of cultural expression.[81] But unfettered feelings conflicted with white Southerners' drive for control. Public masks still shaped Southern culture as whites sought to reassert social and domestic authority. Desires for regeneration and social reconstruction increasingly obscured the continued personal pains experienced by defeated Confederates. The passions generated by war had to be properly channeled. Mary Bayard Clarke once again is instructive in explaining Southerners' strides toward emotional balance and moderation.

An accomplished writer, Mary — writing under pseudonyms such as Tenella because of her sex and her father's strong disapproval of her writing—had published poems, columns, and stories in Southern newspapers, periodicals, and books. She understood all too well the importance of maintaining face in Southern society. In August 1866, writing under the pseudonym Stuart Leigh, she published "The South Expects Every Woman to Do Her Duty" in the *Old Guard*. Vance had asked for the piece, and its claims dovetailed with his vision for postwar North Carolina. Emotional control as a form of political power figures prominently in her writing. She began by announcing "that the women of the Southern Confederacy were the unrecognized 'power behind the throne,' during its whole existence."[82] Mary thus made clear women's influence on and contributions to the Confederate nation. But she continued, in a coy tone, by nodding to Victorian stereotypes, which maintained that women had "been more bitter and uncompromising than men" in the postwar period because "they are women, and seldom let the head dictate to the heart. Where one woman acts from policy, one thousand act from impulse."[83] Mary knew well the gendered perceptions of Southerners, who styled men "as practical and conciliatory and women as intemperate and hysterical."[84]

Visceral reactions now worried former Confederates, and Mary called for women's self-censorship. Only with moderation could women maintain a political platform. Turning to women's interactions with Federal soldiers—a famous (or infamous) arena of contact between the sexes—Mary asked women to act not out of hatred but rather with emotional control. "Make the United States' officer as uncomfortable as you please," she wrote, "but do it so as not to disgrace yourself and your country."[85] Concluding, she pleaded, "You gave yourself heart and soul to the Southern Confederacy, gloried in its success and mourned over its defeat as only a true woman could glory and mourn; and will you now shirk its humiliations? Will you leave your lovers, your fathers, brothers and husbands to bear their burden alone?"[86]

Concerned for their future, white Southerners would only retain control of their fates if they properly harnessed the raw emotions generated by civil war. Although individuals certainly continued to express their personal pains privately, broader social needs demanded different public expressions. Many Southern whites, intimately connected by suffering, found that medium through a new language of restraint and moderation, grounded in the shared experiences of wartime sacrifice. Indeed, as Vance maintained, "It is a noble thing to die for one's country; it is a higher and a nobler thing to *live for it*. The best test of the best heroism now, is a cheerful and loyal submission to the powers and events established by our defeat."[87]

Veterans' Communities

During their military service, Southern men had been mustered into regiments, drilled in formations, and encamped together, thus giving rise to tightly knit communities. Many Confederates had become members of a band of brothers.[88] Historian Susannah J. Ural's case study of the Texas Brigade, for example, illuminates how determined Confederate veterans were to maintain ties in the postwar era. Brigade connections advanced business interests, underpinned support networks, and fostered social connections.[89] The bonds among men clearly transcended the war years, especially as many civilians were left with more questions than answers as to why the men they knew before the conflict had changed so much. As such, veterans looked to fellow combatants for understanding. Job Smith related to his friend Cadwallader "Wad" Jones his haunting returns to the battlefield. "Sometimes in my sleep," he wrote, "my mind wanders to the sad Battlefield lying down in the line & thin as a chip, half frightened out of my wits, expecting any moment the Command of forward."[90] Smith's night terrors are similar to those experienced by another Confederate, who recorded while in the army, "I've had great and exciting times at night with my dreams since the battle; some of them are tragedies and frighten me more than ever the fight did what I was wide awake."[91] Smith now took great solace in sharing these feelings through letters or receiving letters from friends. Together, he imagined, they could "cheer" each other in life and find peace during a period of "degredation" and "trouble."[92] The most "profound transformation for many Confederate soldiers," Drew Gilpin Faust writes, "was deeply personal."[93] Wartime experiences and battlefield horrors left these men exposed and frightened—emotions they shared with friends who underwent similar ordeals.

Smith was part of an expanding group of men who looked to other veterans for comfort, demonstrating that the bonds formed in camp and on campaign had forged lasting friendships. Little in antebellum culture had prepared Southern whites for the shock of defeat or the sheer terror of battle. As veterans tried to process these traumas, they often turned to each other for understanding, and men who had served in the same wartime regiments searched for each other throughout the 1860s and 1870s—the desire to retain these connections contributed to the reunion impulse of the late nineteenth century.[94] At times an old commanding officer provided the clearest line of communication and means to sustain wartime connections. William Henry Tripp, commanding officer of Company B, Fortieth North Carolina

Infantry, received numerous letters from former soldiers looking to discuss their old comrades and current dilemmas. T. E. Vann, for instance, wrote to his "old Captain" lamenting the great changes since the war, none of which "seem to bring better times." Distress, he continued, "is an occupant of every home, or at least has been such in some families so long, that, they have become accustomed to such and no longer grieved."[95] War had partially shattered the forbidding veneer of a closed Southern culture. Southern men, forever changed by that conflict, sought out ways to express and examine their new emotions. Vann easily reached out to his old commanding officer, seeking solace and guidance from a man who had proved himself a bulwark against the trials of war.

The emotions felt and expressed in 1865 and beyond, anxiety, depression, and fear, were born from and deeply shaped by the experience of war; yet these feelings must be historicized. Grounded in veterans' communal knowledge, whites continued their wartime emotional communities, sharing the legacies and burdens of war and defeat. The bonds that brought these men together also promoted the exchange of ideas and feelings.[96] How many times such sentiments were privately exchanged between lovers, or husbands and wives, is impossible to say, but it was probably quite frequent. But it is also apparent that many Southern men were now more willing to express themselves freely to other veterans. This behavior was a marked departure from the strictures of the antebellum era, in which whites' carefully groomed personas defined public postures and stifled emotional revelation.[97] Men freely disclosed themselves to women only.[98] Now, though, men who had once enjoyed mastery deeply questioned themselves and the war they had just fought and lost, which they willingly related to other men.

As Confederate veterans grew into old men, they continued to affiliate with, write to, and think about their wartime friends. Soldiers' homes and Confederate reunions served as prominent venues for public association or celebration, as scholars have so ably documented.[99] Yet a rich and thriving private discourse undergirded these more public interactions, demonstrating that the Civil War remained vivid and alive in soldiers' minds and hearts.[100] Some men would encounter each other years after the war as long-lost friends, whereas others were thrown together because of unresolved issues from the past or the demands of the present. Most veterans embraced each other—either physically or through letters—as intimate comrades-in-arms, though this was not always the case. Two examples illuminate the range of encounters and demonstrate the many ways in which the Civil War continued to shape Southern men. A desperate W. C. Fraley looked to his old commanding general Bryan Grimes in an 1880 letter, recalling an incident from the war in which Fraley charged Grimes with taking a lady's brass pin he possessed. Fraley now wrote to the general some fifteen-plus years after the incident because he was "very hard up." He rather grandly charged, "i think nothing more than right you aught to eather send me the pin or pay me for it for i stuck to you 4 long years threw think & thin from Gariesburg till we had to Surrender at Apomatox court house VA."[101] Thus, an impoverished soldier turned to his old officer to rectify a wrong and receive some relief. Conversely, J. B. Lindsey read with great "interest and pleasure" Randolph A. Shotwell's work *Three Years in Battles and Three in Federal Prisons*. Himself a prisoner of war at Fort Delaware like Shotwell, Lindsey felt connected to the writer because of the experience he endured and because he, too, was a chronicler of the war.[102] Thus, on different terms and for different reasons, these men were reconnected in the postbellum years. Such interactions were fleeting, while others proved more enduring; regardless, comradeship and the Confederacy connected these men well past the war's close.

Wartime comradeship and the Confederacy continued to define veterans such as South Carolinian Munson Buford, whom one twentieth-century observer described as the "personification of the Confederacy."[103] Having enlisted at age sixteen in the South Carolina cavalry, Buford served in the Department of South Carolina, Georgia, and Florida before being transferred to Virginia in 1864. Between 1865 and his death, Buford maintained a diary that included an extensive calendar between 1877 and 1881. He served in the militia and attended Masonic meetings (activities that likely included veterans, given the extent of wartime mobilization), as well as participating in a host of veteran- and war-related events. In early September 1879, for example, he was present at the "Survivors reunion and Barbecue of the 3rd S. C. Regiment," and in June 1880 he "went to Newberry to attend the unveiling of the monument in honor of the dead from Newberry County who was killed & died while in the late Confederate Army."[104] Surrounding himself with former Confederates and recounting the deeds of the Civil War, Munson showed that the conflict and its participants continued to shape him well past the Confederacy's defeat.

The experiences of war were not easily forgotten. Martial men celebrated their wartime service. Combat had been exhilarating and their military records were a point of pride. The sights and sounds of the battlefield had scarred other veterans. They suffered from depression and remained traumatized after the conflict's end. Despite these divergent reactions, both groups turned to paper to reconnect with their old comrades-in-arms and recount their service in the Confederate army. Veterans' behavior demonstrates one of the shifts in Southern masculinity during the postbellum era. Feelings that had once been confined to confessional diaries were now expressed in letters to other men and freely discussed among the war's survivors. The creation of both formal and informal veterans' communities marked a legacy of civil war and a reshaping of Southern masculinity.

Public Confederacies

A bevy of masculine activities such as militia musters, Masonic rituals, and Grange meetings directed Confederate veterans' sense of self and underpinned an emotional support network that had been started with their wartime service. Many of the men on whom veterans relied during the war provided support afterward. Reunions, musters, and meetings bolstered a sense of belonging and reinforced a broader corporate identity.[105] By their associations, old soldiers continually shaped veterans' perceptions and conceptions of the war. Carlton McCarthy recounted that in the army, "the young man learned to value men for what they were . . . and so his attachments, when formed, were sincere and durable, and he learned what constitutes a man and a desirable and reliable friend."[106] Having passed through the trial of war together, many of these men continued their friendships well past military service. Buford was greatly excited, for instance, to receive a letter from William G. Austin, "an old dear Army friend." Buford hoped that the two men could plan a visit soon to "talk and fight [their] old Battles over."[107] Julius A. Lineback—a former North Carolina regimental musician—felt "drawn, during and since the war," to Daniel T. Crouse, a member of his regiment.[108] Soldiers engaged each other because of prolonged familiarity. Having lived together in war, many continued to enjoy geographic proximity in the postbellum era. More deeply, only another soldier could relate to combat's emotional toll, the rigors of prolonged outdoor living, and, when applicable, the physical pain from old wounds.

Veterans sought each other out because white Southern men continued to struggle over their personal and public self-identities. Performative statements, comforting words, and public rituals explained, indeed constructed, a particular reality that glorified the Civil War and its lasting legacy.[109] This look backward was especially vital during a period when many veterans had become infirm, were suffering from poverty, or were no longer in positions of power.[110] Although veterans had relied on their army fellows throughout the 1860s, corporate identity became increasingly urgent during Reconstruction as white Southerners angrily witnessed social, racial, and economic transformations. Veterans' reunions, monument dedications, and informal gatherings marked the public manifestations of the Confederacy's postwar life and a reaction against Reconstruction. For white Southerners, these ephemeral communities provided a critical way to gain psychological solace after the horrors of war and to continue the wartime networks so important to their self-identities. Importantly, these associations also gave rise to Lost Cause mythology, ensured an afterlife for the defeated Confederacy, and appropriated public spaces. Veterans' gatherings represented the increasingly public face of their personal reconstructions.

CHAPTER SIX

Violence

Writing to Randolph A. Shotwell—newspaperman, veteran, and Democrat—a Gaston County, North Carolina, Klansman related the order's charge to him upon initiation. "My Brother," he wrote, "you are one of our number" and "entitled to all the benefits of protection and otherwise which belong to the order." When he first joined, it looked like a "military organization," and "every man was charged to furnish himself with a gun and pistol."[1] In the Ku Klux Klan, white brotherhood met paramilitary violence. It was the fullest and most dangerous manifestation of Southern racism and a continuation of Confederates' wartime communities. The very name Ku Klux reflected the importance of mutual cooperation, as it was likely derived from a corruption of the Greek word *kuklos*, meaning "circle or band." Adding "Klan" completed the alliteration and further advanced the notion of mutual association.[2]

Embracing a martial manhood and gripped by feelings of anger, frustration, and hatred, members of the Ku Klux Klan used violence to assert white dominance in the postbellum South's new racial order.[3] Drawing on Confederate imagery and joining armed bodies that intended to assert control over the South's political, economic, and social life, whites placed themselves in positions of power that contributed to the reassertion of their masculinity.[4] Confederate "ghosts" violently attacked and oppressed freedpeoples as Federal troops and Republicans attempted to realize a postslavery world. Gender and emotions shaped white Southerners' reactions, and indeed Reconstruction, as much as political commitments and entrenched racism, for feelings of anger and excitement propelled white men who employed terrorism to advance political, social, and sexual aims.[5] Positing these assertions does not diminish the importance of race; rather, it widens the range of personal feelings, cultural mores, and historical memories that drove whites' behavior while revealing the Klan's cultural function.[6]

The performative elements of the Ku Klux created avenues for the construction and dissemination of a particular brand of political ideology that supported the Democratic Party and white supremacist doctrine.[7] Klan dens provided a venue for the articulation of these ideas among like-minded men, thus fostering the growth of a masculinity predicated on violence for political advancement.⁸ White Southern manhood remained in flux during the Reconstruction era as men looked backward toward "the patriarchal violence of the antebellum years and the chivalric violence of the war" and presaged "the public lynchings of the Progressive Era," as historian Elaine Frantz Parsons explains.⁹ Klansmen used ritual and decree to communicate their liminal position but also to reify whiteness and manhood. Taking emotions seriously sheds light not only on Klan members' actions but also on their ideas and connections to the Civil War because the Confederate communities created during the war underpinned the formation of many orders of the Ku Klux. Careful attention to emotional expression, as witnessed in Klan initiation rituals, reveals a range of feelings, from rage to fear, that bound Klansmen together and served as a mode of communication.¹⁰ These linkages were critical to the Klan's campaigns of terror. Although never as organized and centralized as their twentieth-century counterparts, nineteenth-century Klan orders proliferated across the South, drawing in white men from different social classes. The horrific results of their actions were well documented, especially in the voluminous African American and white Republican testimony given to Congress in 1871–72.

Vigilante violence underpinned white masculinity in the Democratic South's campaign for "redemption." Race played a prominent role in the establishment of this new white manhood, which operated through savagery. This mode of behavior represented a distinctive emotional community composed of men who shared similar feelings rooted in the past and reactive to the present.¹¹ The men under study—hooded midnight raiders who terrorized white Unionists, African Americans, and the socially marginalized—depended on anonymity. Their acts, while condoned by many whites, were legally condemned. Unmasking these midnight raiders reveals connections between Klan membership and Confederate veterans, while also demonstrating white Southerners' broader engagement in, and understanding of, the process of Reconstruction to which the reclamation of white Southern manhood was central.¹² As men strove to regain mastery over both self and society, they also had to confront the emotional and psychological consequences of civil war.¹³ How men publicly and personally negotiated and responded to these forces shaped the reconstruction of manhood—a process that was neither uniform nor universal—and influenced their emotional lives. The Ku Klux Klan served as one model for an outwardly aggressive, unrestrained, warrior-like masculinity that politically targeted African Americans and white Republicans to "restore" authority.¹⁴

A long history of scholarly and popular works describes the Klan's infamy. Sympathetic histories written in the nineteenth century produced an interpretative tradition that emphasized Klansmen's supposedly understandable reaction to intolerable oppression.[15] Scholars gradually revised such orthodoxy, resulting in two prominent arguments. First, there are those historians who concluded that the Klan's inherent racism appealed to Southern whites.[16] Second, scholars have contended that Klan violence connected to whites' broader campaigns of political insurgency.[17] Recent scholarship, especially that grounded in cultural history and gender studies, has broadened our understanding of the meaning behind the purpose and precedent of the Ku Klux Klan. These historians have demonstrated that racism and political ideology alone do not adequately explain why the Klan targeted particular individuals (especially women and children), engaged in certain behavior (simulated sex acts), referenced and used popular cultural forms (carnival, costuming, ritual), or created a sense of corporate identity rooted in the ideology of the Lost Cause.[18] As Hannah Rosen cautions, "Night rider violence was, in fact, so seemingly instrumental and so explicitly targeted for political ends that it is difficult to resist reducing its meaning entirely to its apparent function. Yet this violence also took striking forms seemingly unrelated to function that were consistent across a wide region and over several years."[19] Scholars must therefore consider gender and emotion in conjunction with race and cultural forms as underpinning political practices.

Rituals and Oaths

Shotwell had served with the Eighth Virginia Infantry during the Civil War. After briefly studying law, he threw himself into the newspaper business. Although his various publishing schemes proved financially unsuccessful, he became a prominent political voice in North Carolina, where he had moved in 1865.[20] A conservative Democrat, he knew many white North Carolinians who were active in the Ku Klux; indeed, he himself had ties to the organization that resulted in his imprisonment until President Ulysses S. Grant pardoned him. Southern military defeat had emboldened men such as Shotwell who angrily reacted to Reconstruction, a period he deemed a "dreadful decade."[21] In a common refrain, Shotwell charged that North Carolina's White Brotherhood stood "as a defensive association to protect the women of the South against personal assault at the hands of Negro assailants, who were protected by the United States representatives."[22] Having endured the hardships of war and remained steadfast to the cause of Southern independence, Shotwell watched in horror as North Carolina was held "captive" between 1865 and 1875.[23] Embittered Confederate veterans like Shotwell sought personal and social redemption through the Ku Klux Klan.

Group cohesion was essential to the integrity of the Klan orders and the performance of their heinous acts. A series of well-documented initiation rituals performed in the Carolinas will be examined to access the systems of feeling underpinning some orders of the Ku Klux. Although it is extremely difficult to determine the frequency of and rates of participation in these rites, they symbolically communicated larger ideas about Southern white men's emotional and cultural worlds.[24] The Klan's rites instilled the order with secrecy and monitored membership.[25] So too were initiations intended to elicit emotional reactions from incoming members, as the orchestrated performances created confusion, promoted fear, and elicited revulsion—symbolic communication that tested men's mettle. Although not all Klansmen went through direct rituals of initiation, those who did were admitted by standing members only. Initiates were required by oath to uphold the order's secrets, assist distressed members, and ensure law and order—that is, white social order. Failure to do so would result in death, or so many oaths decreed. Thus, oath-bound men composed the Ku Klux Klan and joined the order to become part of a brotherhood that defined itself against the revolutions of emancipation and war and protected members and their families.[26]

As whites banded together, their tightly knit fraternities underpinned the growth of a corporate identity and contributed to the embrace of a mutual martial manhood. Like wartime military units, Klansmen wielded power and acted aggressively to achieve positions of race-based mastery. The Klan was not structured as a centralized organization; rather, states of the former Confederacy hosted dozens of unconnected "orders" or "dens" of the group. Nomenclatures and organizational lines are confused and difficult to track. Reports of Klan activity in one geographic area often inspired the formation of new organizations. North Carolina featured the White Brotherhood, the Constitutional Union Guard, and the Invisible Empire, the last being an order that appeared also in South Carolina, in addition to the Chester Conservative Clan and others.[27] Klan membership was diverse and included white men from every rank and class.[28] These men shared a generational legacy of military defeat, and the Ku Klux Klan, however loosely constituted, enforced domination and submission.[29]

Fraternal orders and the rituals practiced therein offered young Victorian men solace and psychological guidance during their passage into manhood.[30] The sociocultural function of fraternities proves useful when considering how Southern whites sought to regain manhood and reestablish "self" through secret societies such as the Klan, which mimicked fraternal orders; both organizations, for example, privileged secrecy and undying loyalty.[31] Shotwell maintained that the methods of the Masons and other fraternities "were laid under contribution for the organic features of the White Brotherhood."[32] By joining the Klan, whites entered a deeply protective, highly secretive venue that fostered social cohesion similar to that shared by soldiers during war. Many of the cultural and social mechanisms that bound together antebellum men were also employed after the war to establish a sense of corporate and political identity.

While initiation rites were performed unevenly and in different ways throughout the South, a number of similar features emerged.[33] Rituals left new members exposed so that they could be reborn into the order. Moreover, initiation procedures were symbolic performances composed of distinct phases that the novice had to negotiate successfully for final passage into the order. Shotwell's thorough account of a rite of initiation performed in North Carolina illustrates the components of these ornate performances. A man seeking to join the Klan was given instructions to meet at a specific, remote location deep in the night—an environment and situation "full of ghostly suggestions."[34] Upon the man's arrival, disguised men descended from the woods. A series of signs and countersigns were offered before the man was guided forward. Now blindfolded, the inductee and his guides were asked a formalized series of questions before gaining entry into the outer rim of the "Circle of Fraternity." A large, costumed body of men was already assembled; they removed the man's blindfold. Before him stood two tall, looming figures wearing long red gowns. The men wore hideous masks, "two feet high, with eye-holes bound in black, and tall horns, formed of red flannel, stuffed with cotton." Each man held a knife in one hand and a pistol in the other. One was pressed to the initiate's head, the other at the breast as he took the oath.[35] Upon his taking the oath, men emerged from the trees in all directions. "Swarms of white robed, ghostly figures, shaking their horns, and presenting pistols at the breast of the startled neophyte! Then, forming a circle, —still with pistols presented—they pronounced in low tones:— "DEATH! DEATH!! DEATH!!! *We have heard; and we will remember!*"[36]

North Carolinian James E. Boyd described similar practices in North Carolina's White Brotherhood, though only one member had admitted Boyd, demonstrating great discrepancy in practice. According to Boyd, the inductee was placed in a large ring composed of disguised men. The man was brought into the circle's center and then left alone. The crowd descended on the

KU KLUX COSTUMES IN NORTH CAROLINA

[*From engraving (after a photograph) in G. B. Raum's "The Existing Conflict," and used by permission. The original photograph was made in 1870 for J. G. Hester, deputy U. S. Marshal in North Carolina, who captured the disguises.*]

This engraving captures both the Ku Klux Klan's elaborate costuming and its symbolic rituals. *Ku Klux Costumes in North Carolina*, 1906-7. Image courtesy of the Schomburg Center for Research in Black Culture, Jean Blackwell Hutson Research and Reference Division, The New York Public Library. *The New York Public Library Digital Collections.*

initiate, making "curious noises" and rubbing him with their horns. Boyd noted that these acts were intended to frighten the neophyte as much as possible before the administering of an oath. As in Shotwell's description, the oath prescribed a penalty of death.[37] Other documented rites in North Carolina symbolically communicated death through the use of a rope. A new member would have a rope tied around his neck, which was tightened until the inductee was asphyxiated slightly—a procedure loosely reminiscent of a Masonic ritual.[38]

Although the evidence is limited, it is clear that the North Carolina Klan rituals cited by Shotwell and Boyd were intended to evoke fear, test mettle, and forge brotherhood. It is notable that key elements in their descriptions—

large bodies gathered for induction, the practice of secrecy, and the use of oaths—are detailed in John C. Lester and D. L. Wilson's early history of the Ku Klux Klan, thereby suggesting the reach of such practices; Lester was a part of the original Pulaski, Tennessee, group.[39] As in fraternal societies, Klan rituals were both concealing and revealing.[40] Initiations marked the passage from one social status to another. New members moved through formalized spaces and underwent personal trials before gaining final acceptance.[41] In the ceremony's beginning, the blindfolded inductee probably felt great anxiety and curiosity as he was brought before the order. Once unmasked, the man did not meet known faces but rather disguised men—further obfuscation. Many Klansmen wore elaborate masks that combined familiar elements, such as tongues, horns, and eyes, into grotesque forms, thus rendering the natural unnatural.[42] Ku Klux costuming evoked the European charivari tradition, as historian Lisa Cardyn notes, thereby representing the blending of old and new cultural forms.[43] Depending on the specific ritual, the inductee either was ritualistically attacked by the crowd before taking an oath or took an oath before the symbolic assault. The attack signaled the display of a rugged, competitive masculinity.[44] The inductee surely felt fear as the large, disguised crowd came upon him, brandishing weapons, making strange noises, and assaulting his person. But the neophyte had to withstand this attack by publicly displaying his manliness. With the successful navigation of these trials—an experience shared, presumably, by at least some standing members—the inductee now had access to the secrets, passwords, and protection of the Ku Klux Klan.

Threats of death, the presence of weapons, ghastly figures, and the use of skulls and skeletons (real or depicted) made death a key feature in rites of initiation. Violence and death were normalized through ritualistic devices and physical actions. New members' bravado and self-control established their willingness to embrace a savage, but directed, masculinity. Representations of death reminded members of the consequences of betrayal but also communicated their rebirth into a secret order.[45] The feelings conjured during the initiation process—fear, anxiety, confusion, and anger—were the same emotions felt by Southern white men during the personal and political crises of Reconstruction. Moreover, the presence of weapons, the use of bleached bones, and the threat of attack echoed features encountered repeatedly on Civil War battlefields, at least for Klansmen who were also veterans. The order not only offered an avenue to express these feelings, however unconsciously, but also presented a vehicle for the reestablishment of a familiar social order.[46]

Oath-bound men, bonded through rite and ritual, operated in concert within the confines of an extended "brotherhood." If a fellow Klansman was engaged in a fight, he made a distress signal; other "brothers" were bound to go to his assistance.[47] Two documents from South Carolina demonstrate the gendered dimensions of Klan politics. The first is a description of an anonymous initiation ritual from 1870 that, while not definitively attributed to the Klan, contains many features of other Ku Klux materials.[48] In the antebellum era, armed collective action upheld white men's mastery over the public and private spheres. The revolutions of Reconstruction undercut white authority and challenged the construction of coalitions.[49] Secret orders perceived these changes as an affront to the South's "natural" social order. As recorded in the document describing the initiation rite, a ranked officer would present this narrative to a new member. The officer announced, "When ignorant depraved men . . . are illegally and unjustly forced upon a people as rulers . . . it is the duty of the people thus oppressed and threatened to oppose this monstrous wrong." To reestablish order and resurrect white manhood, the officer recommended action. He continued, "You must know that there now exists a necessity for organization to prevent the evils threatened[.] Having confidence in you we have invited you to meet us and now ask your active cooperation." The inductee symbolically knelt throughout this speech, with one gloved hand tied behind his back, and then he took an oath very similar to those administered by Klansmen in Tennessee and North Carolina. His passive position not only reflected the same one held by past "brothers" during their initiations but also placed him "in the same position individually that [they were] all in politically."[50] Ritualistic submission made tangible white men's emasculation. But once men joined together in concerted action, they had recourse to rectify perceived wrongs. Through decree and ritual, this South Carolina secret society articulated the politics of white manhood.

The second document, an order from the Grand Cyclops of one of South Carolina's dens (most likely the Chester Conservative Clan), recognized that collective strength wielded power most effectively.[51] The Grand Cyclops ordered, "Whenever it may be necessary to act, let us do it deliberately, firmly, with concentrated power and strength, demoralizing our opponents by the overwhelming display of our strength and with an eye single to the good of our Cause and Country." The use of surgical attacks, the men's deportment, and the group's ideological underpinnings upheld the cause's righteousness in whites' eyes. It was further decreed, "No Klan or members of this organization (unless in very urgent cases not admitting of delay) will undertake to redress grievances of a general character or act in any manner calculated to produce a breach of the peace without orders from these Hd Qrs."[52] This call, while not always heeded, was essential for upholding the moral high ground, according to whites.

Claims of "legitimate" authority became key in the rhetorical battle over political Reconstruction, for white recalcitrance had received national censure.[53] The Reconstruction Act of 1867, passed after the former Confederate states refused to ratify the Fourteenth Amendment and failed to protect African Americans and white Republicans from violence, signaled congressional control over Reconstruction.[54] Georgian George Anderson Mercer angrily denounced "the solemn farce of an election under the Military Reconstruction Bill of Congress," as "crowds of ignorant negroes from the country came in to exercise their franchise."[55] White Southerners deemed both the black franchise and racial equality impossibilities. White manhood, and by default a "proper" social order, could only be restored through "respectable" action and properly channeled aggression. Defenders of the Ku Klux, such as Shotwell, went to great lengths to legitimize the order by emphasizing that "hundreds of our best citizens of all social grades and professions, became members of it" and by claiming that some of the "noblest women [he] ever knew not only approved of the order, but were informed of its operations." Violent acts were credited to "a great many wild, reckless young men" who had "gained admittance to the Order." Shotwell further explained that there were "hundreds of *false* Ku Klux; that is, men who learned enough about the working of the Order to enable them to put on disguise, and gratify personal malice at its expense."[56] The spurious analysis employed by white Southerners attempted to mask their unconstitutional attempt to restore an antebellum social and racial order.[57]

The rituals of the Ku Klux Klan reflected the transitional nature of postwar Southern masculinity. Initiation ceremonies suspended the differences between the sacred and the profane, the living and the dead. These rites turned the social world upside down, thus symbolically communicating to inductees and standing members their current social position. By constructing an emblematic dream world, men not only exorcised the legacy of military defeat but also shaped a path for resolution. With their rebirth into the Ku Klux Klan, men could indulge in sexual and violent behavior typically deemed inappropriate.[58] Thus, performance, symbol, and ritual within the Klan defamiliarized the familiar but did so to teach about the value of being disorderly. While the model of manhood crafted through the Ku Klux Klan would never become normative, it served as a crucial means in whites' broader campaign for the reestablishment of a social and political "self."[59]

Ghosts of the Confederacy

Despite white Southerners' attempts to legitimate their dangerous reactions to Reconstruction, elaborate costumes and intricate oaths betrayed members' rhetoric. The Ku Klux's members managed the tensions between their everyday actions and violent attacks by constructing the dual identity of Christian gentleman and damned soul.[60] Although Klansmen assumed multiple identities—moon men, animals, or foreigners—they often proclaimed themselves to be the ghosts of Confederate soldiers.[61] By linking the Confederacy to the South's Invisible Empire, the Klan resurrected its failed nationalist project and ensured that its soldiers did not die in vain. Confederate dead were ideal figures to revive the antebellum South's racial and social order, for these men had given their lives for its preservation.[62] The Ku Klux Klan symbolically invoked the white South's fallen warriors to once again walk among the living and transform the unrelenting humiliation that came with military defeat into revenge, hatred, and anger.[63]

Southern men's continued engagement with the Civil War and Confederate military service is manifest in the Klan's organization. Most famously, the six men who founded the Ku Klux in Pulaski, Tennessee, were Confederate veterans.[64] From these roots grew Confederate vines. In a compelling case study of Alamance County, North Carolina, for example, historian Scott Reynolds Nelson found that former Confederates in Companies F and K of the Sixth North Carolina Infantry Regiment were among the important leaders called "Chiefs."[65] Chiefs chose victims to be tortured and issued privates orders to be followed.[66] The foot soldiers of the Confederacy became the shock troops of the Ku Klux.[67] Prominent Confederate officers once again led Southern men. Nathan Bedford Forrest—the tenacious wartime cavalryman—served as the first and only Grand Wizard, while famed general John B. Gordon acted as Grand Dragon of the Georgia Klan. Confederate links thus became central to the organization of the Ku Klux Klan.[68]

Klansmen's former military lives directly shaped protocol and order. Former Confederate officers such as Forrest instilled military protocol in early Klan dens. As historian Walter L. Fleming explains, "The ex-Confederates under the command of Forrest, Grand Wizard of the Invisible Empire, were obeying the first law of nature and were bound to reveal nothing to injure the cause, just as when Confederates under Forrest, Lieutenant-General of the Confederate Army, they were bound not to reveal military information to the hostile forces."[69] Sentinels who required signs and countersigns for entry guarded secluded meetings.[70] Raids were often conducted in military-like fashion. Whistles were used to coordinate movements, convey messages, and foster anonymity.[71] Disguised men were often assigned numbers and referenced only by that conferred identity.[72] Rally cries and distress signals often recalled the war. One member of North Carolina's White Brotherhood testified that they used the word "Shiloh" to mobilize comrades.[73] These measures not only bolstered the Klan's effectiveness but also reaffirmed the martial identity of its members. Quasi-military campaigns regenerated white manhood and attempted to resurrect antebellum racial hierarchies.[74]

The militaristic character of the Ku Klux had a practical function, for the United States Army—often supported by state militias—remained a presence throughout the South during Reconstruction. Tennessee governor William G. Brownlow used members of the Twenty-Ninth U.S. Infantry and state militia, for example, to dramatically curtail Klan violence.[75] By operating at night, maintaining secrecy, and wearing disguises, the Ku Klux attempted to thwart military countermeasures. Ghostly apparitions did not fool Brigadier General Alfred H. Terry, commander of the Department of the South, who reported to Secretary of War John A. Rawlins after a two-month investigation, "There can be no doubt of the existence of numerous insurrectionary movements known as the 'Ku Klux Klans,' who, shielded by their disguise[s], by the secrecy of their movements, and by the terror they inspire, perpetrate crime with impunity."[76] Armed conflict between the Ku Klux Klan and state and federal authority in both North and South Carolina led to widespread arrests, the impeachment of North Carolina's governor, and the Republican Party's imperilment in the seaboard states.[77]

The starched white robe emblazoned with an encircled cross, seared into public consciousness by the Klan's hateful acts in the twentieth century, little resembles the motley assortment of costumes and regalia worn in the Reconstruction era. Long robes of red, yellow, black, brown, and white were seen together in some orders, while others were barely costumed. Members of some orders wore elaborately constructed headpieces, which included beards, horns, and exaggerated tongues, while others wore crudely constructed hoods.[78] White North Carolina conservative David Schenck commented that the Ku Klux dressed in white, moved noiselessly at night, and carried skulls and skeletons, thereby giving "themselves an unnatural character."[79] Costuming, masks and hoods in particular, concealed one identity and constructed another.[80] Disguised men indulged in inappropriate behavior.[81] In a fascinating reading of the Thomas Dixon trilogy, literary scholar Judith Jackson Fossett questions the performative function of Klan costuming. She writes, "Dixon's narratives unwittingly call into question the authenticity of white male privilege. If authentic whiteness can be derived only from the wearing of white cloth, does that cloth in fact cover or rather hide a real, but ultimately inferior and flawed white skin?"[82] Fossett's question confronts whites' use of disguise in their quest for social control. Yet Southern men used masking—both figurative and literal—as a means of controlling perception and wielding power.[83]

The Ku Klux Klan employed a variety of tactics to announce their arrival either within a community or at a specific household. References to the military and the supernatural abound. The broadest campaigns involved the sudden appearance of written notices or public parades, not the burning crosses emblematic of the twentieth-century Klan.[84] South Carolina's Conservative *Yorkville Enquirer* printed this notice, similar to ones issued throughout the South:

> K.K.K. DEAD-MAN'S HOLLOW,
> SOUTHERN DIV. Midnight,
> March 30 [1868].
>
> *General Order, No. 1.*
>
> REMEMBER the hour appointed by our Most Excellent Grand Captain-General. The dismal hour draws nigh for the meeting of our mystic Circle. The Shrouded-Knight will come with pick and spade; the Grand Chaplain will come with the ritual of the dead. The grave yawneth, the lightnings flash athwart the heavens, the thunders roll, but the Past Grand Knight of the Sepulcher will recoil not.
>
> By order of the Great Grand Centaur. SULEYMAN, G.G.S.[85]

A combination of the nonsensical and the fantastic, such advertisements were intended to instill fear in local blacks and rally white supporters.[86] But the advertisement's phrasing also had another function. By claiming to be ghosts, acting during the night only, and weaving mystery through printed materials, the members of the Ku Klux were attempting to fictionalize themselves and their order. It was essential to popular representations that the Klan's existence remained in doubt. And, indeed, the effectiveness of such tactics can be seen throughout newspapers and diaries that questioned the order's existence.[87] South Carolinian and former Confederate officer Ellison Summerfield Keitt, for instance, maintained a scrapbook of newspaper clippings about the Ku Klux Klan. One article, taken from the New York *Evening Post*, proclaimed, "The Radical party have, for its own interests, and with a view to the perpetuity of its power, created, fostered and exaggerated a Ku-Klux organization in the States of the South."[88] The incredulity of the writer was not unusual. Historian Elaine Frantz Parsons has gone to great lengths to document how, despite major newspaper coverage and national investigations, "the most fundamental question about the Ku-Klux—whether it existed at all—remained unsettled even in mainstream public discourse."[89]

Paper propaganda often worked in conjunction with parades. These performances presented the Klan as a spectacle to be witnessed, and served as overt demonstrations of power.[90] Lester and Wilson recorded in their sympathetic history of the Klan that Tennessee whites agreed to stage a series of parades on the night of July 4, 1867. Drawing from events in Pulaski, the authors described the scene. That morning, papers announcing the parades were spread throughout town. By evening, the men "donned their robes and disguises and put covers of gaudy materials on their horses." After a signal, the "different companies met and passed each other on the public square in perfect silence; the discipline appeared to be admirable." By marching and countermarching, the Klan created an appearance of vast numbers.[91] Witnesses in Alabama (who at first mistook the men for the advance for a circus company) and Mississippi spoke of similar events, whereas Shotwell complained of "similar societies" that assumed "Ku-Klux colors to mystify the public, and marched into villages in masked processions, with stuffed elephants and other grotesque animals. Even circuses burlesqued Ku-Klux Klans by extravagant performances."[92] These tactics awed and intimidated audiences before the use of coercive force. Ultimately, though, orders of the Klan were too fragmented, its hierarchies too dispersed, to arrange parades with any frequency. Instead, the vast majority of African Americans and whites encountered the Klan intimately, under the cloak of darkness.

The dirt roadways of the South, once under cover of darkness, became deadly arteries canvassed by hooded men searching out African Americans and white radicals for the purposes of intimidation or violence. Upon nearing the victim's home, Klansmen announced their presence through loud commotion, house attacks, and demands of entry. Sometimes the attackers proclaimed themselves to be Confederate dead from hell. Approaching the home of black South Carolinian Andy Timons, Klansmen cried out, "Here we come—we are the Ku Klux. Here we come, right from hell."[93] Dick Wilson testified that after inquiries into his son's location, he responded politely to the "gentlemen," stating that he did not know his son's whereabouts. One man snapped back, "Don't call me any gentleman; we are just from hell fire; we haven't been in this country since Manassas."[94] Individuals would pose one of their group as a fallen hero from the battlefield. In one instance, the ghost was called Stevens. The Klan summoned one African American after another for questioning. They asked, "Was this one of your murderers, Stevens?" He responded yes. "And they would say, 'Well, take him off,' and another would be brought out, and he would answer, 'Yes,' and they would take him off."[95] These elaborate performances and assigned identities resurrected the Confederacy and restored, if temporarily, an antebellum social order dominated by Southern whites.

Elaborate tricks were practiced to advance ghostly identities further. Quite often, as Katharine Du Pre Lumpkin—a writer and sociologist reared in the Lost Cause—recalled from stories of her father's own involvement in the Georgia Klan, a body of disguised men would ride to the home of an African American who had either voted Republican or been "insufferably impudent" to a white man or woman. As the black man approached, the hooded crowd talked of former exploits during the Civil War. One might describe "how he had died at Gettysburg or some other battle and how thirsty he got in hell." The men would then ask the African American for multiple buckets of water, which were quickly consumed, or so it appeared through trickery, until the man supposedly trembled in fear at the supernatural occurrence.[96] So, too, would Klansmen use constructed devices to augment height; others developed an internal framework beneath their costuming that supported a false head or a fake arm, which could be removed in the presence of an African American.[97] Grotesque figures and whites' chicanery created confusion during raids and increased the mystery of the Ku Klux Klan.

Southern blacks quickly unraveled the Klan's performances and recognized its members' deliberate subterfuge.[98] Many blacks, rather than being scared into believing that they were among ghosts, tried to uncover the curious specters before them. One North Carolinian related, "They always said in my country that a man could not kill a Ku-Klux; they said that they could not be hit; that if they were, the ball would bounce back and kill you. I thought though that I would try it, and see if my gun would hit one."[99] Another man, well versed in Klan appearances, actively interrogated the situation upon the Ku Klux's arrival. He wrote, "I went into this thing when they came to my house; they said they had risen from the dead; I wanted to see what sort of men they was; I went a purpose to see who they were; whether they were spirits, or whether they were human; but when I came to find out, they was men like me."[100] By unmasking the Klan and questioning its tactics, African Americans deduced the Klan's real character. In the words of black South Carolinian John Patterson Green, they "wore masks to conceal their cowardly faces."[101]

Scholars have posited a number of different reasons why the Ku Klux Klan posed as Confederate dead.[102] Early histories of the order commonly asserted that whites used ghost disguises to trick and scare blacks, whom they disparagingly described as naive and overly superstitious.[103] Scholarship locating African Americans' reactions to Klan raids has revised the jaundiced perspective of early historians.[104] As many of the accounts examined here relate, armed African Americans were more than willing to test the mettle of the undead. Further, to suggest that blacks were frightened by grotesque disguises proves nothing, for fear and caution are sensible attitudes for anyone confronting gangs of armed, masked men arriving in the dead of night and behaving in a curious manner.[105] The costuming and performance of the Ku Klux has attracted scholars of gender and culture who have argued that "specific popular cultural forms" were borrowed to advance white Southerners' revolt against Reconstruction.[106] Minstrel shows, carnivals, and Mardi Gras reflected the cultural roots of the Klan's inversion performances, while their violent acts were "an expression of white southern men's sense of disempowerment and failure as patriarchs after the war," writes Parsons.[107] Spectral disguises also reflected white Southerners' engagement with a burgeoning Lost Cause mythology.[108] The ghosts, rather than deified heroes, were restless spirits from hell who wreaked havoc among the living. By invoking the Confederate dead and inverting the land of the living, the Ku Klux Klan deliberately created a symbolic world, for the reclamation of white manhood was achieved through actions neither honorable nor gentlemanly.[109]

The resurrection of the dead became a mechanism to both inextricably link the Klan to the Confederacy and distance the order from the chivalrous ideals of Southern gentlemen—such tensions pronounced the transitional nature of white masculinity during the Reconstruction era. By acting as ghosts, Klansmen engaged in symbolic performance and recalled memories of the war. On the one hand, disguises and assumed personas created purposeful theatrics that attempted to bolster whites' position. Klansmen temporally controlled a public stage and conferred an idealized portrait of the South's social and political landscape. This portrait looked backward to the Confederacy and the antebellum era, periods devoid, at least in white people's minds, of politicized African Americans and white radicals. Such deception attempted to conceal white Southerners' political impotence and embattled position, while bolstering their strides toward social control.[110] On the other hand, by portraying the dead among the living, whites conveyed, however unconsciously, their ambiguous position. Such figures, suspended between realms, wanted revenge to redeem a lost social order. Southern men may have been "dead" to the social world, but they were alive to the asocial world.[111] Federal troops, not former Confederates, were the only armed bodies legitimated in the postwar South. Klan warnings often describe the passage of ghosts from one realm to another.[112] The Confederate dead, once among the living, could seek revenge.[113] While the Klan's acts were dishonorable, its members chose to create a "Shadowed Brotherhood" of "murdered heroes" to make right what was now wrong, and by so doing both recall and help create a heroic, idealized vision of Southern manhood.[114]

Landscapes of Terror

Contests over power were central to the South's reconstruction, and given the lasting consequences of who wielded control, emotions ran high.[115] The actions of the Ku Klux were intended to provoke strong feelings among all parties—viewers, victims, and participants. A deadly combination of uncontrolled anger, personal loss, and intense hatred among white Southerners became physically manifest in violent actions that, in turn, created landscapes of terror meant to intimidate and control.[116] Men's visceral reactions fed directly into these encounters and whites' broader campaigns of terror.[117] But the Klan also represented more than white supremacy; it revealed Southerners' fears.[118] Lester, a member of the Klan in Pulaski, Tennessee, maintained that the Ku Klux illustrated "how men, by circumstances and conditions, in part of their own creation, may be carried away from their moorings and drifted along in a course against which reason and judgment protest."[119] While Lester's sentiments clearly reveal a man seeking to be remembered kindly despite his reprehensible actions, his words also illuminate how emotions played a central role in men's actions. The Ku Klux Klan, while calculating and deliberate, also represented white masculinity unmoored in a violent reign of terror. Fortunately, African American resistance and the federal government's investigation destroyed the Ku Klux, thereby holding Southern white men accountable for their actions and forcing them to define and assess their emotional reactions, however grudgingly.

Reconstruction-era violence elicited shock and revulsion.[120] As historian Lisa Cardyn explains, Klansmen's systematic molestation and violation of their victims attempted "to reinstantiate white male dominance in its antebellum form."[121] Stories of the Ku Klux immediately attracted the attention of the national press, offering a useful narration about power and control in the postbellum South.[122] Although reactions certainly varied, some white Southern Republicans were shocked by what they saw unfolding. Ku Klux violence demonstrated humanity at its worst. Amos T. Akerman, longtime Georgia resident, former Confederate officer, and U.S. attorney general during the Grant administration, sought understanding through analogy. After reading Ambrose Spencer's *Narrative of Andersonville*, Akerman maintained that the "temper which induced those atrocities is now active in Ku Kluxery."[123] In this comparison, cruelty, anger, and monstrosity governed Southern white men and resulted in barbarous acts. Reverdy Johnson, engaged by the government during the prosecution of the Ku Klux Klan trials in South Carolina, found the testimony stupefying. At one point he intervened during the hearings to pronounce, "I have listened with unmixed horror to some of the testimony which has been brought before you. The outrages proved are shocking to humanity; they admit of neither excuse nor justification; they violate every obligation which law and nature impose upon men: they show that the parties engaged were brutes, insensible to the obligations of humanity and religion."[124] The words of Akerman and Johnson reflect the stinging visceral reactions produced by Klan violence. The cruelty displayed in such inhumanity connected to the temperament and disposition of Southern whites. As Albion Winegar Tourgée argued, the "blood and torture" of the Ku Klux were grounded in "slavery's barbarity," thus connecting white men's postwar cruelties to their prewar lives.[125]

Masculinity was central to Reconstruction-era conflict. White men, in trying to establish their own dominance, attempted to subvert blacks' strides to fulfill their own manhood. Although it is hearsay, African American farmer Essic Harris of Chatham County, North Carolina, related the story of freedman Anthony Davis, a "mighty man" who talked "about his manhood."[126] Davis had heard stories of the abuse of black women and said that he would "hate to see a man come and butcher up his wife like he had heard tell of their butchering other people." The Ku Klux Klan "got hold of that and came there."[127] J. B. Eaves related that Aaron Biggerstaff was beaten because he was "a very bold man" and talked "more than he ought to"; he would "very often make threats."[128] Southern whites hoped to assuage their humiliation, alleviate the pains of defeat, and channel their emotional tumult by reconstructing the postwar South in their own vision and, by so doing, reconstruct their own manhood.

The events of the Jim Crow era suggest that Reconstruction-era violence and repression resolved for many whites the uncertainty engendered by Confederate defeat. The deliberate balance between violence and restraint, so vital to the antebellum master class, fell away among Ku Kluxers who governed through force only.[129] The resultant masculinity was aggressively outward and swayed more by raw feelings than by self-control. North Carolina conservative and sometime Klansman David Schenck articulated the thoughts of many whites when he wrote, "Fear is the only avenue to a negroes conscience—it is worth all the kindness." He continued by positing that blacks could be ruled with severity only—"Nothing else will answer the purpose"; these beliefs guided larger systems of behavior that attempted to manipulate the feelings of African Americans while bolstering their own moral and cultural superiority.[130] Bound by blood oath, the Ku Klux often operated through roaming groups of men who fed off each other's emotions. "It has become no unusual thing," one North Carolina witness described, "to see groups of 40 to 50 . . . Ku Klux rowdying up and down through the streets of this village [Chapel Hill]."[131] Although still cloaked by anonymity, the Ku Klux marked the rise of a new white masculinity that would shape the Jim Crow South.

During active periods in Klan violence, whites nightly tortured African Americans; Ku Kluxers privileged white masculinity over black bodies.[132] Attacks were intended to inflict physical and psychological harm but also leave outward reminders of the Klan's presence, as reflected in whites' desire for control through the injuries they inflicted on freedpeoples. A North Carolina Republican reported that he had "seen several pistol-shot wounds" and "quite a number of colored men with their backs severely lashed." He also related the "mangled appearance" of one man's body. "On his breast," he remarked, "were two marks or wounds, which he said had been produced in this way: They jabbed him with the muzzle of a double-barreled gun, and his breast exhibited two small circular wounds." Furthermore, he had a badly bruised body.[133] As during the antebellum era, whites deemed the scars on black bodies signifiers of "disruptive" or "unruly" men and women.[134] African Americans who embraced radicalism, voted Republican, or conducted themselves in any way that Southern whites found disagreeable were terrorized.[135] By so doing, whites reinvented antebellum techniques of control and punishment—efforts aimed at the maintenance of white male supremacy—that also reflected their fears over political and social displacement.

Whippings were a common occurrence. Green described the bullwhip and rawhide as "instruments of . . . torture, and made to produce arguments which none dared refute."[136] Harris recalled that at the height of Klan violence, blacks were whipped weekly. Deep, agonizing pain afflicted not only individual victims but also black communities. As Harris further related, "A good many that they have whipped—a heap of them—have gone off."[137] Night raids inflicted terror and were aimed at controlling behavior. James Boyd related that the Klan would "whip a little, and go about the houses of the negroes and tell them if they went to election they would meet them on the way. It was understood that on the night before election the KuKluks would turn out *enmasse*, and visit the houses of the colored people."[138] These tactics constructed a rhetoric of power and symbolically enacted social and racial norms.[139] The Klan intended to remake the South by constructing landscapes controlled by fear and governed by hate. Brutal lashings were dispensed to men, women, and children of all ages and were intended to shame victims into submission.[140] Blacks' assertion of personal dignity became a mortal risk.[141] Often, attackers would represent their violence as retribution for blacks' conduct. Participation in the Union League, military service, and economic success, for instance, were considered flagrant violations.[142]

Attacks came quickly, under the cloak of darkness. James M. Justice testified that the Klan's members "usually commit[ted] their depredations about midnight, between midnight and daylight."[143] Hidden by night skies and arrayed in ghoulish disguises, Ku Kluxers inflicted mental and physical terror on their victims. Black North Carolinian Daniel Jordan, a man accused of stealing, experienced what might be considered a typical raid. A party of some nine or ten disguised men formed and went to the home of Jordan. They arrived sometime between nine and ten o'clock in the evening. The party broke down Jordan's door and advanced to his bed. They led him outside, clothed in only his drawers and a shirt. Jordan escaped once but was returned. The men took turns hitting him, sometimes striking two or three times. Greatly frightened, the group hit Jordan some forty or fifty times with switches of a "tolerable size."[144] Often the Klan tried to cow its victims through aggressive behavior. Disguised men led Gadsden Steel into his yard, where they locked arms with him, grabbed his collar, and put a gun against him, marching to meet one of the disguised men, referred to as number 6. Sitting on a horse, 6 bowed his head and asked Steel, "How do you do." He then "horned [Steel] in the breast with his horns." Steel recounted, "I jumped back from him, and they punched me, and said 'Stand up to him, G—d d—n you, and talk to him.'"[145]

Humiliation often came with physical abuse, thereby contributing further to blacks' dread. Victims were often stripped of their clothing and debased.[146] One woman from North Carolina, after being stripped, was whipped with a board. The men then burned the hair around her genitals and cut her with a knife.[147] Such brutality was not atypical. After whipping Nathan Trollinger, his attackers made him take out his penis and stabbed it with a knife.[148] Acts of sexual terror, while political, also reflected the sadistic desires and uncontrolled feelings of the Ku Klux Klan's members.[149] Such unleashed fury had horrendous consequences. Aaron Biggerstaff, taken from his home around midnight, was whipped so badly that "he was helpless the next day, his back, from his shoulders down, was almost raw; you could hardly lay your hand upon a spot that had not been hit."[150] Historian Lisa Cardyn has argued that the "imprint of Klan terror has persisted in collective memory," contributing to lasting gender and racial subordination.[151]

The Ku Klux Klan did not typically ambush victims on roadways or mete out punishment publicly in villages. Instead, intimate attacks occurred in domestic spaces. Harris recounted a visit from the Klan during the Christmas season of 1870 in which his gun, shot, and powder were seized. Sometime later—perhaps a week or two, he recollected—Harris and his wife were awoken in the night by their dog's barking. Harris leaped out of bed and ran to his door, only to see a yard full of men. He quickly closed and fastened the door, doused the fire, and retrieved a firearm. Quickly thereafter, Harris's window was knocked open and shots poured into the room. The white man for whom Harris worked, Ned Finch, entered the crowd and begged them not to harm Harris or his wife, as he was "a hard-working nigger" and didn't "bother anybody."[152] Despite the continued pleas of Finch and his sister Sally, the Klan continued shooting. Harris estimated that fifty guns were aimed at his house, and for "an hour and a half, and there was not five minutes when they were not shooting."[153] Harris shot and wounded two men, which led to the party's eventual dispersal. Harris himself was hit nine times—his wife and children survived unharmed, though perhaps his inability to protect his family was more harmful than his physical wounds.[154] Several Klansmen were arrested for this incident, but they were discharged after providing alibis.[155]

A Savage Masculinity

Social setting gives shape to emotions and their expression.[156] The Ku Klux Klan represented a distinct, albeit short-lived, emotional community of terror, fear, and anger. The emotive forces behind Klansmen's actions and the feelings produced by their acts are central to the broader narrative of Reconstruction. Visceral reactions, lingering traumas, and burning hostility fed directly into the hundreds of violent encounters that reshaped the postwar South.[157] Not all whites engaged in this behavior or condoned such practices. Moreover, the feelings expressed and the actions exhibited by disguised men under the mask of darkness were but one part of a broader range of emotions.[158] It is essential, however, not to undermine or diminish these monstrous displays and their very real consequences. The Ku Klux Klan's expressions of hatred and racism projected a distinct image of what shape the changing South should take. Emotional reactions and potent feelings were used to regain political power and control labor.

Although the Reconstruction-era Klan had dissolved by the early 1870s, the order's consequences echoed for decades. Whites' attempts to resurrect an antebellum culture and labor system through violent displays of power in public settings shaped the New South. The Ku Klux Klan had spearheaded a reactionary movement of former Confederates who were not ready to put down their guns for the cause of white liberty.[159] Whites' successful regulatory measures were a critical part of a longer campaign in the public reestablishment of manhood and control. Traditions of extralegal violence reveal cultural forms that appealed to Southern whites. These performances engaged broader cultural messages about race, gender, and civilization, which invested the Klan with deeper meaning and fostered its growth.[160] Specifically, white Southerners publicly framed their actions as a response to "disorderly" blacks, social tumult, and the aftershock of war. Public action on the ground, while certainly in response to very real discord, was also a symbolic act. By visibly organizing themselves into armed bodies, Southern men established imagined communities that privileged pugnacity and strength.[161]

Whites cobbled together elements of their past—traditions of extralegal violence and ritual life—with their more immediate experiences—the memories and consequences of civil war—in the ghoulish construction of the Ku Klux Klan. These cultural materials proved so effective because they were so familiar to Southern white men. A quest to reestablish white manhood and a potent emotional universe shaped the Klan's actions, and indeed Reconstruction. This epoch represented but one phase in white men's broader transformation. During this period, anger, excitement, loss, and despair propelled Southerners as they employed terrorism to advance political, social, and sexual aims.[162] As demonstrated through behavior and experience, the Klan starkly revealed whites' continued confrontation with the experiences of civil war and military defeat. Instead of dwelling on feelings of loss, however, whites actively manipulated the past to re-create the present. The shifting discourses about race and manhood, the historical processes that shaped men's cultural and emotional lives, directly contributed to the South's social and political life.

Conclusion

In 1893 George Anderson Mercer delivered a speech on the Georgia volunteer. In it he recalled the "gallant" actions of the First Georgia Regiment, which had "on many a stricken field displayed its constancy and courage." Continuing, Mercer charged that "it does us good sometimes to catch the echoes of that eventful period" and recall how the drums of war had roused white Georgians from lethargy. Although mournfully recollecting the dead, Mercer also celebrated the Civil War and Confederates' heroics.[1] Looking backward, he explicitly linked the state militia of the late nineteenth century to George Washington's belief in "a well regulated Militia" the century before. Georgians had not only fought nobly and died on Civil War battlefields but were also proud members of the United States' martial tradition. Nearly thirty years earlier, Mercer was less secure in what the American Civil War had meant and less than celebratory of military service. In late March 1865, during the Confederacy's darkest days, he feared being "reduced from competence to poverty" and worried about facing "beggary and a miserable future, with a wife and child dependent upon me."[2] Less than a month later, Mercer entered "a period of deep depression." After he left the army, he returned to Savannah, a city "greatly depressed." Confederate defeat seemed imminent and a Northern victory ensured.[3]

Mercer's uncertainty during the tumultuous days of civil war had transformed into certitude by the last decade of the 1800s. The fact that Mercer neatly ordered his wartime experiences in the postwar era is neither revealing nor surprising. Rather, it aligns with what scholars have long contended. In the postbellum era, Civil War soldiers turned to paper and to speeches to recount the triumphs, and sometimes tribulations, of their youth. In the first fifteen years after the war, historian David Blight explains, "ex-soldiers groped for ways to express the trauma of their personal experience as well as its larger legacies." By the early 1880s, American culture welcomed soldiers' stories, though the war had already started making its way into the books.[4] Most memoirs, recorded years after the conflict from memory and scattered notes, ordered past events to create meaningful accounts for the present. Indeed, as Paul Fussell remarks, a world of "conversions, metamorphoses, and rebirths is a world of reinvigorated myth."[5] Perhaps no society was more desperate for a story of rebirth than the defeated white South. How veterans recorded their memoirs and continued to discuss the Confederacy reflected how they came to conceive of the Civil War and their role in it.

To examine Mercer's differing reactions to war through the lens of memory, however revealing, offers an incomplete narrative. The phases of Mercer's life can also be seen as shifting emotional regimes. Feelings are decipherable cultural products, and this book has recounted the models of expression white Southerners employed to understand and convey personal change, civil war, and social reconstruction. During the antebellum era, men such as Mercer were raised in a society with strict expectations for men's public personas. Guided by Christian gentility but also wielding immense power and control because of their gender and race, white men guarded their interactions with others to uphold a carefully maintained public face. Examining their emotions is difficult because feelings had to be suppressed. Yet men felt joy and sadness, love and anxiety. Southerners' fluid masculinities and emotional lives were written on the pages of their diaries and seen through their relationships with and letters to women and family. Once the public and private faces of Southern manhood are combined, men appear at once pugilist and antagonist but also introspective and vulnerable. They were entirely prepared for war but less ready for its consequences.

White Southerners sought to ensure the continuation of their racial order and labor systems through the Confederacy. Men from across the South excitedly welcomed secession and viewed military service as the fulfillment of obligations to family and nation. Antebellum culture had seemingly prepared men well for this enterprise. What happened instead was both shocking and unexpected. The authoritarian regime that governed soldiers' lives in camp and on campaign clashed with an independent, self-directed manhood. Chivalric notions of dying on a glorious battlefield eroded as Confederates watched in horror the dismemberment of their fellows on unearthly battlefields. Men reacted with uncertainty as they reeled from civil war. They turned to their comrades-in-arms for emotional support, creating tightly bound soldier communities. Soldiers expressed great love for their families but also abiding admiration for their fellows. A range of feelings once selectively revealed became the guiding forces in letter after letter home. Civil war had changed Southern men, altered their familial and personal relationships, and widened their means of self-expression.

Military defeat engendered raw emotions. Feelings went unchecked as Confederates mourned the loss of cause and comrades but also excitedly looked forward to familial reunions and a return to prewar pursuits. Men also expressed anger and rage at military occupation and the beginnings of Reconstruction. Some veterans never regained self-control, succumbing to deep depression or even contemplating suicide. Others, driven by a commitment to the reassertion of an antebellum social order, channeled raw emotions into extralegal violence and reactionary political stands against the federal government and African Americans. Men's intimate associations with their fellows underpinned the Ku Klux Klan, which marked a dangerous postbellum manifestation of wartime communities. The feelings engendered by the vast changes of the late 1860s and early 1870s were written into oaths and initiations governing orders of the Klan. Southern men were keenly aware of what they felt, even if they had trouble expressing it publicly. Instead, they acted decisively, with devastating consequences for African Americans and white Republicans.

The panoply of emotions elicited by civil war, emancipation, and reconstruction seldom appeared in the public discourse of the postbellum era. Northerners and Southerners buried the war's varied meanings and lingering traumas for the causes of reconciliation, reunion, and white supremacy.[6] During the rise of the "New South," a new generation of Southerners, too young to have participated in the war, shaped society and increasingly controlled the public discourse. Historian Paul M. Gaston's definitive study of this group describes the transformation. Southerners "expressed reverence for the civilization that had existed in the South, but conceded that it had passed irrevocably into history, had become an 'Old South' that must now be superseded by a new order."[7] As nineteenth-century Americans moved toward the cause of national reunion in the 1870s and beyond, vigorous public celebrations and a rich body of literature created a portrait of the Civil War in which romance and sentimental remembrance triumphed over reality.[8]

The public accounts of the postbellum era became the final records of white Southerners' perceptions of the war. Once-proud men became paper soldiers. The sanitized version of the war, so often present in published accounts, masked the lingering traumas and uncertainties first experienced in war. Mercer expressed on paper his poignant emotions, but the personal contours of his private life, like those of most white Southerners, received little public disclosure. These contrasts were compounded by the unique position Confederate veterans came to occupy in the years after the Civil War. Southerners maintained, writes James Marten, "an almost mystic regard for Confederate veterans."[9] The image of honorable, unsullied heroes overshadowed the ambiguities provoked by war. Public portraits that emphasized strides toward stability, shared social suffering, and individual heroism masked the confusion and sadness that privately consumed many men. By emphasizing national reunion and battlefield heroics, moreover, veterans distanced themselves from the racialized violence that defined the postbellum era. Many whites came to agree about a narrative of the war that left the legacies of slavery and racism unresolved.

The trauma of the Civil War certainly lingered, but the means of expression had changed. Many veterans turned inward, communicating to family or other former soldiers about their experiences as they had done during the war itself. With time, though, even these confidants were lost. In June 1885 Mercer, after his wife's death, once again turned to his diary. Though he had written scores of careful entries since boyhood, as he grew older, Mercer wrote less frequently. This traumatic event, though, drew him back to the pages where he had made sense of his life. Deeply pained, he wrote, "Now what I set down is written with the lacerated and bleeding edges of my heart. At ten minutes past seven o'clock on the morning of Tuesday last the 16th inst., my darling wife passed peacefully from time into eternity." The night before, he sat with his wife as she lay dying. With "breaking heart," he recalled their "long years of mutual confidence, trust, and love, and her unstinted devotion and affection as wife and mother." The experience pushed Mercer to the limits of his endurance. "I did not realize in advance that my nature was hard enough to live through such an ordeal, but great grief stuns and stupefies rather than destroys. The bruises sooner or later disappear from the surface, where they are seen, and sink into the soul, where they are felt."[10] As a broken man no longer with the woman he loved, Mercer drifted until meeting his own end in 1907.

Notes

Abbreviations

DU	David M. Rubenstein Rare Book and Manuscript Library, Duke University, Durham, N.C.
ECU	East Carolina University, J. Y. Joyner Library, Greenville, N.C.
FSNMP	Fredericksburg-Spotsylvania National Military Park, Fredericksburg, Va.
HNOC	Williams Research Center, Historic New Orleans Collection, New Orleans.
LSU	Louisiana and Lower Mississippi Valley Collections, Louisiana State University Libraries, Baton Rouge.
NCSA	North Carolina State Archives, Raleigh.
OR	United States War Department. *The War of the Rebellion: A Compilation of the Official Record of the Union and Confederate Armies.* 128 vols. Washington, D.C.: Government Printing Office, 1880-1901.
SHC	Southern Historical Collection, Wilson Library, University of North Carolina-Chapel Hill.
TU	Special Collections, Howard-Tilton Memorial Library, Tulane University, New Orleans, La.
USC	South Caroliniana Library, University of South Carolina, Columbia.
UVA	Albert and Shirley Small Special Collections Library, University of Virginia, Charlottesville.
VHS	Virginia Historical Society, Richmond.
WM	Special Collections Research Center, Swem Library, College of William and Mary, Williamsburg, Va.

Introduction

1. "Harry" Wells to "Mollie" Long, June 20, 1863, Folder 2, Harrison Wells Papers, SHC.

2. Faust, *Mothers of Invention*, 3-4.

3. See especially Wiley, *Life of Johnny Reb*; Mitchell, *Civil War Soldiers*; McPherson, *For Cause and Comrades*; Sheehan-Dean, *Why Confederates Fought*; Phillips, *Diehard Rebels*; Manning, *What This Cruel War*; and Sheehan-Dean, *View from the Ground*.

4. Two very important works in Civil War-era emotions history that influenced this project immensely are Berry, *All That Makes a Man*; and Woods, *Emotional and Sectional Conflict*.

5. Recorded words, public acts, and emotional expression are viewed as translatable products of Southern culture. The works of Rhys Isaac deeply influenced my approach to doing history. For a clear distillation of his methodology, see Isaac, "Ethnographic Method in History."

6. Woodward, *Burden of Southern History*, 189-91.

7. See, for example, Gaston, *New South Creed*, prologue and chap. 1; Foster, *Ghosts of the Confederacy*, 15-35, specifically; Roark, *Masters without Slaves*, chap. 4. See also Carmichael, *Last Generation*, chap. 8.

8. See, for example, Maddex, *Reconstruction of Edward A. Pollard*; Rose, *Victorian America*; Kantrowitz, *Ben Tillman*; Poole, *Never Surrender*; McClurken, *Take Care of the Living*; Marten, *Sing Not War*; and Megan Kate Nelson, *Ruin Nation*.

9. McClurken, *Take Care of the Living*; Sommerville, "'Will They Ever Be?'"; Silkenat, *Moments of Despair*. See also Marten, *Sing Not War*; and Gannon, *Won Cause*.

10. Susan-Mary Grant, "Lost Boys," 235.

11. On this historiographical trend, see Sternhell, "Revisionism Reinvented?" For a reaction against this trend, see Gallagher and Meier, "Coming to Terms," 492-93.

12. Frances M. Clarke, *War Stories*, 2.

13. On this approach and its potential insights, see Carmichael, "Soldier-Speak," 273-74; and Wickberg, "What Is the History?," 669.

14. Kenneth S. Greenberg, *Honor and Slavery*, 24-31.

15. Wyatt-Brown, *Southern Honor*, 275-81, 363-65; McCurry, *Masters of Small Worlds*, 6-7, 85-91; Faust, "Christian Soldiers," 73-74; Glover, "'Let Us Manufacture Men,'" 29; Laver, "Refuge of Manhood," 4. Mastery certainly connects to an ideal of honor that pervaded Southern culture, but recent historians of masculinity have been careful to disentwine the two concepts. That said, scholars of the Confederacy have fruitfully invoked the paradigm as a means of understanding soldiers' reactions to military service. And, as Kenneth Greenberg holds, although the language of honor connected directly to slavery, it was "spoken almost universally by the white men of the South." Greenberg, *Honor and Slavery*, xii.

16. Laskin, "Good Old Rebels," 106. For the importance of honor in shaping Confederate ideology, see Wyatt-Brown, *Shaping of Southern Culture*, 208-18.

17. On the culture of sacrifice among Civil War soldiers, see Mitchell, *Civil War Soldiers*, 17-18; and Frances M. Clarke, *War Stories*.

18. Dean, *Shook over Hell*, 90.

19. William J. Clarke to Mary Bayard Clarke, May 23, 1861, in Mary Bayard Clarke, *Live Your Own Life*, 74.

20. See, respectively, March 6, 7, and 9, 1868, Clarke Diary, Volumes, Box 2, William J. Clarke Papers #153, SHC.

21. William J. Clarke to "Sir," July 7, 1874 [speech fragment?], Folder 21, Box 1, Clarke Papers, SHC.

22. For Clarke's biographical overview, which supplemented the content of this paragraph, see Powell, "Clarke, William John."

23. Cashin, introduction, 353; Clawson, *Constructing Brotherhood*, 10; Bederman, *Manliness and Civilization*, 5-15.

24. The classic statement on Southern honor remains Wyatt-Brown, *Southern Honor*. See also Kenneth S. Greenberg, *Honor and Slavery*; Baptist, *Creating an Old South*; and Baptist et al., "Looking Back."

25. Woodward, *Burden of Southern History*, 189-91. For the emotional consequences of defeat, see Wyatt-Brown, "Death of a Nation" and "Honor Chastened," in Wyatt-Brown, *Shaping of Southern Culture*. T. J. Jackson Lears isolates a pervasive sense of doubt that shaped postwar life despite a public optimism, which he partially roots in the presence of Civil War veterans. Lears, *No Place of Grace*. In a later work Lears describes this as the "long shadow of Appomattox." Lears, *Rebirth of a Nation*, 12-50.

26. Faust, "Christian Soldiers," 69.

27. On the broader methodology, see especially Stowe, *Intimacy and Power*; Berry, *All That Makes a Man*; and Carmichael, *Last Generation*.

28. Glatthaar, *General Lee's Army*, 30-31; Carmichael, *Last Generation*, 145-47; and Manning, *What This Cruel War*, 32-3. In his study of the Tennessee Civil War Veterans Questionnaire, historian Fred Arthur Bailey makes a strong case for the Confederacy's collapse as a "miscarriage of military strategy but also a failure of culture." The South's upper classes, most committed to the cause, could not sustain the support of small farmers and poor whites after the realities of war proved too daunting and too difficult. These assertions bolster my argument pertaining to the study group examined herein but also create an additional layer of consideration when discussing broader commitment to the Confederacy. Bailey, *Class and Tennessee's Confederate Generation*, 104, but see also 77-104.

29. Jason Phillips has offered some of the best methodological alternatives to positive social science approaches. His writing both influenced and solidified my own thinking on the subject. Phillips, "Battling Stereotypes," 1418. See also Kohn, "Social History," 560.

30. Faust, *Southern Stories*, 1.

31. Constructions of hegemonic culture create, in Lears's words, "some forms of experience readily available to consciousness while ignoring or suppressing others." Lears, "Concept of Cultural Hegemony," 577. On elite whites' social ethnocentrism, see Bailey, *Class and Tennessee's Confederate Generation*, 67-70.

32. McCurry, *Confederate Reckoning*, 11-37, 77, 124.

33. Phillips, "Battling Stereotypes," 1414.

34. Glatthaar, *General Lee's Army*, xv.

35. Singal, *War Within*; Berry, *All That Makes a Man*.

36. Geertz, "Deep Play," 449.

37. Rosenwein, "Worrying about Emotions in History," 837; see also 842-43.

38. On this approach, see Eustace, *Passion Is the Gale*; and Eustace, "AHR Conversation," 1503-4.

39. Reddy, "Against Constructionism," 333.

40. Many scholars have used this period to either conclude or begin their studies. *Private Confederacies* joins recent scholarship in locating this critical period of change in the broader spectrum of Southern history. See, for example, Carmichael, *Last Generation*; and Rubin, *Shattered Nation*.

41. Sommerville, "'Burden Too Heavy to Bear,'" 455-57; Sommerville, "'Will They Ever Be Able to Forget?,'" 322-23.

42. On emotions history, see especially Lewis and Stearns, *Emotional History*; Lewis, *Pursuit of Happiness*; and Rosenwein, "Worrying about Emotions in History."

43. The classic statement on this topic remains Wyatt-Brown, *Southern Honor*. See also Kenneth S. Greenberg, *Honor and Slavery*; Baptist, *Creating an Old South*; and Baptist et al., "Looking Back."

44. Berry, *All That Makes a Man*, 11.

45. See, for example, Carmichael, *Last Generation*; and Rubin, *Shattered Nation*.

46. Gary W. Gallagher and Kathryn Shively Meier question the usefulness of a "long Civil War" lens, noting that Confederate military forces did surrender, slavery was destroyed, and millions of citizen-soldiers demobilized. Gallagher and Meier, "Coming to Terms," 493.

47. This approach is deeply influenced by Isaac, *Transformation of Virginia*, 5-7, 323-57; Turner, *Process, Performance, and Pilgrimage*; and Geertz, *Interpretation of Cultures*.

48. See especially Edwards, *Gendered Strife and Confusion*; Wyatt-Brown, *Shaping of Southern Culture*; Bercaw, *Gendered Freedoms*; Berry, *All That Makes a Man*; and Glover, *Southern Sons*.

49. The rationale for why men fought in the Civil War is highly debated. For the parameters of this debate, see especially Linderman, *Embattled Courage*; McPherson, *For Cause and Comrades*; Berry, *All That Makes a Man*; and Sheehan-Dean, *Why Confederates Fought*.

Chapter One

1. George Anderson Mercer Diary, n.d. [ca. January 1, 1851], Box 1, Volume 1, SHC.

2. On narrative and constructions of identity, see Isaac, "Stories and Constructions of Identity." On the use of diaries and other reflections of self, see Hoffman, Sobel, and Teute, *Through a Glass Darkly*.

3. For the best summation, see Reddy, *Navigation of Feeling*, 3-8.

4. Mercer Diary, September 12, 1851, Box 1, Volume 1, SHC.

5. The powerful analytical framework of honor—a vision that has dominated interpretation for the past three decades, though it goes back much further—is now posited as an ethos central to manliness, but only part of masculinity. Instead, historians have insisted on the primacy of gender analysis in interpreting Southerners and their self-identities. Contradictions within men's gender regime preclude a singular interpretation of manhood and instead point to competing but also complementary models of masculinity. On constructions of masculinity, see Bederman, *Manliness and Civilization*, 6-7.

6. Cash, *Mind of the South*, 99.

7. Letters, although outside the purview of this chapter, have been utilized for similar ends. See especially Berry, *All That Makes a Man*.

8. On the limitations and virtues of this type of source, see Cott, *Bonds of Womanhood*, 16-18.

9. Faust, *Southern Stories*, 1-2.

10. Mercer Diary, December 17, 1865, Box 1, Volume 5, SHC; Myers, *Children of Pride*, 1623. Johnny Mercer, the famed musician and composer, was grandson to George Anderson Mercer, thus extending the family successes into the twentieth century.

11. Most importantly, see Berry, *All That Makes a Man*; Friend and Glover, *Southern Manhood*; and Carmichael, *Last Generation*.

12. With that said, female diarists and religious journals have received substantial attention. Moreover, Civil War diaries are very popular forms of evidence, though more for content as opposed to function. This is not the case for historians of the eighteenth century who have extensively considered the diary as evidence. See, for instance, Isaac, *Landon Carter's Uneasy Kingdom*.

13. As Drew Gilpin Faust remarks, "Writing is inescapably an act of discovery; autobiographical writing inevitably produces new exploration and understanding of the self. It is as much a process of self-creation as of self-description." Faust, *Mothers of Invention*, 162.

14. Clement Daniel Fishburne Diary [1854-55], [April] 20, [1854 or 1855], Box 1, Papers of the Fishburne Family, UVA.

15. Fishburne Diary, [March] 16, [1854], Box 1, Papers of the Fishburne Family, UVA.

16. Hodes, *Sea Captain's Wife*, 28. See also Kierner, *Beyond the Household*, 151-53.

17. D. Appleton and Company, *Appleton's Complete Letter Writer*, ix. See also Hodes, *Sea Captain's Wife*, 28-29.

18. Stowe, *Intimacy and Power*, 102-6, 126-28.

19. Fishburne Diary, 1854, Box 1, Papers of the Fishburne Family, UVA.

20. Lewis, *Pursuit of Happiness*, 209-16.

21. Lewis, quote on 214; also see 212-16. The best investigation of an eighteenth-century diary of this ilk remains Ulrich, *Midwife's Tale*. For a different model of analysis in a work of similar power, see Isaac, *Landon Carter's Uneasy Kingdom*. On eighteenth-century conceptions of self and identity, see Hoffman, Sobel, and Teute, *Through a Glass Darkly*.

22. McPherson, *Battle Cry of Freedom*, 19-20.

23. William J. Clarke to Frances Miller, February 24, 1856, in Mary Bayard Clarke, *Live Your Own Life*, 43-45.

24. Mercer Diary, September 4, October 18, and November 4, 1859, respectively, Box 1, Volume 2, SHC.

25. Mercer Diary, October 18, 1859, Box 1, Volume 2, SHC.

26. Mercer Diary, November 4, 1859, Box 1, Volume 2, SHC.

27. Kierner, *Beyond the Household*, 143. See also Pryor, *Reading the Man*, 80-81.

28. Nanny C. Waller, January 5, 1850, Nanny C. Waller Diary, 1849-51, WM.

29. Cott, *Bonds of Womanhood*, 15-17. See also Nylander, "Everyday Life," 95.

30. Consider, for example, the diaries of James Henry Hammond, the South Carolina politician and planter. See Faust, *James Henry Hammond*; and Hammond, *Secret and Sacred*.

31. Pryor, *Reading the Man*, 84–85.

32. Josiah Gorgas, entry for February 26, 1858, in Gorgas, *Journals of Josiah Gorgas*, 16.

33. Mercer Diary, April 29, 1855, Box 1, Volume 1, SHC.

34. Edmund Kirby-Smith Diary, November 19, 1849, Edmund Kirby-Smith Papers, SHC.

35. Stowe, *Intimacy and Power*, 49.

36. Faust, *James Henry Hammond*, 18–19; Berry, *All That Makes a Man*, 19–40. A thorough treatment of the public and the private is found in Benn and Gaus, *Public and Private*.

37. On Hammond's diary, see Faust, *James Henry Hammond*; and Hammond, *Secret and Sacred*. Also see Byrd, *Secret Diary of William Byrd*.

38. Mercer Diary, n.d. [ca. January 1851], Box 1, Volume 1, SHC; John Burgwyn MacRae Diary, ca. 1866, Series 3, Folder 14, John Burgwyn MacRae Papers, SHC; Martin Witherspoon Gary, diary entry, ca. January 1851, MSS/Volumes, Martin Witherspoon Gary Papers, 1851–1927, USC.

39. Kirby-Smith Diary, November 19, 1849, Kirby-Smith Papers, SHC.

40. Pryor, *Reading the Man*, 192; Rotundo, "Learning about Manhood," 36–37.

41. Timothy J. Williams, *Intellectual Manhood*, 1–3.

42. Lewis, *Pursuit of Happiness*, 155–56.

43. Gorgas, entry for July 1, 1860, in Gorgas, *Journals of Josiah Gorgas*, 35.

44. Kirby-Smith Diary, [December] 5, [1849], Kirby-Smith Papers, SHC.

45. Fishburne Diary, March 11, 1854, Box 1, Papers of the Fishburne Family, UVA.

46. Kirby-Smith Diary, [November] 20, [1849], Kirby-Smith Papers, SHC.

47. Gorgas, entry for January 12, 1857, p. 5; entries for February 12 and 26, 1858, p. 16; and entry for July 1, 1858, p. 22, in Gorgas, *Journals of Josiah Gorgas*.

48. Pryor, *Reading the Man*, 192.

49. Laskin, "Good Old Rebels," 186.

50. Lears, "Concept of Cultural Hegemony," 571.

51. Mercer Diary, April 29, 1855, Box 1, Volume 1, SHC.

52. Kirby-Smith Diary, [November] 23, [1849], Kirby-Smith Papers, SHC.

53. Kirby-Smith Diary, [November] 23, [1849], Kirby-Smith Papers, SHC.

54. Kirby-Smith Diary, [December] 5, [1849], Kirby-Smith Papers, SHC.

55. Mercer Diary, April 29, 1855, Box 1, Volume 1, SHC.

56. Mercer Diary, March 17, 1855, Box 1, Volume 2, SHC.

57. Stowe, *Intimacy and Power*, 147.

58. Rose, *Victorian America*, 145.

59. Gorgas, entry for January 28, 1857, in Gorgas, *Journals of Josiah Gorgas*, 5.

60. Gorgas, 6. On white Southerners' dreams of slaveholding, see Johnson, *Soul by Soul*.

61. Rose, *Victorian America*, 145.

62. Gorgas, entry for January 12, [1857], in Gorgas, *Journals of Josiah Gorgas*, 4.

63. Gorgas, entry for June 3, 1860, in Gorgas, *Journals of Josiah Gorgas*, 34.

64. Sarah Woolfolk Wiggins, prologue to *Journals of Josiah Gorgas*, by Gorgas, xxxviii.

65. Jabour, *Marriage in the Early Republic*, 55.

66. Smedes, *"She Hath Done,"* 9.

67. Jabour, *Marriage in the Early Republic*, 45-58. On the limitations of women's power in nineteenth-century marriages, see Lebsock, *Free Women of Petersburg*, 52-53.

68. Kirby-Smith Diary, [November] 23, [1849], Kirby-Smith Papers, SHC.

69. Edmund K. Smith to Maj. [Putnam], January 20, 1853 [1854], Box 2, Folder 16, Kirby-Smith Papers, SHC.

70. Lebsock, *Free Women of Petersburg*, 16.

71. Lebsock, 17-53. For a thoughtful examination of the companionate ideal at work in one relationship, see Jabour, *Marriage in the Early Republic*.

72. Berry, *All That Makes a Man*, 85.

73. Waller Diary, February 2, 1850, WM.

74. Lewis, *Pursuit of Happiness*, 222.

75. Mercer Diary, April 29, 1855, Box 1, Volume 1, SHC.

76. For instance, Mercer Diary, September 12, 1851, and April 29, 1855, Box 1, Volume 1, SHC.

77. On men's emotional command, see Glover, "'Let Us Manufacture Men,'" 34-35; and Berry, *All That Makes a Man*.

78. Mercer Diary, April 29, 1855, Box 1, Volume 1, SHC.

79. Gorgas, entry for December 13, 1857, in Gorgas, *Journals of Josiah Gorgas*, 13.

80. Cornelia P. Spencer, journal entry for January 7, 1865, Cornelia P. Spencer Volumes, Volume 2, Box 14, Cornelia Phillips Spencer Papers, SHC.

81. Lewis, *Pursuit of Happiness*, 79. See also Faust, *This Republic of Suffering*; and Schantz, *Awaiting the Heavenly Country*.

82. Waller Diary, July 24, 1849, WM.

83. Mercer Diary, September 24, 1850, Volume 1, SHC.

84. See especially Bruce, *Violence and Culture*, 233; Cash, *Mind of the South*; Wyatt-Brown, *Southern Honor*; Proctor, *Bathed in Blood*; and Ownby, *Subduing Satan*.

85. Andrew, *Wade Hampton*, 27.

86. This reading relies on Geertz, "Deep Play," 417-21, especially.

87. Bruce, *Violence and Culture*, 233; Ownby, *Subduing Satan*.

88. Wyatt-Brown, *Southern Honor*; Franklin, *Militant South*. See also Hackney, "Southern Violence"; and Ayers, *Vengeance and Justice*. For an excellent comparison between early twentieth-century Northern and Southern violence, see Adler, "Murder, North and South."

89. Bruce, *Violence and Culture*, 196.

90. Ownby, *Subduing Satan*, 21-27. On women in hunting and sport, see Struna, "Beyond Mapping Experience"; and Parratt, "Athletic 'Womanhood.'"

91. See, for instance, the early accounts of Lawson, *New Voyage to Carolina*; and Beverley, *History and Present State*. See also Beilein, *Bushwhackers*, 144.

92. Hahn, *Roots of Southern Populism*, 58.

93. On slaves' hunting and fishing, see Genovese, *Roll, Jordan, Roll*, 62-63. On firearm ownership among free blacks before Turner's Rebellion, see Ely, *Israel on the Appomattox*, 181-82 especially.

94. McCurry, *Masters of Small Worlds*, 15; Hundley, *Social Relations*, 37-38, 343.

95. Cash, *Mind of the South*, 30.

96. Proctor, *Bathed in Blood*, 1, 12-13.

97. Hahn, *Roots of Southern Populism*, 59; McCurry, *Masters of Small Worlds*, 105-6.

98. Isaac, *Transformation of Virginia*, 131; Faust, *James Henry Hammond*, 75, 104-5; Proctor, *Bathed in Blood*, 76-98, 104-18.

99. Elliott, *Carolina Sports*, 191.

100. Marks, *Southern Hunting*, 28-37; Elliott, *Carolina Sports*, 254-58; McCurry, *Masters of Small Worlds*, 7-16.

101. Proctor, *Bathed in Blood*, 13, 34.

102. Wyatt-Brown, *Southern Honor*, 195-96.

103. Bruce, *Violence and Culture*, 197. On men's devotion to and interest in these dogs, see, for instance, Alexander, *Fighting for the Confederacy*, 22; and Kirby-Smith, "English Setter's Lineage," n.d. [ca. 1859], Volume 1, Kirby-Smith Papers, SHC.

104. Proctor, *Bathed in Blood*, 99-100.

105. Elliott, *Carolina Sports*, 173-74. See also Ownby, *Subduing Satan*, 24; and Proctor, *Bathed in Blood*, 106-8.

106. Elliott, *Carolina Sports*, 174.

107. Elliott, 164.

108. Mercer Diary, May 9, 1855, Box 1, Volume 2, SHC.

109. Alexander, *Fighting for the Confederacy*, 3; Proctor, *Bathed in Blood*, 44.

110. Franklin, *Militant South*, 69.

111. Browning, *Forty-Four Years*, vi.

112. Berry, *All That Makes a Man*, 21.

113. Elliott, *Carolina Sports*, 282.

114. Proctor, *Bathed in Blood*, 72; Wyatt-Brown, *Southern Honor*, 191, 196.

115. John W. Daniel, "Oration on the Illustrious Dead," June 28, 1859, Box 13, Folder 1859, Speeches, John W. Daniel and the Daniel Family Papers, 1816-1936, UVA.

116. Daniel.

117. Daniel.

118. Franklin, *Militant South*, 227-49.

119. Berry, *All That Makes a Man*, 166.

120. See especially Franklin, *Militant South*; and McWhiney and Jamieson, *Attack and Die*.

121. Wyatt-Brown most clearly articulates his vision on the latter point in Wyatt-Brown, *Hearts of Darkness*, xiii-xvi.

Chapter Two

1. Ruffin Thomson to Pa, January 10, 1862, Box 1, Folder 5, Ruffin Thomson Papers #3315, SHC.

2. Although I do not actually use objects in this analysis, material culture methodology has been invaluable. My interests tend toward what Jules David Prown deems "soft material culture," which renders "the artifact as part of a language through which culture speaks its mind." Prown, *Art as Evidence*, 237. In particular, see Prown, 73-74; and Deetz, *In Small Things Forgotten*.

3. On descriptive references, see especially Wiley, *Life of Johnny Reb*, 108-22; Linderman, *Embattled Courage*, 114-5; Mitchell, *Civil War Soldiers*, 92; Glatthaar, *General Lee's Army*, 215-16; and Pryor, *Reading the Man*, 402-3. As a methodology, material culture has transformed from a nascent idea into a serious field of study. For an introduction, see especially Prown, *Art as Evidence*, 69-95; and Schlereth, *Material Culture Studies in America*. For the importance of clothing, see Isaac, *Transformation of Virginia*, 43-44; Roach and Eicher, *Visible Self*; and Baumgarten, "Leather Stockings and Hunting Shirts," 252-54.

4. Notable exceptions include Glatthaar, *General Lee's Army*, 66-77, 220-27, especially; and Wiley, *Life of Johnny Reb*, 151-73.

5. DeGruccio, "Letting the War Slip," 27. See also Nelson, *Ruin Nation*.

6. Beilein, "Guerrilla Shirt," 156.

7. Shortly after drafting a provisional constitution and appointing Jefferson Davis as provisional president, the Confederate Congress created the post of quartermaster general. Further, the Confederate government acknowledged its duties to clothe troops in March 1861. Wilson, *Confederate Industry*, 4-5. The 1861 *Uniform and Dress of the Army of the Confederate States* established the Confederacy's official uniforms, though regulations were never followed exactly. See Confederate States of America, War Department, *Uniforms and Dress*.

8. Wilson, *Confederate Industry*, 5.

9. See especially Linderman, *Embattled Courage*, 35-41; McPherson, *For Cause and Comrades*, 86-89; and Glatthaar, *General Lee's Army*, 36, 50-51, 76. For a broader context, see Keegan, *Face of Battle*; and Shils and Janowitz, "Cohesion and Disintegration."

10. Thomas Ruffin Jr. to Father, May 26, 1862, Box 30, Folder 450, Thomas Ruffin Papers, SHC.

11. Several recent scholars have developed complex portraits of Southern masculinity. See in particular Carmichael, *Last Generation*; Berry, *All That Makes a Man*; Sheehan-Dean, *Why Confederates Fought*; and McClurken, *Take Care of the Living*.

12. Wiley, *Life of Johnny Reb*, 108.

13. Wiley, 108; Confederate States of America, Secretary of War, *Regulations*, 255-56.

14. Fussell, *Uniforms*, 3-4.

15. Wiley, *Life of Johnny Reb*, 108.

16. McCarthy, *Detailed Minutiae*, 16, 17. See also Redwood, "Fortunes and Misfortunes."

17. George [Battle] to Mother, July 22, 1861, in Battle and Battle, *As You May Never*, 4.

18. Shotwell, *Three Years in Battle*, 314-15.

19. Wilson, *Confederate Industry*, 13.

20. "AN ACT to Provide for the Public Defense," March 6, 1861, in OR, series 4, vol. 1, pp. 126, 295.

21. Wilson, *Confederate Industry*, 13.

22. Jensen, "Survey."

23. Bohannon, "Dirty, Ragged," 106.

24. "General Orders, No. 100," December 8, 1862, in *OR*, series 4, volume 2, p. 229. See also Wiley, *Life of Johnny Reb*, 110; Jensen, "Survey"; and Bohannon, "Dirty, Ragged," 106-7.

25. Thomas Ruffin Jr. to Thomas Ruffin, May 26, 1862, Box 30, Folder 450, Ruffin Papers, SHC.

26. Thomas Ruffin to [Thomas Ruffin Jr.], May 21, 1862, Box 30, Folder 450, Ruffin Papers, SHC.

27. W[illiam] H. Joyner to "Dear Wife," December 2, 1861, Box 1, Folder 5, Joyner Family Papers #4428, SHC.

28. Faust, *Mothers of Invention*, 46.

29. "A Homespun Party," *Southern Field and Fireside* (Augusta, Ga.), January 14, 1860, p. 270, c. 2.

30. Julia to Grandma, November 4, 1861, Lenoir Family Papers, SHC.

31. On the perceptions and realities of Confederate women's efforts, see Rubin, *Shattered Nation*, 53-64. See also Faust, *Mothers of Invention*, 47-48; and "JOINT RESOLUTION of Thanks to the Patriotic Women of the Country for Voluntary Contributions Furnished by Them to the Army," April 11, 1862, in *OR*, series 4, volume 1, p. 1055.

32. Hill Fitzpatrick to Amanda, September 15, 1863, in Fitzpatrick, *Letters to Amanda*, 87; Faust, *Mothers of Invention*, 46-47.

33. Faust, *Mothers of Invention*, 51.

34. Hill Fitzpatrick to Amanda, September 10, 1863, in Fitzpatrick, *Letters to Amanda*, 85.

35. See, respectively, R. G. Joyner to "Dear Mother," March 21, 1862, Box 1, Folder 6; I. Sidney Joyner to "Dear Mother," April 25, 1862, Box 1, Folder 7; W. H. Joyner to "Dear Wife," May 2, 1862, Box 1, Folder 7; and J. S. Joyner to "Dear Mother," December 3, 1862, Box 1, Folder 9, Joyner Family Papers, SHC.

36. W. J. O'Daniel to "Friend Torrence," December 11, 1862, Subseries 1.2, 1862, Folder 21, L. C. Glenn Papers #3052, SHC.

37. M. Hill Fitzpatrick to Amanda, December 4, 1862, in Fitzpatrick, *Letters to Amanda*, 33.

38. TNS to Mary Simpson, April 24, 1862, in Simpson and Simpson, *"Far, Far from Home,"* 117.

39. John N. Cocke to "Dear Father & Mother," September 30, 1862, Folder 1862 September 30, Cocke Family Papers, 1794-1981, VHS.

40. John N. Cocke to "Dear Father & Mother," September 30, 1862, Folder 1862 September 30, Cocke Family Papers, VHS.

41. William Henry Cocke to "Dear Parents," September 30, 1862, Folder 1862 September 30, Cocke Family Papers, VHS.

42. Glatthaar, *General Lee's Army*, 167, 209-10, 445.

43. Glatthaar, 208.

44. On the material needs of a wealthy officer, see Ruffin Thomson to Pa, January 13 and 18, [1864], and March 14, 1864, Box 1, Folder 8, Thomson Papers, SHC.

45. See, for instance, the correspondence among the Joyner Family, Series 1, Folders 5-19, Joyner Family Papers, SHC.

46. Ruffin Thomson to Pa, August 27, 1863, Box 1, Folder 7, Thomson Papers, SHC.

47. Faust, *Mothers of Invention*, 51.

48. George M. Waddy to "My Dear Aunty," April 9, 1863, Box 2, Folder 1, Civil War Collection, WM.

49. Leonidas Torrence to "Dear Sister," June 8, 1862, Subseries 1.2, 1862, Folder 21, Glenn Papers, SHC.

50. M. Hill Fitzpatrick to Amanda, November 7, 1862, in Fitzpatrick, *Letters to Amanda*, 30.

51. M. H. Fitzpatrick to Amanda, September 10, 1863, in Fitzpatrick, *Letters to Amanda*, 85.

52. Pryor, *Reading the Man*, 402.

53. McCarthy, *Detailed Minutiae*, 26. See also Linderman, *Embattled Courage*, 114-15. Clothing reveals much about social values, individual and group psychologies, and cultural aesthetics. What people wear and how they wear it carries messages and meanings. On the broader significance of costuming, see Baumgarten, "Leather Stockings and Hunting Shirts," 251-55.

54. M. H. Fitzpatrick to Amanda, September 10, 1863, in Fitzpatrick, *Letters to Amanda*, 85. See also Linderman, *Embattled Courage*, 183-84.

55. James A. Graham to Mother, March 19, 1862, in Graham, *James A. Graham Papers*, 119.

56. W[illiam] H. Joyner to "Dear Wife," March 20, 1862, Joyner Family Papers, SHC.

57. J. D. Joyner to "Dear Mother," March 29, 1863, Joyner Family Papers, SHC; Harman A. Hiner to Miss Victoria Jane Wilson, March 29, 1863, Box 2, Folder 1, Civil War Collection, WM.

58. Jensen, "Survey."

59. Blackford, *War Years with Jeb Stuart*, 99.

60. Richard [Waldrop] to "Moether," May 27, 1862, Box 1, Folder 1, Richard Woolfolk Waldrop Papers, SHC.

61. J[ulia] H. Joyner to "Dear Son," April 24, 1862, Series 1, Folder 7, Joyner Family Papers, SHC.

62. Baumgarten, "Leather Stockings and Hunting Shirts," 253.

63. Gallagher, *Confederate War*, 58-59.

64. Fremantle, *Three Months*, 293.

65. Barry and Burt, *Suppliers to the Confederacy II*, 171, 172.

66. J. Gorgas, February 3, 1863, in OR, series 4, volume 2, pp. 382-83.

67. Pritchard and Huey, *English Connection*, 456.

68. Barry and Burt, *Suppliers to the Confederacy II*, 171, 172.

69. Sheehan-Dean, *Why Confederates Fought*, 58.

70. McCarthy, *Detailed Minutiae*, 194.

71. McCarthy, 194.

72. On each point respectively, see McCarthy, *Detailed Minutiae*, 1-9, 178-80.

73. "Emotional community" is borrowed from Rosenwein, "Worrying about Emotions in History," 842-43.

74. Mitchell, *Vacant Chair*, 158-59; McPherson, *For Cause and Comrades*, 77-89; Sheehan-Dean, *Why Confederates Fought*, 58-60.

75. See in particular Gallagher, *Confederate War*; Glatthaar, *General Lee's Army*; and Laskin, "Good Old Rebels," as well as Laskin, "'Army Is Not Near,'" 92–93. On Confederate dissent, see especially Escott, *After Secession*; and Noe, *Reluctant Rebels*.

76. In an excellent historiographical essay on antebellum Southern masculinity, Craig Thompson Friend and Lorri Glover demarcate scholars' distinctions between mastery and honor. As they explain concisely, mastery was forged largely through family and household, whereas honor operated through community-based expectations. These different perspectives rarely overlap in the scholarship, which now tends to discuss competing masculinities. Friend and Glover's insights have significantly influenced my understanding of these configurations. See Friend and Glover, "Rethinking Southern Masculinity: An Introduction," in Friend and Glover, ed., *Southern Manhood*, vii-xvii. On honor, see especially Cash, *Mind of the South*; Franklin, *Militant South*; Bruce, *Violence and Culture*; Wyatt-Brown, *Southern Honor*; Greenberg, *Honor and Slavery*; Baptist, *Creating an Old South*; and Baptist et al., "Looking Back." On mastery, see especially McCurry, *Masters of Small Worlds*; and Burton, *In My Father's House*.

77. Berry, *All That Makes a Man*, 181. This particular point seems an aberration in an otherwise compelling portrait of Southern men and their inner lives with which I generally agree; moreover, it is a work to which I am intellectually indebted greatly.

78. Blight, "No Desperate Hero," 61.

79. These conceptualizations were informed by the methodological approaches found in, respectively, Bourdieu, *Field of Cultural Production*, and Cantwell, *Ethnomimesis*.

80. Krick, foreword, xvii.

81. Faust, "Christian Soldiers," 77. See also Bailey, *Class and Tennessee's Confederate Generation*, 78. For the Union perspective regarding class contests, see Foote, *The Gentlemen and the Roughs*.

82. On camp vices and immorality, see Wiley, *Life of Johnny Reb*, 175; Faust, "Christian Soldiers," 68–69; Woodworth, *While God Is Marching On*, 184–85; and Glatthaar, *General Lee's Army*, 228–34. Despite the widespread immorality witnessed in Confederate camps especially before the revivals, Kent T. Dollar argues religiosity still prevailed in the early part of the war. Dollar, "'Strangers in a Strange Land.'"

83. E. B. Mendenhall to "cousin Mary" [M. E. Torrence], Wilmington, N.C., 28th NC, January 1, 1862, Subseries 1.2, 1862, Folder 21, Glenn Papers, SHC.

84. According to Joseph T. Glatthaar, 80 percent of the men who entered service in 1861 and ultimately served in the Army of Northern Virginia were born and lived in the same state. Many of these men lived in the same community, an area of no more than a twenty-mile radius. Glatthaar, *General Lee's Army*, 36. See also McPherson, *For Cause and Comrades*, 80.

85. Glatthaar, *General Lee's Army*, 66–77.

86. Dooley, *John Dooley*, 5.

87. Shotwell, *Papers of Randolph Abbott Shotwell*, vol 1, 94–95.

88. Ruffin Thomson to Pa, June 30, 1861, Box 1, Folder 4, Thomson Papers, SHC.

89. Ruffin Thomson to Pa, May 24, 1862, Box 1, Folder 5, Thomson Papers, SHC.

90. J. D. Joyner to "Dear Mother," October 11, 1862, Series 1, Folder 9, Joyner Family Papers, SHC.

91. Nelson, "'Right Nice Little House[s],'" 184; Reeves and Geier, "Under the Forest Floor," 201.

92. Stevens, *Reminiscences of the Civil War*, 92.

93. Leonidas Torrence to "Dear Sister," April 12, 1863, Folder 22, Glenn Papers, SHC.

94. James W. Albright Diary, October 16, 1864, Volume 1, James W. Albright Diary and Reminiscences, SHC; [Richard Waldrop] to Mother, December 23, 1864, Box 1, Folder 2, Waldrop Papers, SHC. See also Meier, *Nature's Civil War*, 106-7.

95. Ruffin Thomson to Pa, February 2, 1863, Box 1, Folder 6, Thomson Papers, SHC.

96. Reeves and Geier, "Under the Forest Floor," 214.

97. Reeves and Geier, 213.

98. Ruffin Thomson to Pa, May 24, 1862, Box 1, Folder 5, Thomson Papers, SHC.

99. Ruffin Thomson to Pa, March 14, 1864, Box 1, Folder 8, Thomson Papers, SHC.

100. For instance, R. W. Waldrop to "Dear little Sister," January 22, 1862, and Richard to Mother, August 27, 1862, Waldrop Papers, SHC.

101. Richard W. Waldrop Diary, [September] 18 and 23, [1863], Box 1, Folder 4, Waldrop Papers, SHC.

102. Ruffin Thomson to Pa, December 4, 1862, Box 1, Folder 5, Thomson Papers, SHC.

103. Dooley, *John Dooley*, 72.

104. Fredrickson, *Racism*, 81.

105. Brasher, *Peninsula Campaign*, 132-33.

106. Confederate States of America, War Department, *Regulations*, 11.

107. Linderman, *Embattled Courage*, 235.

108. Ruffin Thomson to Pa, February 10, 1863, Box 1, Folder 6, Thomson Papers, SHC.

109. TNS to Anna Tallulah Simpson, January 15 and July 27, 1862, and TNS to Mary Simpson, October 12, 1862, in Simpson and Simpson, *"Far, Far from Home,"* 105, 139, 153. See also McCarthy, *Detailed Minutiae*, 38.

110. James A. Graham to Father, March 7, 1862, in Graham, *James A. Graham Papers*, 116.

111. M. H. Fitzpatrick to Amanda, January 5, 1863, in Fitzpatrick, *Letters to Amanda*, 49; [John Charles Gaines] to Ruff, April 16, 1864, Box 1, Folder 8, Thomson Papers, SHC.

112. Ruffin Thomson to Pa, April 3, [1862], Box 1, Folder 5, Thomson Papers, SHC.

113. Ruffin Thomson to Pa, February 10, 1863, Box 1, Folder 6, Thomson Papers, SHC.

114. M. H. Fitzpatrick to Amanda, April 17, 1863, in Fitzpatrick, *Letters to Amanda*, 62.

115. Rubin, *Shattered Nation*, 53-64.

116. See especially Mitchell, *Civil War Soldiers*, 17; Sheehan-Dean, *Why Confederates Fought*, 152-53; and Silber, *Gender and the Sectional Conflict*, 3-4, 6-11.

117. Silber, *Gender and the Sectional Conflict*, 12-16.

118. R[ichard] W. Waldrop to Father, May 19, 1861, Waldrop Papers, SHC.

119. Leonidas Torrence to "Dear Mother," April 12, 1863, Subseries 1.2, Folder 22, Glenn Papers, SHC.

120. An excellent discussion of this process among men from another army is found in Martin, *Napoleonic Friendship*, 75-79, especially.

121. Katz, *Love Stories*, 6. As Jonathan Ned Katz also relates, the nineteenth-century bed-sharing habits of some men developed into more intimate sexual relationships. It is difficult to document such encounters among Civil War soldiers, though the possibilities are extremely intriguing.

122. RWS to Caroline Virginia Taliaferro Miller, August 17, 1861, and RWS to Caroline Virginia Taliaferro Miller, February 3, 1862, in Simpson and Simpson, *"Far, Far from Home,"* 61, 108-9.

123. James A. Graham to Mother, April 22, 1861, in Graham, *James A. Graham Papers*, 103.

124. Ruffin Thomson to Pa, March 30, 1862, Box 1, Folder 5, Thomson Papers, SHC.

125. Dooley, *John Dooley*, 70-71. See also RWS to Caroline Virginia Taliaferro Miller, August 17, 1861, and RWS to Caroline Virginia Taliaferro Miller, February 3, 1862, in Simpson and Simpson, *"Far, Far from Home,"* 61, 108-9.

126. J. M. Doyle to Dear Sir [Josiah Knighton], May 24, 1862, Box 1, Folder 3, Josiah Knighton and Family Papers, LSU.

127. W. J. O'Daniel to "Mrs Torrence," July 20, 1863, Folder 22, Glenn Papers, SHC.

128. McCarthy, *Detailed Minutiae*, 89.

129. Melville, *Moby Dick*, 54.

130. Shotwell, *Papers of Randolph Abbott Shotwell*, 1:133.

131. Jackman, entry for July 2, 1863, in Jackman, *Diary of a Confederate Soldier*, 78.

132. Albright Diary, November 23, 1862, Volume 3, Albright Diary and Reminiscences, SHC.

133. TNS to Anna Tallulah Simpson, September 24, 1862, in Simpson and Simpson, *"Far, Far from Home,"* 146.

134. Ruffin Thomson to Mama, December 1, 1862, Box 1, Folder 5, Thomson Papers, SHC.

135. Ruffin Thomson to Mama, December 1, 1862, Box 1, Folder 5, Thomson Papers, SHC; TNS to Mary Simpson, December 2, 1862, in Simpson and Simpson, *"Far, Far from Home,"* 160.

136. See especially Faust, "Christian Soldiers," 74; and Dollar, "'Strangers in a Strange Land,'" 148, 157-62.

137. I am indebted to Benedict Anderson for this concept. Anderson, *Imagined Communities*.

138. Jackman, entry for August 18, 1862, in Jackman, *Diary of a Confederate Soldier*, 5.

139. Alexander, *Fighting for the Confederacy*, 37.

140. Thomas O. Moore to L. P. Walker, May 7, 1861, in OR, series IV, vol. I, 295.

141. Glatthaar, *General Lee's Army*, 34-35, 42, 50-52; Mitchell, *Civil War Soldiers*, 57-60; Berry, *All That Makes a Man*, 176-77.

142. John Forman to "sister," December 20, 1861, Box 1, Folder 2a, Robert A. Newell Papers, LSU.

143. Wyatt-Brown, *Shaping of Southern Culture*, 215.

144. Wiley, *Life of Johnny Reb*, 68-89; Linderman, *Embattled Courage*; McPherson, *For Cause and Comrades*, 30-45.

145. As Joseph Glatthaar writes, "The drill and discipline pulled units together. It hardened them for the battlefield experience and it created an élan within companies, regiments, and even brigades. Soldiers, who already identified with their companies from recruitment on the local level, began to see themselves as a group. . . . For all to achieve, each individual component must succeed, and each person must rely on everyone else to perform effectively." Glatthaar, *General Lee's Army*, 51; see also 76. See also McPherson, *For Cause and Comrades*, 46-61.

146. TNS to Mary Simpson, June 18, 1862, in Simpson and Simpson, *"Far, Far from Home,"* 129. See also Dooley, *John Dooley*, 59-60; and Eggleston, *Rebel's Recollections*, 82.

146. Eggleston, *Rebel's Recollections*, 82.

147. Glatthaar, *General Lee's Army*, 316.

148. On the important wartime role of Confederate officers, see Carmichael, *Last Generation*, 149-77. On officers' roles in battle, see McPherson, *For Cause and Comrades*, 54-61; and Glatthaar, *General Lee's Army*, 197-99.

149. Carmichael, *Last Generation*, 149-77.

150. Bledsoe, *Citizen-Officers*, xii.

151. Sheehan-Dean, *Why Confederates Fought*, 1-5, 152-53; Carmichael, *Last Generation*, 149-77.

152. Laskin, "Good Old Rebels," 420-21. See also Pryor, *Reading the Man*, 403-5.

153. On soldiers' fears of the effects of curtailed freedom, see Mitchell, *Civil War Soldiers*, 59.

154. J[oseph] D. Joyner to "Dear Mother," October 11, 1862, Series 1, Folder 9, Joyner Family Papers, SHC.

155. J. T. Thompson to "Dear Mother and sisters," March 26, 1862, in James Thomas Thompson, "Georgia Boy," 322.

156. Neely, Holzer, and Boritt, *Confederate Image*, 209.

157. Neely, Holzer, and Boritt, 210.

158. Neely, Holzer, and Boritt, 209.

159. Jackman, entry for June 30, 1862, in Jackman, *Diary of a Confederate Soldier*, 47. See also McCarthy, *Detailed Minutiae*, 204.

160. Confederate States of America, War Department, *Regulations*, 52. On the importance of a camp's location and men's interactions with these spaces, see Meier, *Nature's Civil War*, 105-8.

161. Confederate States of America, War Department, *Regulations*, 53.

162. On the Forty-Sixth Virginia Infantry and the men portrayed in the watercolor, see Collins, *46th Virginia Infantry*.

163. Ruffin Thomson to Mama, December 1, 1862, Box 1, Folder 5, Thomson Papers, SHC.

164. Ruffin Thomson to Pa, November 11, 1863, Box 1, Folder 7, Thomson Papers, SHC.

165. T. W. Harriss to "Uncle," January 23, 1862 Box 2, Folder 1, Civil War Collection, WM.

166. J. T. Thompson to "Dear Mother and sisters," March 26, 1862, in James Thomas Thompson, "Georgia Boy," 322.

167. Laskin, "Good Old Rebels," 186.

168. Gallagher, *Confederate War*, 71-74; Sheehan-Dean, *Why Confederates Fought*, 157; Carmichael, *Last Generation*, 193-94.

Chapter Three

1. Dooley, *John Dooley*, 102.
2. On this incident, see Dooley, 104; and Stewart, *Pickett's Charge*, 141.
3. Dooley, *John Dooley*, 105.
4. Dooley, 107.
5. For an overview of soldiers' varied reactions to and actions during battle, see Guelzo, *Gettysburg*, 276-78.
6. Reardon, *Pickett's Charge*, 15.
7. "Emotional community" is borrowed from Rosenwein, "Worrying about Emotions in History," 837; see also 842-43.
8. Gallagher, *Confederate War*, 71-75. On the Army of Northern Virginia's remarkable degree of cohesion, see especially Sheehan-Dean, *Why Confederates Fought*, 1-5, 152-53; Glatthaar, *General Lee's Army*, 358; and Carmichael, *Last Generation*, 149-77.
9. Carmichael, "Soldier-Speak," 276.
10. On emotional control more broadly, see Reddy, "Against Constructionism," 335.
11. See, for instance, Wiley, *Life of Johnny Reb*; Barton, *Goodmen*; McPherson, *For Cause and Comrades*; Costa and Kahn, *Heroes and Cowards*; and Glatthaar, *General Lee's Army*.
12. I use the phrase "metaphysical confusion" to highlight the traumatic and transformative nature of war, as manifest in emotions and expressions. Although this chapter makes few attempts to grapple with bigger ideas, this phase of men's lives underpins later chapters that deal more explicitly with Southerners' intellectual culture. Ultimately, though, as Louis Menand so eloquently puts it, the American Civil War "tore a hole" in the lives of its participants. Menand, *Metaphysical Club*, x.
13. Walter Clark to Mother, September 26, 1862, in Clark, *Papers of Walter Clark*, 1:80.
14. Robert Wallace Shand Diary, January 1, 1863, Robert Wallace Shand Papers, USC.
15. See especially Faust, "Christian Soldiers"; Sheehan-Dean, *Why Confederates Fought*, 109-10; McPherson, *For Cause and Comrades*, especially chap. 5; Mitchell, *Civil War Soldiers*, 173-74; Carmichael, *Last Generation*, 207-10; and Frances M. Clarke, *War Stories*, 18-19.
16. Shand Diary, January 1, 1863, Shand Papers, USC.
17. E. B. Mendenhall to "cousin Mary" [M. E. Torrence], January 1, 1862, Subseries 1.2, 1862, Folder 21, L. C. Glenn Papers, SHC.
18. James Thomas Thompson to "Dear Mother and sisters," March 26, 1862, in Thompson, "Georgia Boy," 322.
19. Schantz, *Awaiting the Heavenly Country*, 38.

20. Faust, *This Republic of Suffering*, 30.
21. James T. Thompson to "Mother and sisters," August 12, 1861, in Thompson, "Georgia Boy," 316.
22. James T. Thompson to "Mother and sisters," August 12, 1861, in Thompson, "Georgia Boy," 316.
23. Faust, "Christian Soldiers," 72, 83-86.
24. George Battle to "Dear Mother," July 31, 1861, in Battle and Battle, *As You May Never*, 7.
25. T. W. Harriss to "Uncle," January 23, 1862, Box 2, Folder 1, Civil War Collection, WM.
26. Henry W. Smart to "Sister," May 26, 1862, Box 2, Folder 1, Civil War Collection, WM.
27. Nelson, *Ruin Nation*, 163.
28. Leonidas Torrence to "Dear Pa," July 20, 1861, in Torrence, "Road to Gettysburg," 480.
29. Leonidas Torrence to "Dear Mother," June 8, 1862, Subseries 1.2, 1862, Folder 21, Glenn Papers, SHC.
30. Leonidas Torrence to "Dear Mother," May 7, 1863, Subseries 1.2, Folder 22, 1863-64, Glenn Papers, SHC.
31. This reading is influenced deeply by Carmichael, "Soldier-Speak," 276-79.
32. Sommerville, "'Burden Too Heavy,'" 487.
33. Linderman, *Embattled Courage*, 160.
34. Faust, "Christian Soldiers," 69.
35. Glatthaar, *General Lee's Army*, 268.
36. Gallagher, *Confederate War*, 85.
37. Alexander, *Fighting for the Confederacy*, 222.
38. Glatthaar, *General Lee's Army*, 269. See also Pryor, *Reading the Man*, 389.
39. Glatthaar, *General Lee's Army*, 269; Sheehan-Dean, *Why Confederates Fought*, 121.
40. Charles A. Wills to "Dear Wife" [Mary], June 12, 1863, Wills Papers, WM.
41. Wm. H. Thomson to Ruffin [Thomson], July 2, 1863, Box 1, Folder 7, Ruffin Thomson Papers, SHC.
42. R. E. Lee to Mary Custis Lee, March 9, 1863, quoted in Pryor, *Reading the Man*, 366.
43. TNS to Mary Simpson, June 26, 1863, in Simpson and Simpson, *"Far, Far from Home,"* 249.
44. William Beverley Pettit to Arabella, [June 15, 1863], in Spears and Pettit, *Civil War Letters*, 1:121.
45. Shotwell, *Three Years in Battle and Three in Federal Prisons*, vol. 1, 475.
46. For examples, see TNS to Mary Simpson, June 18, 1862, in Simpson and Simpson, *"Far, Far from Home,"* 129; Dooley, *John Dooley*, 59-60; and Eggleston, *Rebel's Recollections*, 82.
47. Faust, "Christian Soldiers," 73.
48. On the Union counterpart, see Foote, *The Gentlemen and the Roughs*, chap. 6.
49. Shotwell, *Papers of Randolph Abbott Shotwell*, 1:478.

50. Leonidas Torrence to Mother, June 17, 1863, in Torrence, "Road to Gettysburg," 508.

51. Torrence, diary entries for June 5 and 12, [1863], in Torrence, "Road to Gettysburg," 509, 510.

52. Joe to "Dear wife," June 17, 1863, in Hoyle, *"Deliver Us,"* 124.

53. Carmichael, "Soldier-Speak," 276.

54. Joe to "Dear wife," June 17, 1863, in Hoyle, *"Deliver Us,"* 124.

55. William Beverley Pettit to Arabella, [June 25, 1863], in Spears and Pettit, *Civil War Letters*, 1:127.

56. TNS to Caroline Virginia Taliaferro Miller, June 28, 1863, in Simpson and Simpson, *"Far, Far from Home,"* 250.

57. [John Futch] to "Dear & loving Wife," June 29, 1863, Futch Letters, 1861-1863, NCSA. Futch, from New Hanover County, enlisted in the Third North Carolina Infantry on February 1, 1862. Manarin et al., *North Carolina Troops*, 118; Perry, *Civil War Courts-Martial*, 169.

58. Forth, *Masculinity in the Modern West*, 130; Butler, "Performative Acts," 526.

59. R. E. Rodes, 1863, in *OR*, series 1, vol. 27, pt. 2, p. 550.

60. Clarke, *War Stories*, 19-20, 54.

61. Meier, *Nature's Civil War*, 126.

62. Shotwell, *Papers of Randolph Abbott Shotwell*, 1:485.

63. TNS to Caroline Virginia Taliaferro Miller, June 28, 1863, in Simpson and Simpson, *"Far, Far from Home,"* 250.

64. Joe to "dear wife," June [24], 1863, in Hoyle, *"Deliver Us,"* 126.

65. Dooley, *John Dooley*, 96.

66. For a survey of the depravations faced on the march, see Adams, *Living Hell*, 37-59.

67. RWS to Anna Tallulah Simpson, June 13, [1861], in Simpson and Simpson, *"Far, Far from Home,"* 13.

68. M. Hill Fitzpatrick to Amanda, August 1, 1862, in Fitzpatrick, *Letters to Amanda*, 21.

69. James A. Graham to Mother, March 15, 1862, in Graham, *James A. Graham Papers*, 118; William McLean to "Dear Ma," July 15, 1864, Box 2, Folder 1, Civil War Collection, WM.

70. Fletcher, *Rebel Private*, 19-20.

71. J. D. Joyner to "Dear Papa," September 30, 1862, Series 1, Folder 9, Joyner Family Papers, SHC.

72. Ditz, "New Men's History," 3.

73. TNS to Caroline Virginia Taliaferro Miller, June 28, 1863, in Simpson and Simpson, *"Far, Far from Home,"* 252.

74. TNS to Mary Simpson, June 26, 1863, in Simpson and Simpson, *"Far, Far from Home,"* 249.

75. TNS to Caroline Virginia Taliaferro Miller, June 14, 1863, in Simpson and Simpson, *"Far, Far from Home,"* 247.

76. Shotwell, *Papers of Randolph Abbott Shotwell*, 1:500-501.

77. J. D. Joyner to "Dear Mother," June 29, 1863, Folder 12, Joyner Family Papers, SHC.

78. Glatthaar, *General Lee's Army*, 292-95.

79. M. H. Fitzpatrick to Amanda, August 1, 1862, in Fitzpatrick, *Letters to Amanda*, 21; TNS to Sister, December 2, 1862, in Simpson and Simpson, *"Far, Far from Home,"* 163.

80. Ruffin Thomson to Pa, November 11, 1863, Box 1, Folder 7, Thomson Papers, SHC.

81. Coddington, *Gettysburg Campaign*, 3-25; Guelzo, *Gettysburg*, 33-35; Glatthaar, *General Lee's Army*, 269.

82. Shotwell, *Papers of Randolph Abbott Shotwell*, 1:486.

83. Laskin, "Good Old Rebels," 196.

84. This approach to understanding battle is influenced by Lynn, *Battle*.

85. John Warwick Daniel, "Memoir of the Battle of Gettysburg, Pa., and Subsequent Withdrawal of the Confederate Army of Northern Virginia, 1-4 July 1863," John Warwick Daniel Memoir, VHS. It is very certain from dating techniques that this account was written after the fact, despite its appearance of having been conceived in the moment. It is my suspicion that the account was conceived shortly after the battle and recorded as a rough draft in 1863 but modified sometime between 1863 and the early 1870s, for in 1875 Daniel published *The Campaign and Battles of Gettysburg*. Importantly, much of the account's ambiguity, meditations on the Union dead, and horror over the battle were removed entirely from *The Campaign and Battles of Gettysburg*, which reads as a conventional battle narrative.

86. Glatthaar, *General Lee's Army*, 414. Futch, from New Hanover County, enlisted in the Third North Carolina Infantry on February 1, 1862. Manarin et al., *North Carolina Troops*, 118; Perry, *Civil War Courts-Martial*, 169.

87. Daniel, "Memoir." On the position of Lee's army before the battle, see Guelzo, *Gettysburg*, 127-28.

88. Daniel, "Memoir."

89. On the prewar Victorian mind-set, see Singal, *War Within*, 3-33; Rose, *Victorian America*, 7-8; and Carmichael, "Soldier-Speak," 276.

90. On expression over experience, see Eustace, *Passion Is the Gale*; and Eustace, "AHR Conversation," 1503-4.

91. Faust, *This Republic of Suffering*, 267. Americans' shifting ideas became manifest in diverse ways. In her study of war-themed poetry, for example, Franny Nudelman contends that those representations that "resist narration or contextualization" communicate "the alien and incomprehensible nature of wartime suffering," thereby suggesting an abandonment of prewar thinking. Nudelman, *John Brown's Body*, 99.

92. Daniel, "Memoir."

93. Daniel, "Memoir."

94. On the importance of the dead's countenance, see Faust, *This Republic of Suffering*, 20-22. This scene brings to mind Timothy O'Sullivan's dead Confederate "sharpshooter" at Devil's Den. According to William A. Frassanito, the body, initially posed with both a blanket underneath and a knapsack for a pillow (the knapsack remained, but a later image reveals the blanket was removed), supported a story formulated as

Notes to Chapter Three 175

Alexander Gardner pondered the scene. The "dying boy evidently laid himself down to stoically await his end" and appears almost sleeping in the final image. Frassanito, *Gettysburg*, 192.

95. William M. Reddy deploys emotives as "instruments for directly changing, building, hiding, intensifying emotions." He later continues, "Where emotives have their greatest effects and are subject to their greatest failures is in situations of what I will call intense ambivalence. Cultural or conventional action patterns often come into play both in producing such situations and in helping actors navigate them." Reddy, "Against Constructionism," 331, 333.

96. Clark, *Histories of the Several Regiments*, 1:195.

97. Pfanz, *Gettysburg*, 293–94.

98. John Futch to "My Dear Wife," August 6, 1863, Futch Letters, NCSA.

99. Daniel, "Memoir."

100. On this drive to control circumstances, see Rose, *Victorian America*, 240–42.

101. Dooley, *John Dooley*, 99.

102. Dooley, 99.

103. Carmichael, "Soldier-Speak," 279.

104. Sheehan-Dean, *Why Confederates Fought*, 123.

105. [Joseph Hoyle] to "My Dear wife," July 1863, in Hoyle, *"Deliver Us,"* 129.

106. Dooley, *John Dooley*, 106.

107. [Joseph Hoyle] to "My Dear wife," July 1863, in Hoyle, *"Deliver Us,"* 129.

108. Dooley, *John Dooley*, 107.

109. Joseph to "Dear Mother," August 12, 1863, Folder 12, Joyner Family Papers, SHC.

110. William Beverley Pettit to "My darling wife," July 26, 1863, in Spears and Pettit, *Civil War Letters*, 140.

111. Glatthaar, "Common Soldier's Gettysburg Campaign," 28.

112. Charley related in October 1861 that John had sent letters, presumably by his own hand, but "not a one that could read them" in either the Third or Fortieth North Carolina. This suggests that John was semiliterate at best. Charley Futch to "Brother," October 16, 1861, Futch Letters, NCSA.

According to historian Joseph T. Glatthaar, "Private John Futch was a small slaveholder and father of two who had joined the 3rd North Carolina with his three relatives." In 1860 Futch, then twenty-eight years old, resided with his father and was listed as "farmer." Thus, Futch may be defined as a yeoman farmer who was, at best, poorly educated. Glatthaar, *General Lee's Army*, 414; Ellis, *North Carolina English*, 234. See also Records to John Futch, in North Carolina, Hanover County, 1860 U.S. Census, 842; and Records to John Futch, in North Carolina, Hanover County, 1860 U.S. Slave Census, 282.

113. John Futch to "Kind Wife," July 12, 1863, Futch Letters, NCSA.

114. Schantz, *Awaiting the Heavenly Country*, 67.

115. John Futch to Wife, July 19, 1863, Futch Letters, NCSA.

116. John Futch to "Dear Wife," July 31, 1863, Futch Letters, NCSA.

117. Broomall, "'Band of Brothers.'"

118. John Futch to "Dear Wife," August 2, 1863, Futch Letters, NCSA.

119. On these conditions, see John Futch to Martha A. Futch, August 6 and 16, 1863, Futch Letters, NCSA.
120. John Futch to "Dear Wife," August 2, 1863, Futch Letters, NCSA.
121. Sommerville, "'Burden Too Heavy,'" 464.
122. Berry, *All That Makes a Man*, 47-80 especially.
123. Sommerville, "'Burden Too Heavy,'" 487.
124. Faust, *This Republic of Suffering*, 10.
125. John Futch to "My Dear Wife," August 6, 1863, Futch Letters, NCSA.
126. Faust, *This Republic of Suffering*, 267.
127. See especially Faust, "Christian Soldiers"; Sheehan-Dean, *Why Confederates Fought*, 109-10; McPherson, *For Cause and Comrades*, chap. 5; Mitchell, *Civil War Soldiers*, 173-74; Carmichael, *Last Generation*, 207-10; and Clarke, *War Stories*, 18-19.
128. Gannon, *Won Cause*, 137.
129. John Futch to "Dear Wife," August 2, 1863, Futch Letters, NCSA.
130. Carmichael, "Soldier-Speak," 276.
131. Futch's reactions contribute to my overall understanding of the war's profound emotional toll that, among some, negated nationalism. I am here informed by Faust's argument, "As the emotional and physical deprivation of Southern white women escalated, the Confederate ideology of sacrifice began to lose its meaning and efficacy." Faust, "Altars of Sacrifice," 1225.
132. John to [Parents], July 11, 1863, Folder 1863 July 11, Cocke Family Papers, VHS. William's letter is referenced within and does not survive.
133. C. W. Avery to Dear Sir [T. R. Caldwell], July 18, 1863, Box 1, Folder 6, Tod Robinson Caldwell Papers #128, SHC.
134. John, July 11, 1863, Folder 1863 July 11, Cocke Family Papers, VHS.
135. Joe to "Dear wife," July 9, 1863, in Hoyle, *"Deliver Us,"* 126-27.
136. W. J. O'Daniel to "Mrs Torrence," July 20, 1863, Folder 22, Glenn Papers, SHC.
137. Linderman, *Embattled Courage*, 216-65.
138. Dean, *Shook over Hell*, 72.
139. Reardon, *Pickett's Charge*, 2.
140. Gallagher, "Lee's Army," 1.
141. Laskin, "Good Old Rebels," 223.
142. Joe to "Dear wife," July 9, 1863, in Hoyle, *"Deliver Us,"* 127. This aligns with Aaron Sheehan-Dean's observation that soldiers' accounts of Gettysburg emphasized balance and mutual destruction rather than an irreversible turning point. Sheehan-Dean, *Why Confederates Fought*, 125.

Chapter Four

1. Appomattox stands as a clear breaking point between war and peace; see, for example, Catton, *Stillness at Appomattox*; and Manning, *What This Cruel War*. Works that quickly close the war at Appomattox include William C. Davis, *Honorable Defeat*; and Marvel, *Lee's Last Retreat*. Dan T. Carter's *When the War Was Over* stands as an excellent exception to this general historiographical trend. Indeed, Carter's study begins at the end and uses Appomattox as a point of departure to examine Southern

self-reconstruction, a failed venture. See also the very important study by Gregory P. Downs, *After Appomattox*.

2. Neely, Holzer, and Boritt, *Confederate Image*, 68.

3. Alexander, *Fighting for the Confederacy*, 544. William B. Holberton describes a pervasive feeling of good cheer among Northern and Southern soldiers: Holberton, *Homeward Bound*, 90-92.

4. Grant, *Grant*, 741; Waugh, *U. S. Grant*, 99. As historian Caroline E. Janney has noted, however, "No contemporary diarists recalled this order; instead they wrote of the mad revelry that followed the news that the Union had finally been secured." Janney, *Remembering the Civil War*, 43.

5. Downs, *After Appomattox*, 11.

6. Guelzo, *Fateful Lightning*, 514; Downs, *After Appomattox*, 236.

7. See, for example, Levin, "'When Johnny Comes,'" 85-86; and Greenough, "Aftermath at Appomattox."

8. Mark L. Bradley examines in great detail the prolonged negotiations leading up to Johnston's eventual surrender. See Bradley, *This Astounding Close*, 157-222. For the Department of the Trans-Mississippi, see Kerby, *Kirby-Smith's Confederacy*, 424-27. On the Confederate Cherokees and the war in the West, see Gaines, *Confederate Cherokees*. For feelings of loss and liberation postdefeat, see Winter, "Brutal Heroes," 194-95 especially.

9. Nye, "Western Masculinities," 417.

10. R. E. Lee, General Orders, No. 9. HQ, ANV [Army of Northern Virginia], April 10, 1865, in OR, series 46, vol. 1, p. 1267; J. E. Johnston, General Orders, No. 22, May 2, 1865, in OR, series 47, vol. 1, p.1061.

11. For the importance of honor, see Chamberlaine, *Memoirs of the Civil War*, 92; and Shotwell, *Papers of Randolph Abbott Shotwell*, 1:221.

12. Kirby-Smith to Col. [Sprague], May 30, 1865, Box 3, Folder 47, Edmund Kirby-Smith Papers, SHC.

13. E. Kirby-Smith, "Memorandum for Col. Sprague," [1865], Box 3, Folder 47, Kirby-Smith Papers, SHC.

14. Sternhell, *Routes of War*, 155-56.

15. McCarthy, *Detailed Minutiae*, 192.

16. For similar problems in documenting the spring and summer of 1865, see Phillips, *Diehard Rebels*, 5. See also Marten, *Sing Not War*, 10.

17. Phillips, *Diehard Rebels*, 176-81.

18. William Ellis Diary, April 10, 1865, William H. Ellis Papers, LSU.

19. James Edward Whitehorne Diary, April 2, 1865, SHC.

20. Reid, "Excluding the Rebel," 464.

21. Whitehorne Diary, April 16, 1865, SHC.

22. Joseph Frederick Waring Diary, April 22, 1865, Box 1, Folder 4, Joseph Frederick Waring Papers, SHC.

23. Phillips, *Diehard Rebels*, 173.

24. W. L. Alexander to Mother, July 9, 1865, Series 1.2, Box 2, Folder 12, William Alexander Hoke Papers, SHC. For similar reactions, see McClurken, *Take Care of the Living*, 66.

25. Julius A. Lineback Diary, [June/July 1865], Box 1, Volume 2, Folder 2-N, J. A. Lineback Papers, SHC.

26. "War-Worn Veterans," *Intelligencer* (Atlanta, Ga.), May 10, 1865.

27. Whitehorne Diary, April 9, 1865, SHC.

28. April 9, 1865, marked the date of Lee's surrender to Grant. For the next three days, Lee's men, numbering over twenty-eight thousand, were paroled. Most waited for the official paroles—still, scores departed immediately. Jay Winik offers a narrative account of the exchanges between, and then meeting of, Grant and Lee. See Winik, *April 1865*, 173-99. For a more straightforward, if still highly useful, reading, see Cauble, *Surrender Proceedings*.

29. Scores of accounts describe an unwillingness to surrender in the weeks before Appomattox. Once the surrender was official, many soldiers resigned themselves to an uncertain fate with profound sadness. Historian J. Tracy Power describes 1864 as a year of "unprecedented" destruction that led many soldiers to conclude that "1865 would be the last year of the conflict." By the spring, Power contends, many of Lee's men had a loss of purpose. Power, *Lee's Miserables*, 234. See also Powers, chaps. 8, 9.

30. Richard W. Waldrop Diary, April 9, 12, and 18, 1865, Folder 4, R. W. Waldrop Papers, SHC.

31. Whitehorne Diary, April 13, 1865, SHC.

32. Whitehorne Diary, April 16 and 22, 1865, SHC.

33. On changes in the household, see Whites, *Crisis in Gender*; and McClurken, *Take Care of the Living*.

34. Kena King Chapman Diary, April 17, 1865, SHC.

35. Chapman Diary, April 20, 1865, SHC.

36. Chapman Diary, April 23, 1865, SHC.

37. Rolle, *Lost Cause*, 50; Kerby, *Kirby-Smith's Confederacy*, 424.

38. Edmund Kirby-Smith to Robert Rose, May 2, 1865, quoted in Kerby, *Kirby-Smith's Confederacy*, 415.

39. Edmund Kirby-Smith to the Trans-Mississippi Department, Proclamation Draft, [May 26, 1865], Kirby-Smith Papers, SHC.

40. [Edmund Kirby-Smith to Cassie Selden Kirby-Smith, June-July 1865], Folder 48, Kirby-Smith Papers, SHC. See also Kerby, *Kirby-Smith's Confederacy*, 428-29.

41. [Edmund Kirby-Smith to Cassie Selden Kirby-Smith, June-July 1865], Folder 48, Kirby-Smith Papers, SHC.

42. [Edmund Kirby-Smith], [June-July 1865], Folder 48, Kirby-Smith Papers, SHC.

43. Stephen Berry deeply influenced this methodology. See Berry, *All That Makes a Man*, especially 11.

44. [Edmund Kirby-Smith to Cassie Selden Kirby-Smith], August 21, 1865, Folder 49, Kirby-Smith Papers, SHC.

45. [Cassie Selden Kirby-Smith to Edmund Kirby-Smith], August 15, 1865, Folder 49, Kirby-Smith Papers, SHC.

46. [Edmund Kirby-Smith to Cassie Selden Kirby-Smith], August 21, 1865, Folder 49, Kirby-Smith Papers, SHC.

47. [Cassie Selden Kirby-Smith to Edmund Kirby-Smith], August 15, 1865, Folder 49, and [Edmund Kirby-Smith to Cassie Selden Kirby-Smith, October 2, 1865], Folder 50, Kirby-Smith Papers, SHC.

48. [Edmund Kirby-Smith to Cassie Selden Kirby-Smith, October 4, 1865], Folder 50, Kirby-Smith Papers, SHC.

49. [Edmund Kirby-Smith to Cassie Selden Kirby-Smith, October 2, 1865], Folder 50, Kirby-Smith Papers, SHC.

50. Rister, "Carlota."

51. Carl Coke Rister, in his article on Carlota, holds that, despite good fortune, most "former Confederates felt bitter about being exiles from the land of their birth." Rister, "Carlota," 45.

52. Reynolds quoted in Rolle, *Lost Cause*, 128.

53. Rolle, 54-55.

54. Foster, *Ghosts of the Confederacy*, 15-17; Rubin, *Shattered Nation*, 173; Phillips, *Diehard Rebels*, 181-82; Rolle, *Lost Cause*; Rister, "Carlota"; Weaver, "Confederate Emigration to Brazil"; Sutherland, "Exiles, Emigrants, and Sojourners."

55. Guterl, *American Mediterranean*, 91.

56. John Taylor Wood, June 19, 1865, Personal Diary, Volume 3, John Taylor Wood Papers, SHC.

57. Robert Cantwell's work heavily influenced this formulation of movement and culture. See Cantwell, *Ethnomimesis*, introduction especially.

58. Marten, *Sing Not War*, 61-64; Phillips, *Diehard Rebels*, 182.

59. The most thorough treatments of violence in the spring of 1865 include Carter, *When the War Was Over*, 6-23; Greenough, "Aftermath at Appomattox"; Bradley, *This Astounding Close*; and Wyatt-Brown, *The Shaping of Southern Culture*, 230-46. The mechanics of military demobilization are thoroughly explored in Holberton, *Homeward Bound*. The best overall work on 1865 remains Ash, *Year in the South*.

60. Carter, *When the War Was Over*, 10.

61. In interrogating the consequences of violence, Franny Nudelman contends that narratives of national unity through bloodshed must be viewed in conjunction with discussions about the devastating consequences of combat—"the ruin of body, mind, and spirit." Nudelman, *John Brown's Body*, 2. On veterans' role in violence, see Logue, *To Appomattox and Beyond*, 105. In the North, the Civil War's close also marked a spike in crime and violence. Abbott, "Civil War."

62. Wyatt-Brown, *Southern Honor*, 370-71. See also Hackney, "Southern Violence"; and Ayers, *Vengeance and Justice*. For an excellent comparison of early twentieth-century Northern and Southern violence, see Adler, "Murder, North and South."

63. Kantrowitz, "One Man's Mob," 67-68.

64. On Confederate veterans' involvement in the Klan, see Nelson, *Iron Confederacies*, 109-10; and Hahn, *Nation under Our Feet*, 268. For linkages between the war's effects on men and Klan membership read, Jacob Alson Long Recollections [typed copy], Jacob A. Long Papers, SHC. On the alienating effects of war more broadly, see Stiles, *Jesse James*, 161.

65. On continued discord and a turn to racial violence in North Carolina, see Bradley, *Bluecoats and Tar Heels*, chaps. 4, 8, 9; and Paludan, *Victims*, 99-133. For South Car-

olina, see Zuczek, *State of Rebellion*, 47-108 especially; Poole, *Never Surrender*, chaps. 5, 6; and Poole, "Religion, Gender," 573-77. For the broad view, see Hahn, *Nation under Our Feet*, chap. 6; Foner, *Reconstruction*, 342-45 and 425-59 especially; and Rable, *But There Was No Peace*.

66. Winter, "Brutal Heroes," 194-95 especially. On military unit cohesion, see McPherson, *For Cause and Comrades*, 85-92.

67. John Hampden Chamberlayne to Edward Pye Chamberlayne and Lucy Parke (Chamberlayne) Bagby, April 12, 1865, in Chamberlayne, *Ham Chamberlayne— Virginian*, 320. For an excellent discussion of Chamberlayne in the postwar years, see Carmichael, *Last Generation*, chap. 8.

68. Joseph E. Johnston quoted in Jefferson Davis, *Papers of Jefferson Davis*, 2:548.

69. Dooley, *John Dooley*, 177.

70. "From Grant's Army. The Process of Paroling—Sentiment of the Rebel Officers and Privates," *Milwaukee Daily Sentinel*, April 25, 1864.

71. Alexander, *Fighting for the Confederacy*, 531-32. An interesting discussion of guerrilla warfare is found in Winik, *April 1865*, 144-63.

72. On April 4, 1865, Davis issued a decree that argued the war had assumed a new phase and the Confederacy was "relieved from the necessity of guarding cities and particular points." He urged, "It is . . . unwise and unworthy of us, as patriots engaged in a most sacred cause, to allow our energies to falter." Jefferson Davis, Public Proclamation, April 4, 1865, in Jefferson Davis, *Papers of Jefferson Davis*, 2:502. This proclamation appeared in Northern newspapers as well. The *Philadelphia Inquirer*, for instance, printed the document on April 17. "The Dying Confederacy," *Philadelphia Inquirer*, April 17, 1865. William B. Feis offers a compelling examination of this document and a brief historiographical discussion of its interpretation by scholars. He argues that Davis was not encouraging guerrilla warfare, as Lee's army was still active and attempting to join Johnston's command. Feis, "Jefferson Davis." Michael B. Ballard contends the opposite. He posits that the "desperate president was proposing a war of persistent guerrilla-type harassment and was personally pledging never to give up." Ballard, *Long Shadow*, 57. While Feis's argument is intriguing, Davis's retreat, the continual reestablishment of Confederate capitals, and his unwillingness to see Confederate field commanders surrender suggest that he desired to prolong the struggle indefinitely. The actual terms of the engagement are debatable; however, the open discussion of guerilla warfare among Confederate officers indicates Davis had, at the very least, considered the option, even if his prose in the public decree of April 4 did not directly indicate the idea. See also Gallagher, *Confederate War*, 140-53; and Rubin, *Shattered Nation*, 130-34.

73. Such bands impeded some soldiers' progress home; see Marten, *Sing Not War*, 42-44.

74. See Phillips, *Diehard Rebels*, chap. 5, conclusion, for his rich description of this ethos in the war's close and beyond.

75. Scott Reynolds Nelson describes the rail lines linking Richmond, Danville, Greensboro, and Charlotte as in sad repair, though recently constructed. These thoroughfares were epicenters of activity and violence in the immediate aftermath of Lee's surrender. As Nelson's study demonstrates, this trend continued well beyond

the postwar years because of the profound socioeconomic changes enacted by the railroads. Nelson, *Iron Confederacies*.

76. Merrill, *Campaigns*, 374-75.

77. Ayers, *Vengeance and Justice*, 142.

78. *Chronicle and Sentinel* (Augusta Ga.), n.d., quoted in the *Tri-weekly Telegraph* (Houston), June 15, 1865, cited in Carter, *When the War Was Over*, 12.

79. The disorder within the town spilled into the countryside throughout April. Union troops from the Twenty-Fourth Corps who were garrisoned in the surrounding area found considerable robbing and pillaging by paroled prisoners. Calkins, *Final Bivouac*, 150.

80. Semmes, *Memoirs of Service Afloat*, 819.

81. Dooley, *John Dooley*, 181.

82. Bertram Wyatt-Brown describes the soldiers' profound loss of purpose with great eloquence. "Most white southerners," he writes, "found their world shattered." Wyatt-Brown, *Shaping of Southern Culture*, 254. See also Reid, *After the War*, especially chap. 34.

83. Dooley, *John Dooley*, 180.

84. Ballard, *Long Shadow*, 69.

85. Augustus Dean, "Reminiscences of Augustus A. Dean," Bound Volume 425, FSNMP.

86. Dooley, *John Dooley*, 180.

87. Trudeau, *Out of the Storm*, 390-91; Marten, *Sing Not War*, 33.

88. Dean, "Reminiscences."

89. Tripp, *Yankee Town, Southern City*, 160.

90. Greenough, "Aftermath at Appomattox," 8.

91. Wyatt-Brown, "Death of a Nation," 254.

92. Author unknown, letter fragment ca. 1865, Series I, Folder 60, Walton-Glenny Family Papers, HNOC.

93. Rosen, *Terror in the Heart*, 180.

94. Bradley, *This Astounding Close*, 150-53.

95. Carter, *When the War Was Over*, 12.

96. Athos [pseud.], "Greensboro in April, 1865," *Greensboro Patriot*, March 23, 1866.

97. Athos [pseud.]. See also Barrett, *Civil War in North Carolina*, 387.

98. Bradley, *This Astounding Close*, 153.

99. Bradley, 153-54.

100. Bradley, *Bluecoats and Tar Heels*, 30-31. On the extent of postwar North Carolina crime and violence, see Carter, *When the War Was Over*, 21.

101. J. Kilpatrick to Lieut. Col. J. A. Campbell, April 30, 1865, in *OR*, series 47, vol. 3, p. 354.

102. There is some confusion as to the event's actual date, as April 27 is crossed out but the entry begins, "On Monday 27th." March 27 fell on a Monday in 1865, which may suggest she was recalling an event from the past month. Elizabeth Collier Diary, [Spring 1865], SHC.

103. Cornelia Phillips Spencer Diary, May 4, 1865, Volume 3, Cornelia Phillips Spencer Papers, SHC. For a general account of disorder in North Carolina after the war, see Schenck, [spring 1865], in *Diary*, 41-43.

104. Jonathan Worth to Addison [Worth], April 22, 1865, Box 1, Folder 7, Jonathan Worth Papers, SHC.

105. Crawford, *Ashe County's Civil War*, 153. For a compellingly deep analysis of violence in western North Carolina, see Paludan, *Victims*. For North Carolina's Lower Cape Fear, see Evans, *Ballots and Fence Rails*.

106. Evans, *Ballots and Fence Rails*, 41.

107. "Mob Violence," *Macon (Ga.) Daily Telegraph*, May 11, 1865.

108. "Mob Violence."

109. Josiah Gorgas, entry for May 3, 1865, in Gorgas, *Journals of Josiah Gorgas*, 163. See also Russell K. Brown, "Post-Civil War Violence." In late May, the *Macon Daily Telegraph* complained of a large number of guns and pistols that were fired daily, day and night, in defiance of a city ordinance that prohibited the use of firearms within three hundred yards of any home. "Firing Guns and Pistols," *Macon (Ga.) Daily Telegraph*, May 30, 1865.

110. Reddy, *Navigation of Feeling*, 52-53; Kleinman, Das, and Lock, *Social Suffering*. For a broader reading on the long-term consequences of defeat, see Lears, *Rebirth of a Nation*, 12-50 especially.

111. Men's eventual retreat from the public arena is well documented. Federal authorities circumscribed the roles of former Confederate soldiers, which thrust Southern women to the fore. Instituted memorial customs, in particular, functioned as public expressions of Confederate sentiments. Scholars such as Gaines M. Foster have viewed Memorial Days as significant acts of commemoration that furthered the process of reunion. William Blair rightly modifies this assessment, contending that these acts also were forms of resistance that perpetuated Confederate identity. Women proved central to the construction of Confederate identity, as David Blight has demonstrated so admirably. Blair complicates this familiar story, recounting that while Federal authorities circumscribed the roles of former Confederate soldiers, thereby allowing women to dominate public spaces, *Cities of the Dead* continued to provide a means for rebel resistance, in Blair's assessment, in the form of guerrilla warfare through mourning. White Southern women made important decisions concerning the content and form of celebrations while always maintaining an eye toward normative gender roles. Once postwar Confederate identity became linked with cemeteries, Blair posits, it assumed a less threatening role that made reunion easier. Blair, *Cities of the Dead*, 77-97. See also Blight, *Race and Reunion*; and Foster, *Ghosts of the Confederacy*.

112. For an account of continued violence in South Carolina, see Clemson, *Rebel Came Home*, 94. On rebuilding the South, see Rubin, *Shattered Nation*, 173.

113. Vance, *Duties of Defeat*, 10.

114. On these processes among Southern women between 1865 and 1866, see Janney, *Burying the Dead*, chaps. 1, 2.

115. Zebulon B. Vance, proclamation of April 28, 1865, quoted in Albright, *Greensboro*, 77.

116. Vance quoted in Albright, *Greensboro*, 77.

117. North Carolina General Assembly, *Public Laws*, 15.

118. J. A. Campbell, General Orders No. 35, May 4, 1865, in OR, series 47, vol. 3, p. 396.

119. David Schenck Diary, n.d. [spring 1865], Folder 6, Volume 5, Box 2, David Schenck Papers, SHC.

120. Schenck Diary, n.d. [spring 1865], Folder 6, Volume 5, Box 2, and July 24, 1865, Folder 6, Volume 5, Box 2, Schenck Papers, SHC. On the military occupation, see Bradley, *Bluecoats and Tar Heels*, 246–47.

121. Evans, *Ballots and Fence Rails*, 68–73; Evans, *To Die Game*, 61–62.

122. Eggleston, "Rebel's Recollections," 663, 667.

123. Eggleston, *Rebel's Recollections*, 181–83.

124. Greenough, "Aftermath at Appomattox," 22.

125. S. B. M. Young to H. W. Halleck, May 15, 1865, in OR, series 1, vol. 46, pt. 3, p. 1157. See also Greenough, "Aftermath at Appomattox," 7.

126. Benjamin Franklin Perry, "Provisional Governorship of South Carolina," n.d., Box 1, Folder 21, B. F. Perry Papers, USC.

127. W. L. T. Prince, W. Allen Benton, and F. Lynch to Benjamin Franklin Perry, October 30, 1865, Box 1, Folder 8, Perry Papers, USC.

128. Litwack, *Been in the Storm*, 367.

129. "Town Ordinances: Adopted by the Mayor and Board of Commissioners for the Town of Goldsboro, to Go into Operation on the 15th Day of February, 1866," University of North Carolina-Chapel Hill, North Carolina Collection, Chapel Hill.

130. John Hope Franklin's *Militant South* remains the most important statement of antebellum Southern militancy. Franklin, *Militant South*. See also Baptist, *Creating an Old South*.

131. Zuczek, *State of Rebellion*; Hogue, *Uncivil War*. The classic statement on Reconstruction-era violence remains Rable, *But There Was No Peace*. See also Lemann, *Redemption*.

132. Hadden, *Slave Patrols*, chap. 6, epilogue; Hahn, *Nation under Our Feet*, 270. See also Lemann, *Redemption*; and Evans, *To Die Game*, 60–61.

133. Zuczek, *State of Rebellion*, 18.

134. Quoted in Bradley, *Bluecoats and Tar Heels*, 74.

135. Charlotte E. Grimes, "Sketches of My Life," Grimes-Bryan Papers, ECU.

136. McCarthy, *Detailed Minutiae*, 192.

137. Shotwell, *Papers of Randolph Abbott Shotwell*, vol. 2:215.

138. W. Scott Poole's recent study *Never Surrender*, while focused on the South Carolina Upcountry, suggests that scholars should reexamine continued resistance and the Lost Cause through cultural forms and expressions. While outside this book's direct purview, Poole's argument has influenced my thinking. Poole, *Never Surrender*.

139. In his provocative 1981 essay "A Generation of Defeat," David Herbert Donald posits that "segregation and disfranchisement should be viewed as the final public acts, the last bequests, of the Southern Civil War generation." Donald holds that white Southerners' simultaneous traumas of defeat and emancipation eventually fa-

cilitated racial segregation and disfranchisement. Donald's conclusions, while more far reaching than my own, suggest how deeply the war affected white Southerners' ideas and identities. Donald, "Generation of Defeat," quote on 334; see also 334-40.

Chapter Five

1. Rufus Barringer Diary, April 10 and April 24, [1865], Box 1, Folder 3, Rufus Barringer Papers, SHC.
2. Papa [Rufus Barringer] to children, June 10, 1865, Box 1, Folder 4, Barringer Papers, SHC.
3. Barringer Diary, August 8, [1865], Barringer Papers, SHC.
4. Foster, *Ghosts of the Confederacy*, 5.
5. Veterans' ambiguous feelings about war and defeat have given rise to competing interpretations of the Civil War's long-term consequences. Historian Diane Miller Sommerville has contended, for example, that the psychological crisis "that grew out of the Civil War also shaped and remapped the cultural and intellectual contours of the region." Both she and David Silkenat charge that whites' attitudes toward suicide shifted, making it more acceptable in the postwar South because it enabled Southerners to "maintain mastery and control." Other historians have contended that Lost Cause mythology reveals whites' firm command of themselves and society in the New South era. Indeed, as Gaines M. Foster writes, Southerners had "remembered the battle but had forgotten its pain, its cost, and its issues." Scholarly emphasis on the war's "dark sides" has created concern among some historians that these "atypical experiences" are cast as "normative ones." See, respectively, Sommerville, "'Burden Too Heavy,'" 487, 489; Foster, *Ghosts of the Confederacy*, 4; and Gallagher and Meier, "Coming to Terms," 492.
6. John Hampden Chamberlayne to Sally Grattan, August 1, 1865, in Chamberlayne, *Ham Chamberlayne*, 333.
7. Marten, *Sing Not War*, 49.
8. On this point, see McCurry, *Confederate Reckoning*.
9. Craig Thompson Friend, "From Southern Manhood to Southern Masculinities: An Introduction," in Friend, ed., *Southern Masculinity: Perspectives on Manhood in the South Since Reconstruction*, ii-viii.
10. On this approach and its potential insights, see Carmichael "Soldier-Speak," 273-74; and Wickberg, "History of Sensibilities?," 669.
11. Eustace, *Passion Is the Gale*; Eustace, "AHR Conversation," 1503-4.
12. See especially Linderman, *Embattled Courage*, 268, 275.
13. See, respectively, Blight, *Race and Reunion*, 149-50; Brian Matthew Jordan, "'Living Monuments,'" 126; and Marten, *Sing Not War*, 10-11. See also, Susannah J. Ural, *Hood's Texas Brigade: The Soldiers and Families of the Confederacy's Most Celebrated Unit* (Baton Rouge: Louisiana State University Press, 2017), 260-61.
14. Janney, *Remembering the Civil War*, 134.
15. As historian Heather Cox Richardson has observed, "Reconstruction is a process, not a time period." Richardson, "North and West," 90. By using the term *reconstruction*, small *r*, I am avoiding a strictly political interpretation of Reconstruction.

For insights on the intellectual dimensions of the shift from civil war to civic peace, see Leslie Butler, "Reconstructions."

16. As William L. Barney has noted, for "all the limits of the biographical approach, it remains indispensable for uncovering the individual choices that transform historical processes into concrete actions." Barney, *Making of a Confederate*, 217.

17. [James] Walton to Amelia [Walton], May 6, 1865, Series I, Folder 58, Walton-Glenny Family Papers, HNOC.

18. Henry to "Parents," June 21, 1865, Box 1, Folder 7, Henry Brown Richardson and Family Papers, LSU.

19. Rubin, *Shattered Nation*, 112-13.

20. On Confederates' unwavering optimism, see Rubin, 123-26.

21. [James] Burdge [Walton] to M. A. [Amelia] Walton, February 6, 1865, Series I, Folder 56, Walton-Glenny Family Papers, HNOC.

22. Carmichael, *Last Generation*, 207; Rubin, *Shattered Nation*, 123-26; Phillips, *Diehard Rebels*.

23. Whites, *Crisis in Gender*, 30; Carmichael, *Last Generation*, 208-9.

24. Burdge to M. A. Walton, February 6, 1865, Series I, Folder 56, Walton-Glenny Family Papers, HNOC.

25. Burdge to M. A. Walton, February 6, 1865, Series I, Folder 56, Walton-Glenny Family Papers, HNOC.

26. [James] B. [Walton] to [family], April 3, 1865, Series I, Folder 57, Walton-Glenny Family Papers, HNOC.

27. Henry to "Parents," June 21, 1865, Box 1, Folder 7, Richardson Family Papers, LSU. See also Anne Sarah Rubin's excellent account of Richardson's oath. Rubin, *Shattered Nation*, 164-65.

28. Eunice Thurston Richardson to Henry Brown Richardson, July 15, 1865, Box 1, Folder 3, Richardson Family Papers, LSU.

29. Henry to "Parents," June 21, 1865, Box 1, Folder 7, Richardson Family Papers, LSU.

30. Josiah Gorgas, May 4, 1865, [typed copy of journal], Josiah Gorgas Papers, SHC.

31. George Anderson Mercer Diary, June 11, 1865, Box 1, Volume 5, Mercer Papers, SHC.

32. Wyatt-Brown, *The Shaping of Southern Culture*, 256.

33. Insights on the relationship between the individual and the social were gained from Flynn, *Sartre*, 1:19-22 especially.

34. Josiah Gorgas, entry for May 4, 1865, in Gorgas, *Journals of Josiah Gorgas*, 167.

35. Gorgas Journal, May 26, 1865, Gorgas Papers, SHC.

36. Josiah Gorgas, entry for August 31, 1865, in Gorgas, *Journals of Josiah Gorgas*, 186.

37. Josiah Gorgas, entry for June 2, 1865, in Gorgas, *Journals of Josiah Gorgas*, 175.

38. Mercer Diary, December 17, 1865, SHC.

39. [James] B. [Walton] to Amelia [M. A. Walton], May 6, 1865, Series I, Folder 58, Walton-Glenny Family Papers, HNOC.

40. Barney, *Making of a Confederate*, 11.

41. [James] B. [Walton] to Amelia [M. A. Walton], May 6, 1865, Series I, Folder 58, Walton-Glenny Family Papers, HNOC.

42. For white men's embrace of family, see Whites, *Crisis in Gender*, 142-44.

43. [James] B. [Walton] to Amelia [M. A. Walton], May 6, 1865, Series I, Folder 58, Walton-Glenny Family Papers, HNOC. For similar sentiments among Southern men, see Whites, *Crisis in Gender*, 140-41.

44. James [B. Walton] to Amelia [M. A. Walton], June 10, 1865, Series I, Folder 59, Walton-Glenny Family Papers, HNOC.

45. James [B. Walton] to Amelia [M. A. Walton], June 10, 1865, Series I, Folder 59, Walton-Glenny Family Papers, HNOC.

46. James [B. Walton] to Amelia [M. A. Walton], June 10, 1865, Series I, Folder 59, Walton-Glenny Family Papers, HNOC.

47. Henry to Mother, December 26, 1865, Box 1, Folder 7, Richardson Family Papers, LSU.

48. Henry to Mother, December 26, 1865, Box 1, Folder 7, Richardson Family Papers, LSU.

49. Henry to Parents, January 31, [1868?], Box 1, Folder 9, Richardson Family Papers, LSU.

50. Henry to Parents, November 30, 1868, Box 1, Folder 9, Richardson Family Papers, LSU.

51. See especially Whites, *Gender Matters*, chap. 5.

52. Bederman, *Manliness and Civilization*, 7.

53. J. B. Mitchell to Ruffin H. Thomson, December 20, 1866, Box 1, Folder 10, Ruffin Thomson Papers, SHC. Mitchell's quote comes from Alexander Pope's *Essay on Man I* (1733), x.

54. J. B. Mitchell to Ruffin H. Thomson, December 20, 1866, Box 1, Folder 10, Thomson Papers, SHC.

55. C. Woodward Hutson to Mother, March 31, 1869, Loose Papers, Box 1, Hutson Family Papers, TU.

56. For a counterargument about the persistence of Confederate loyalty, see Phillips, *Diehard Rebels*, chap. 5, conclusion, for his rich description of this ethos in the war's close and beyond.

57. Rubin, *Shattered Nation*, 141; Logue, *To Appomattox and Beyond*, 105.

58. "The Confederate Soldier," *Yorkville (S.C.) Enquirer*, April 16, 1868.

59. For the public face of white Southerners' efforts at rebuilding, see Rubin, *Shattered Nation*, 172-90 especially.

60. Vance, *Duties of Defeat*, 10.

61. Fox-Genovese, "Anxiety of History," 77.

62. Rubin, *Shattered Nation*, 190.

63. Mercer Diary, June 22, 1866, SHC.

64. Mercer Diary, June 10, 1866, SHC.

65. Mercer Diary, November 11, 1866, SHC.

66. Mercer Diary, November 11, 1866, SHC.

67. Josiah Gorgas, entry for October 15, 1866, in Gorgas, *Journals of Josiah Gorgas*, 201.

68. Josiah Gorgas, entry for January 6, [18]67, in Gorgas, *Journals of Josiah Gorgas*, 203.

69. Dooley, *John Dooley*, 204.

70. Statement of Edward Warren and R. B. Haywood, n.d. [1864], Box 1, Folder 8, William J. Clarke Papers, SHC.

71. "To His Excellency President Davis," n.d., Box 2, Folder 28, Undated Papers, Clarke Papers, SHC. Although the statement is undated, the petition refers to Clarke as being "at present afflicted" with a severe wound and mentions several earlier Civil War battles, thereby suggesting the 1864 date.

72. William J. Clarke to Mary Bayard Clarke, May 23, 1861, in Mary Bayard Clarke, *Live Your Own Life*, 74; William J. Clarke to Mary Bayard Clarke, January 27, 1863, in Clarke, 137.

73. William J. Clarke Diary, March 6, 7, 9, and 26 and April 24, 1868, Box 2, Volumes, Clarke Papers, SHC.

74. The best reference to this pain is found in his personal diary from 1868. See, for instance, March 6, 7, and 26, April 24, and June 15, 1868. He also noted the "anniversary of battle at National Bridge Mexico where [he] was wounded," August 12, 1868, and "wounded at Drewry's Bluff VA in 1864." He mistakes April 15, 1868, for the "anniversary" but then crosses it out and instead notes the date May 15, 1864. William J. Clarke Diary, 1868, Volumes, Box 2, Clarke Papers, SHC.

75. Jeffrey W. McClurken powerfully recounts how disabled veterans, unable to work, turned to the state for aid. McClurken, *Take Care of the Living*, chap. 6.

76. Mary Bayard Clarke to Frank Clarke, November 20, [1866], Box 2, Folder 29, Undated Papers, Clarke Papers, SHC.

77. On this point, see Edwards, *Gendered Strife and Confusion*, 110.

78. On the expansion of women's roles during the war and the readjustment afterward, see Rubin, *Shattered Nation*, 208-9 especially; Faust, *Mothers of Invention*, 248-54; and Whites, *Crisis in Gender*.

79. Mary Bayard Clarke to Frank Clarke, November 20, [1866], Box 2, Folder 29, Undated Papers, Clarke Papers, SHC.

80. Wyatt-Brown, *Shaping of Southern Culture*, 259.

81. See especially Silkenat, *Moments of Despair*, 25-26; and Sommerville, "'Burden Too Heavy,'" 489-91.

82. Stuart Leigh [Mary Clarke], "The South Expects Every Woman to Do Her Duty," August 1866, in Clarke, *Live Your Own Life*, 222.

83. Leigh, 223.

84. Rubin, *Shattered Nation*, 226.

85. Leigh, "South Expects," 226.

86. Leigh, 227.

87. Vance, *Duties of Defeat*, 11.

88. The phrase "band of brothers" is used in two ways. First and most obvious, it is derived from a line in the 1861 Confederate tune "The Bonnie Blue Flag." Outwardly projecting unity, white Southerners utilized such imagery to bolster their cause. Perhaps more importantly, though, is historian Stephanie McCurry's more nuanced use of the phrase, which informs this essay. She asserts, "The idea of the people and the nation as a band of brothers had a long provenance in Southern and American history." The people

and their national building project, McCurry continues, were the exclusive domain of a band of brothers who directly underpinned secession and the Confederate cause. "Secession was an attempt to define a new nation as a band of brothers with similar interests, rights, and duties. But even among 'the people,' the white male voters soon to be soldiers, unity was elusive." McCurry, *Confederate Reckoning*, 34, 77; see also 11-37.

89. Ural, *Hood's Texas Brigade*, 250-82.

90. Job B. Smith to Wad [Cadwallader Jones], February 11, 1866, Folder 5, Box 1, Cadwallader Jones Papers, SHC.

91. Williams, *From That Terrible Field*, 60, also quoted in Faust, "Christian Soldiers," 85.

92. Smith to Wad, February 11, 1866, Folder 5, Box 1, Jones Papers, SHC.

93. Faust, "Christian Soldiers," 90.

94. Foster, *Ghosts of the Confederacy*, 89-95.

95. T. E. Vann to "old Captain" [William Henry Tripp], March 4, 1869, Folder 9, Box 2, William Henry Tripp and Araminta Guilford Tripp Papers, SHC.

96. Rosenwein, "Worrying about Emotions in History," 842-43.

97. Berry, *All That Makes a Man*, 17-44; Glover, "'Let Us Manufacture Men.'"

98. Berry, *All That Makes a Man*, 47-80 especially.

99. See most notably Rosenburg, *Living Monuments*; and Foster, *Ghosts of the Confederacy*, 104-8, 112-14.

100. This assertion counters Gerald F. Linderman, who contends that it was not until around the year 1880 that Americans revived their interest in martial matters. David Blight rightly questions Linderman's strict dichotomy between "hibernation" (1865-80) and "revival" (post-1880) as too schematic, arguing instead for a more fluid periodization. In the first fifteen years after the war, he posits, "ex-soldiers groped for ways to express the trauma of their personal experience as well as its larger legacies." See Linderman, *Embattled Courage*, 275, 266-97; and Blight, *Race and Reunion*, quote on 170. See also Blight, 149-50.

101. W. C. Fraley to General Grimes, February 9, 1880, Correspondence, 1880-1921, Grimes-Bryan Papers, ECU.

102. J. B. Lindsey to R. A. Shotwell, May 13, 1880, Box 4, Folder 27, Shotwell Family Papers, SHC.

103. P. D. Johnson to John G. Barrett, October 3, 1957, Box 2, Folder 7, Munson Monroe Buford Papers, SHC.

104. Munson Monroe Buford Diary, September 4, 1879, and June 30, 1880, Box 1, Folder 3, Buford Papers, SHC.

105. Logue, *To Appomattox and Beyond*, 122.

106. McCarthy, *Detailed Minutiae*, 209.

107. M. M. Buford to Trick [William G. Austin], November 22, 1896, Box 2, Folder 7, Buford Papers, SHC.

108. Julius A. Lineback Diary, February 27, 1904, Box 1, Volume 2, Folder 2-A, J. A. Lineback Papers, SHC.

109. Bourdieu, *Language and Symbolic Power*, 223-26.

110. Logue, *To Appomattox and Beyond*, 121-29.

Chapter Six

1. "To Capt R. A. Shotwell," n.d., Box 4, Folder 28, Shotwell Family Papers, SHC.

2. Lester and Wilson, *Ku Klux Klan*. See also Parsons, *Ku-Klux*, 29-30. Following this logic and several accounts of initiation rituals, historian Allen W. Trelease describes the Tennessee Klan as being similar to a college fraternity in initiation and structure. Trelease, *White Terror*, 4-6; Lester and Wilson, *Ku Klux Klan*, 55, 60.

3. Parsons, *Ku-Klux*, 78.

4. On whites' gendered reaction to defeat, see Whites, *Crisis in Gender*, 133-37, 142-43; Rubin, *Shattered Nation*, 135, 141-47; and Wyatt-Brown, *Shaping of Southern Culture*, 230-46.

5. Insights drawn from Geertz, "Deep Play," 448-53; and Raymond Williams, *Marxism and Literature*, 128-35. For an informative reading of Klan violence through the lens of emotions history, see Harcourt, "Whipping of Richard Moore."

6. This array of forces composes what Daniel Wickberg calls "sensibility." The study of sensibility seeks, in Wickberg's words, to "dig beneath the social actions and apparent content of sources to the ground upon which those sources stand: the emotional, intellectual, aesthetic, and moral dispositions of the persons who created them." Wickberg, "What is the History of Sensibilities?," 669.

7. Foner, *Reconstruction*, 425-26.

8. Rable, *But There Was No Peace*, 94-95. The purpose of the Ku Klux Klan has been heavily contested by scholars. The most overtly political reading of the Klan's function is found in Zuczek, *State of Rebellion*, 55-61 especially.

9. Parsons, *Ku-Klux*, 100-101.

10. On this approach, see Eustace, *Passion Is the Gale*; and Eustace, "*AHR* Conversation," 1503-4.

11. "Emotional community" is Barbara H. Rosenwein's term. She conceives of it as something similar to social communities—i.e., families or neighborhoods. The researcher is searching for systems of feelings and how these communities define and assess such emotions. Rosenwein, "Worrying about Emotions in History," 842-43.

12. Kimmel, *Manhood in America*, 95, 124-25; Wyatt-Brown, *Shaping of Southern Culture*, chaps. 8, 9; Whites, *Crisis in Gender*, 132-59; Bercaw, *Gendered Freedoms*, chap. 3.

13. McClurken, *Take Care of the Living*, 1-2, 65-71, especially; Bercaw, *Gendered Freedoms*, chap. 3.

14. As Gail Bederman has argued, *manhood* is a fluid term that has been "defined quite differently in different times, places, and contexts." Bederman, *Manliness and Civilization*, 5; see also 5-10. On contrasting models of white masculinity during the Reconstruction era, see Friend, *Southern Masculinity*.

15. On this narrative tradition, see Harcourt, "Who Were the Pale Faces?" Earliest works include Lester and Wilson, *Ku Klux Klan*, and "New Light on the Ku Klux Klan."

16. See especially Trelease, *White Terror*; and Rable, *But There Was No Peace*.

17. On this tradition, see especially Escott, *Many Excellent People*; and Lemann, *Redemption*. Scott Reynolds Nelson's revealing work entwines these strands, positing that a potent mix of racism and politics drove whites into the ranks of the Ku Klux. See Nelson, *Iron Confederacies*, 97-99.

18. Cardyn, "Sexualized Racism/Gendered Violence"; Poole, *Never Surrender*, 78-79 especially; Parsons, *Ku-Klux*; and Rosen, *Terror in the Heart*, chaps. 5, 6.

19. Rosen, *Terror in the Heart*, 181.

20. For an overview of Shotwell's life, see Wert, "Shotwell, Randolph Abbott."

21. Shotwell, *Papers of Randolph Abbott Shotwell*, 2:216.

22. Shotwell, 2:235.

23. Shotwell, 2:214.

24. See especially Turner, *Process, Performance, and Pilgrimage*; Isaac, *Transformation of Virginia*; and Geertz, "Deep Play."

25. For the earliest initiations in Tennessee, see Trelease, *White Terror*, 15-19; for more general information, see Trelease, 59-60. Formalized Ku Klux oaths, constitutions, and structure are detailed in Lester and Wilson, *Ku Klux Klan*, 135-86.

26. On secrecy and brotherhood, see Lester and Wilson, *Ku Klux Klan*, 147, 170-73; and Randolph Shotwell, "Ku-Klux Chronicles: Captain Shotwell's Story of the Klans," clipping in Shotwell Scrapbook, Box 4, Folder 29, Shotwell Family Papers, SHC. On how these whites defined themselves against Reconstruction, see Trelease, *White Terror*, chap. 3; and Kantrowitz, *Ben Tillman*, 1-9. On self-defense and protection, see Testimony of Albertus Hope, December 12, 1871, in United States Congress, Joint Select Committee, *Report of the Joint Select Committee to Inquire into the Condition of Affairs in the Late Insurrectionary States* (Washington, D.C.: Government Printing Office, 1871), vol. 5, 1680-85; hereinafter *Report of the Joint Select Committee*.

27. Trelease, *White Terror*, 51, 68, 72; Shotwell, "Ku-Klux Chronicles."

28. Trelease, *White Terror*, 51; Rable, *But There Was No Peace*, 94-95; Randolph Shotwell, "Rutherford Ku Klux Reminiscence," April 15, 1878, newspaper clipping in Shotwell Scrapbook, Box 4, Folder 29, Shotwell Family Papers, SHC. Through a study of manuscript census records in Alamance County, North Carolina, Paul D. Escott concluded that recruitment "brought many neighbors whose farms adjoined each other into the Klan, and family relations were another channel through which membership spread." Escott, *Many Excellent People*, 158.

29. Hahn, *Nation under Our Feet*, 268; Donald, "Generation of Defeat."

30. Carnes, *Secret Ritual and Manhood*, 14; Syrett, *Company He Keeps*, 28-31. On the Klan's connections to fraternal orders, see Harcourt, "Who Were the Pale Faces?," 54-55. Linkages between ritual and manhood are explored in Carnes, *Secret Ritual and Manhood*. For the Klan's dependence on contemporary popular cultural forms, see Parsons, "Midnight Rangers."

31. Syrett, *Company He Keeps*, 33, 44.

32. Shotwell, "Ku-Klux Chronicles." William R. Tickel, when questioned about his connection to the Klan, confessed to giving Jacob A. Long—a Klan chief in Alamance County—a sign. After acknowledging the sign, Long said, "You belong to the first degree. There is three other degrees of which you don't know any thing. You will probably be initiated at some future time." This suggested Masonic-like hierarchies and levels of organization. Testimony of William R. Tickel, September 2, 1870, Box 1, Folder Sept.-Dec. 1870, Klan Papers.

33. Testimony of William R. Tickel, September 2, 1870, Box 1, Folder Sept.-Dec. 1870, Klan Papers, DU.

34. Shotwell, *Papers of Randolph Abbott Shotwell*, vol. 2:372.

35. Shotwell, vol. 2:373. Part of this ceremony mimics a wartime ceremony of induction, according to Shotwell, and also informed the Klan's name. He writes, "At the initiation of members into the 'Q' company, a gun was cocked and pointed at the head of the applicant to test his nerve. The click, click of the lock while the gun was being cocked suggested the words Ku-Klux, and candidates for initiation were finally called subjects to be Ku-Kluxed. The word came into use and was by the disbanded 'Q' men brought into one of the societies of the Invisible Empire." Shotwell, "Ku-Klux Chronicles."

36. Shotwell, *Papers of Randolph Abbott Shotwell*, vol. 2:374. Italics in the original. Stanley F. Horn named Shotwell as chief of Rutherford County's Klan. According to Horn, another initiation oath read, "I promise and pledge myself to assist, according to my pecuniary circumstances, all brothers in distress . . . I promise and swear that I will obey all instructions given me by my chief; and should I ever divulge, or cause to be divulged, any secrets, signs or passwords of the Invisible Empire, I must meet with the fearful and just penalty of the traitor, which is death—death—death, at the hands of the brethren." Horn, *Invisible Empire*, 55.

37. Testimony of James E. Boyd, August 31, [1870], Box 1, Folder Jan.-Aug. 1870, Klan Papers, DU.

38. Scott Reynolds Nelson, *Iron Confederacies*, 111; Duncan, *Duncan's Masonic Ritual*, 28.

39. Lester and Wilson, *Ku Klux Klan*, 63-67.

40. Carnes, *Secret Ritual and Manhood*, 34-36.

41. Turner, *Process, Performance, and Pilgrimage*, 17-18.

42. Turner, 20.

43. Cardyn, "Sexualized Racism/Gendered Violence," 831. See also Parsons, *Ku-Klux*, 77; and Natalie Zemon Davis, "Reasons of Misrule."

44. The Ku Klux Klan represents a specific, and fleeting, venue in which white Southern men displayed a rugged masculinity. For a broader discussion of male aggressiveness, see Ownby, *Subduing Satan*.

45. I garnered numerous insights from Mark C. Carnes's discussion of death symbolism in Masonic rituals in *Secret Ritual and Manhood*, 54-63. As anthropologists have argued, symbolic meaning is connected to cultural context. If we follow the logic of Clifford Geertz, cultural form can be treated as text. Excitement, despair, loss, and risk not only are the emotional results of Klan ceremonies but are also reflective of feelings that that particular society valued. Geertz, "Deep Play," 448-53. See also Turner, *Process, Performance, and Pilgrimage*.

46. For connections between performance and social realities, see Geertz, "Deep Play." For the Klan's cultural function, see Nelson, *Iron Confederacies*; and Parsons, "Midnight Rangers."

47. Testimony of James E. Boyd, August 31, [1870], Box 1, Folder Jan.-Aug. 1870, Klan Papers, DU. Mitchell Snay explores the brotherhood of the Klan through comparative perspective with Union Leagues and Fenians, arguing that the Civil War era was a period of intense nationalism. He includes an excellent description of the military characteristics and means of bonding of each order. Snay, *Fenians*, chap. 2.

48. This first document is rather curious and could be from any number of fraternal orders. But its explicitly political message and its time frame of circa 1870 suggest that this is a document from an order of the Klan. Moreover, sections of this document have distinctive correlations to the Ku Klux Klan "Obligation" or oath detailed in Lester and Wilson, *Ku Klux Klan*, 147. The anonymous, undated document itself is found in the Artemus Darby Goodwyn Papers, Folder 8, Box 1, USC.

49. Kantrowitz, "One Man's Mob," 67-68; Kantrowitz, *Ben Tillman*, 50-60. On South Carolina's antebellum white men, see Ford, *Origins of Southern Radicalism*; and McCurry, *Masters of Small Worlds*.

50. Anonymous, undated document, Folder 8, Box 1, Goodwyn Papers, USC. For other references to kneeling during initiation, see Testimony of Kirkland L. Gunn, December 12, 1871, in *Report of the Joint Select Committee*, vol. 5, 1686; and Testimony of Sam Ferguson, December 13, 1871, in *Report of the Joint Select Committee*, vol. 5, 1740.

51. The second document, well established to be from the Klan, is "Head Quarters Genl Orders! No 1," ca. October 1868, Oversized Folder (1868-1913), Iredell Jones Papers, USC.

52. "Head Quarters Genl Orders!"

53. Kantrowitz, "One Man's Mob."

54. Foner, *Reconstruction*, 276-77.

55. George Anderson Mercer Diary, November 3, 1867, Volume 5, SHC.

56. Shotwell, "Ku-Klux Chronicles." For a broader discussion of Klan denial and skepticism, see Parsons, *Ku-Klux*, 181-214.

57. Kantrowitz, "One Man's Mob," 67.

58. Parsons, "Midnight Rangers," 830.

59. This interpretation relies heavily on an anthropological reading of rituals. See Turner, *Process, Performance, and Pilgrimage*; Geertz, "Deep Play"; and Isaac, *Transformation of Virginia*, especially "A Discourse on the Method."

60. Parsons, *Ku-Klux*, 97.

61. Parsons, 76-78, 81, 84-101.

62. Whites, *Gender Matters*, 92.

63. Wyatt-Brown, *The Shaping of Southern Culture*, 255-58.

64. Parsons, *Ku-Klux*, 30.

65. Nelson, *Iron Confederacies*, 109-10. See also Olsen, "North Carolina," 179.

66. Nelson, *Iron Confederacies*, 111. The elaborate hierarchy envisioned by the Klan, if never fully realized, is detailed in Lester and Wilson, *Ku Klux Klan*, 155-70. A version of the constitution and by-laws, likewise detailing structures of command, is found in Testimony of Kirkland L. Gunn, December 12, 1871, in *Report of the Joint Select Committee*, vol. 5, 1686-87.

67. Testimony of Charles W. Foster, December 12, 1871, in *Report of the Joint Select Committee*, vol. 5, 1700-05. See also Charles Reagan Wilson, *Baptized in Blood*, 112.

68. Wilson, *Baptized in Blood*, 112. See also Fry, *Night Riders*, 145-47.

69. Walter L. Fleming, introduction to *Ku Klux Klan*, by Lester and Wilson, 28.

70. Testimony of James E. Boyd, August 31, [1870], Box 1, Folder Jan.-Aug. 1870, Klan Papers, DU.

71. Testimony of Kirkland L. Gunn, December 12, 1871, in *Report of the Joint Select Committee*, vol. 5, 1689; Lester and Wilson, *Ku Klux Klan*, 59; Scott Reynolds Nelson, *Iron Confederacies*, 110.

72. Testimony of Kirkland L. Gunn, December 12, 1871, in *Report of the Joint Select Committee*, vol. 5, 1689; Testimony of Gadsden Steel, December 12, 1871, in *Report of the Joint Select Committee*, vol. 5, 1718-19.

73. Testimony of James E. Boyd, August 31, [1870], Box 1, Folder Jan.-Aug. 1870, Klan Papers, DU. See also Testimony of William Tickel, April 1, 1870, Box 1, Folder Sept.-Dec. 1870, Klan Papers, DU.

74. Cardyn, "Sexual Terror," 153-54.

75. Foner, *Reconstruction*, 439-40; Bradley, *Army and Reconstruction*, 53.

76. Quoted in Bradley, *Army and Reconstruction*, 56-57.

77. Scott Reynolds Nelson, *Iron Confederacies*, 98.

78. Trelease, *White Terror*, 53. On the cultural significance of Klan costuming, see Parsons, *Ku-Klux*, 79-101. On clothing description, see Testimony of John Caldwell, December 13, 1871, in in *Report of the Joint Select Committee*, vol. 5, 1726-27.

79. David Schenck Diary, April 12, 1868, Folder 7, Volume 6, Box 2, David Schenck Papers, SHC.

80. Carnes, *Secret Ritual and Manhood*, 34.

81. Parsons, "Midnight Rangers," 830.

82. Fossett, "(K)night Riders," 41.

83. Kenneth S. Greenberg, *Honor and Slavery*, 24-31.

84. Schenck Diary, April 12, 1868, Folder 7, Volume 6, Box 2, Schenck Papers, SHC; John Patterson Green, *Recollections of the Inhabitants*; Trelease, *White Terror*, 54-55; Fry, *Night Riders*, 145.

85. *Yorkville (S.C.) Enquirer*, April 2, 1868. See also Trelease, *White Terror*, 71. Similar advertisements were reprinted in Lester and Wilson, *Ku Klux Klan*, 189-96.

86. On the broadest processes of early Klan mobilization, see Trelease, *White Terror*, 49-56.

87. An extensive collection of newspaper clippings from 1867-1876 can be found in Ellison Summerfield Keitt's Reconstruction-era Scrapbook. Keitt's sympathy with the Klan obviously directed what clippings he found interesting, but the stories may be an invaluable marker for Klan deception. Reconstruction-era Scrapbook, 1867-76, Ellison S. Keitt Papers, USC. On Klan rumors and mystery, see Schenck Diary, December 18, 1869, Folder 7, Volume 6, Box 2, Schenck Papers, SHC.

88. "The Evening Post and the So-Called Ku-Klux," n.d., Reconstruction-era Scrapbook, 1867-76, Ellison S. Keitt Papers, USC.

89. Parsons, *Ku-Klux*, 181, but also see 181-214.

90. Parsons, "Midnight Rangers," 817-18; Scott, *Domination*, 85-90.

91. Lester and Wilson, *Ku Klux Klan*, 93.

92. Testimony of John H. Wager, October 14, 1871, in *Report of the Joint Select Committee*, vol. 2, 933; Testimony of Austin Pollard, November 16, 1871, in *Report of the Joint Select Committee*, vol. 12, 1101-02; Shotwell, "Ku-Klux Chronicles"; Parsons, "Midnight Rangers," 817-18. Mark L. Bradley documents the successful intervention of a Freed-

men's Bureau officer in Salisbury, North Carolina, who stopped a planned nighttime parade of the White Man's Club and "Fantastics," or Ku Klux, before elections. Bradley, *Bluecoats and Tar Heels*, 183.

93. Testimony of Andy Timons, December 12, 1871, in *Report of the Joint Select Committee*, vol. 5, 1712.

94. Testimony of Dick Wilson, December 13, 1871, in *Report of the Joint Select Committee*, vol. 5, 1747.

95. Testimony of Simpson Bobo, July 13, 1871, in *Report of the Joint Select Committee*, vol. 4, 803.

96. Lumpkin, *Making of a Southerner*, 91. See also Robuck, *My Own Personal Experience*, 91, 126; Trelease, *White Terror*, 58-59; and Parsons, "Midnight Rangers," 813.

97. Trelease, *White Terror*, 56.

98. On African Americans' resistance to the Klan, see Rosen, *Terror in the Heart*, 188-89. See also Piersen, *Black Legacy*, 142-44.

99. Essic Harris, "Testimony," 89-90.

100. Testimony of Dick Wilson, December 13, 1871, in *Report of the Joint Select Committee*, vol. 5, 1749.

101. Green, *Recollections of the Inhabitants*, 136.

102. Parsons, in particular, has done exceptional work by revealing the way the Klan employed not only the imagery of dead Confederate soldiers but also that of ghosts, foreigners, moon men, and animals. Parsons, *Ku-Klux*, 76-78, 81, 84-101.

103. Cook, *Secret Political Societies*, 21-24; Fleming, *Sequel of Appomattox*, 252-53; Susan L. Davis, *Authentic History*, 8; Lester and Wilson, *Ku Klux Klan*, 98; Horn, *Invisible Empire*, 18-19. For the historical perspective on white attitudes toward African Americans' intelligence, see Jordon, *White over Black*, 8, 187-90.

104. See especially McWhiney and Simkins, "Ghostly Legend"; Trelease, *White Terror*, 56-58; Fry, *Night Riders*, 69-80; Piersen, *Black Legacy*, 142-44; and Parsons, "Midnight Rangers," 813.

105. Piersen, *Black Legacy*, 142.

106. Parsons, *Ku-Klux*, 77.

107. Parsons, 77.

108. On antebellum tactics, see Fry, *Night Riders*, 66-81. Charles Reagan Wilson proposes that the Ku Klux Klan had direct Confederate connections that made it part of the religion of the Lost Cause. Wilson, *Baptized in Blood*, 112-13. So, too, does W. Scott Poole maintain that the Klan's Confederate imagery reinforced the Lost Cause, as he envisions "the spirits of vengeful Confederate soldiers as an act of pious remembrance." Poole, *Never Surrender*, 111. On the other hand, Gaines M. Foster contends that the Klan did very little to shape the postwar Confederate tradition. Foster, *Ghosts of the Confederacy*, 48. In significant ways, D. W. Griffith's reimagining of the Klan proved deeply influential in the early twentieth-century conception and development of Lost Cause mythology.

109. Parsons, "Midnight Rangers," 831.

110. Scott, *Domination*, 50.

111. Turner, *Process, Performance, and Pilgrimage*, 19.

112. Lester and Wilson, *Ku Klux Klan*, 190.

113. Lester and Wilson, 190.

114. "General Orders No. 3," in Lester and Wilson, *Ku Klux Klan*, 192. On Southern manhood, see Zuczek, *State of Rebellion*, 56-57; and Nelson, *Iron Confederacies*, 111.

115. On the importance of emotions history and Reconstruction, see Harcourt, "Whipping of Richard Moore." See also Janiewski, "Reign of Passion," 126.

116. For the groundbreaking study of anger, see Stearns and Stearns, *Anger*.

117. Harcourt, "Whipping of Richard Moore," 268.

118. Ayers, *Vengeance and Justice*, 159. For the emotional consequences of Confederate defeat, see Wyatt-Brown, *The Shaping of Southern Culture*. T. J. Jackson Lears isolates a pervasive sense of doubt that shaped postwar life despite a public optimism, which he partially roots in the presence of Civil War veterans. Lears, *No Place of Grace*. In a later work Lears describes this as the "long shadow of Appomattox." Lears, *Rebirth of a Nation*, 12-50.

119. Lester and Wilson, *Ku Klux Klan*, 49.

120. This section's discussion of violence is deliberately generalized. Parsons has conducted the most detailed and extensive analysis of localized violence—both Ku Klux and otherwise—to date. See Parsons, *Ku-Klux*, 215-302.

121. Cardyn, "Sexualized Racism/Gendered Violence," 677.

122. Parsons, *Ku-Klux*, 144-45; Prince, *Stories of the South*, 65.

123. A. T. Akerman to "Sir," January 1, [1872], Letterbook 1871-76, Amos Tappan Akerman Letter Books, 1871-76, UVA.

124. Reverdy Johnson, December 31, 1871, quoted in Green, *Recollections of the Inhabitants*, 143.

125. Tourgée, *Invisible Empire*, 141.

126. Essic Harris, "Testimony," 95.

127. Harris, 95.

128. Testimony of J. B. Eaves, July 12, 1871, in *Report of the Joint Select Committee*, vol. 2, 170.

129. Kantrowitz, "Two Faces of Domination," 96.

130. Schenck Diary, n.d. [winter 1868-69], Folder 7, Volume 6, Box 2, Schenck Papers, SHC; Trudier Harris, *Exorcising Blackness*, 18-19.

131. James B. Mason to William W. Holden, September 22, 1869, quoted in Trelease, *White Terror*, 196.

132. See, for example, the vivid description of terror in Alamance County, North Carolina, in Trelease, *White Terror*, chap. 12; and Cardyn, "Sexualized Racism/Gendered Violence," 708.

133. Testimony of James M. Justice, July 3, 1871, in Klan Trials, N.C., 103.

134. Johnson, *Soul by Soul*, 145-46; Harcourt, "Whipping of Richard Moore," 271.

135. See, for instance, Testimony of Charles W. Foster, December 12, 1871, in *Report of the Joint Select Committee*, vol. 5, 1701-03.

136. Green, *Recollections of the Inhabitants*, 136.

137. Essic Harris, "Testimony," 98-99. See also Schenck Diary, March 20 and June 10, 1870, Folder 7, Volume 6, Box 2, Schenck Papers, SHC.

138. Testimony of James E. Boyd, August 31, [1870], Box 1, Folder Jan.-Aug. 1870, Klan Papers, DU.

139. Rosen, *Terror in the Heart*, 181.

140. Cardyn, "Sexual Terror," 143-45.

141. Scott, *Domination*, 37.

142. Rosen, *Terror in the Heart*, 189.

143. Testimony of James M. Justice, July 3, 1871, in *Report of the Joint Select Committee*, vol. 2, 103.

144. For the incident, see Testimony of William Tickel, September 1, 1870, Box 1, Folder Sept. -Dec. 1870, Klan Papers, DU; and Testimony of Daniel Whitesell, n.d., Box 1, Klan Papers, DU.

145. Testimony of Gadsden Steel, December 12, 1871, in *Report of the Joint Select Committee*, vol. 5, 233.

146. Testimony of J. B. Eaves, July 12, 1871, in *Report of the Joint Select Committee*, vol. 2, 167.

147. Testimony of A. Webster Shaffer, June 15, 1871, in *Report of the Joint Select Committee*, vol. 2, 36-37.

148. Testimony of John W. Long, August 30, 1870, Box 1, Folder Jan.-Aug. 1870, Klan Papers, DU.

149. Cardyn, "Sexual Terror," 150-51.

150. Testimony of J. B. Eaves, July 12, 1871, *Report of the Joint Select Committee*, vol. 2, 170.

151. Cardyn, "Sexual Terror," 142.

152. Essic Harris, "Testimony," 88.

153. Harris, 90.

154. Scott, *Domination*, 37.

155. Trelease, *White Terror*, 386.

156. Rosenwein, "Worrying about Emotions in History," 837; on "emotional communities," see Rosenwein, 842-43.

157. Harcourt, "Whipping of Richard Moore," 268.

158. On the transfer and display of emotions, see Rosenwein, "Worrying about Emotions in History," 842.

159. Rosen, *Terror in the Heart*; Edwards, *Gendered Strife and Confusion*; Kantrowitz, *Ben Tillman*.

160. Parsons, "Midnight Rangers," 812-13.

161. Rosen, *Terror in the Heart*, 183. Perhaps the most effective, if contested, use of imagination is found in Benedict Anderson's masterful treatment, *Imagined Communities*. Anderson's communities are imagined "because the members of even the smallest nation will never know most of their fellow-members, meet them, or even hear of them, yet in the minds of each lives the image of their communion." Anderson, *Imagined Communities*, 6.

162. Insights drawn from Geertz, "Deep Play," 448-53; and Raymond Williams, *Marxism and Literature*, 128-35.

Conclusion

1. George Anderson Mercer Diary, March 17, 1893, Volume 5, SHC.
2. Mercer Diary, March 19 and 20, 1865, Volume 4, SHC.
3. Mercer Diary, April 16 and 28, 1865, Volume 4, SHC.
4. Blight, *Race and Reunion*, 170. For a different timeline, see Linderman, *Embattled Courage*, 275; also see 266-97.
5. Fussell, *Great War and Modern Memory*, 140.
6. Blum, *Reforging the White Republic*; Blight, *Race and Reunion*.
7. Gaston, *New South Creed*, 25.
8. Blight, *Race and Reunion*, 4. The New South's rise marked a departure from an antebellum social order; yet instead of abandoning old values, New South advocates emphasized the "Southernness" of their movement and romanticized the past out of which it came; see Gaston, *New South Creed*, 25-27, 168-69. On the creation of collective or historical memory, see Brundage, *Southern Past*; and Baker, *What Reconstruction Meant*.
9. Marten, *Sing Not War*, 203.
10. Mercer Diary, June 21, 1885, Volume 5, SHC.

Bibliography

Archives

Louisiana

Louisiana State University, Louisiana and Lower Mississippi Valley Collections, Special Collections, Hill Memorial Library, Baton Rouge
  William H. Ellis Papers
  Josiah Knighton and Family Papers
  Robert A. Newell Papers
  Henry Brown Richardson and Family Papers
Tulane University, Howard-Tilton Memorial Library, New Orleans
  Hutson Family Papers
  Joseph Jones Papers
Williams Research Center, Historic New Orleans Collection, New Orleans
  Walton-Glenny Family Papers

North Carolina

Duke University, David M. Rubenstein Rare Book and Manuscript Library, Durham
  Ku Klux Klan Papers
East Carolina University, J. Y. Joyner Library, Greenville
  Grimes-Bryan Papers
North Carolina State Archives, Division of Archives and History, Raleigh
  Futch Letters
University of North Carolina–Chapel Hill, North Carolina Collection, Chapel Hill
  "Town Ordinances: Adopted by the Mayor and Board of Commissioners for the Town of Goldsboro, to Go into Operation on the 15th Day of February, 1866"
University of North Carolina–Chapel Hill, Southern Historical Collection, Wilson Library, Chapel Hill
  James W. Albright Diary and Remembrances
  Rufus Barringer Papers
  Munson Monroe Buford Papers
  Tod Robinson Caldwell Papers
  Kena King Chapman Diary
  William J. Clarke Papers
  Elizabeth Collier Papers
  L. C. Glenn Papers
  Josiah Gorgas Papers

William Alexander Hoke Papers
Cadwallader Jones Papers
Joyner Family Papers
Edmund Kirby-Smith Papers
J. A. Lineback Papers
Lenoir Family Papers
Jacob Alson Long Papers
John Burgwyn MacRae Papers
George Anderson Mercer Diary
Thomas Ruffin Papers
David Schenck Papers
Shotwell Family Papers
Cornelia Phillips Spencer Papers
Ruffin Thomson Papers
William Henry Tripp and Araminta Guilford Tripp Papers
Richard Woolfolk Waldrop Papers
Joseph Frederick Waring Papers
Harrison Wells Papers
J. E. Whitehorne Diary
John Q. Winfield Letters
John Taylor Wood Papers
Trist Wood Papers
Jonathan Worth Papers

South Carolina

University of South Carolina, South Caroliniana Library, Columbia
Martin Witherspoon Gary Papers
Artemus Darby Goodwyn Papers
Iredell Jones Papers
Ellison S. Keitt Papers
B. F. Perry Papers
Robert Wallace Shand Papers
James F. Sloan Papers

Virginia

Fredericksburg-Spotsylvania National Military Park, Fredericksburg
"Reminiscences of Augustus A. Dean"
University of Virginia, Albert and Shirley Small Special Collections Library, Charlottesville
Amos Tappan Akerman Letter Books
John W. Daniel and the Daniel Family Papers
Papers of the Fishburne Family
Thomas Lafayette Rosser Papers

Virginia Historical Society, Richmond
   Cocke Family Papers
   John Warwick Daniel Memoir
William and Mary, Special Collections Research Center, Swem Library,
    Williamsburg
   Civil War Collection
   Nanny C. Waller Diary
   Wills Papers

Newspapers and Periodicals

Century Illustrated Monthly Magazine (New York)
Chronicle and Sentinel (Augusta, Ga.)
Greensboro (N.C.) Patriot
Intelligencer (Atlanta, Ga.)
Macon (Ga.) Daily Telegraph
Milwaukee Daily Sentinel
Philadelphia Inquirer
Southern Field and Fireside (Augusta, Ga.)
Tri-weekly Telegraph (Houston)
Yorkville (S.C.) Enquirer

Printed and Digitized Primary Sources

Alexander, Edward Porter. *Fighting for the Confederacy: The Personal Recollections of General Edward Porter Alexander*. Edited by Gary W. Gallagher. Chapel Hill: University of North Carolina Press, 1989.

Battle, George Boardman, and Walter Raleigh Battle. *As You May Never See Us Again: The Civil War Letters of George and Walter Battle, 4th North Carolina Infantry; Coming of Age on the Front Lines of the War between the States, 1861-1865*. Edited by Joel Gregory Craig and Sharlene Baker. Wake Forest, N.C.: Scuppernong, 2004.

Beverley, Robert. *The History and Present State of Virginia*. Edited by Louis B. Wright. Chapel Hill: University of North Carolina Press, 1947.

Browning, Meschach. *Forty-Four Years of the Life of a Hunter; Being Reminiscences of Meshach Browning, a Maryland Hunter*. Revised and illustrated by E. Stabler. Philadelphia: J. B. Lippincott, 1859.

Byrd, William. *Histories of the Dividing Line betwixt Virginia and North Carolina*. Edited by William K. Boyd. 1728. New York: Dover, 1967.

———. *The Secret Diary of William Byrd of Westover, 1709-1712*. Edited by Louis B. Wright and Marion Tinling. Richmond, Va.: Dietz, 1941.

Chamberlaine, William W. *Memoirs of the Civil War: Between the Northern and Southern Sections of the United States of America, 1861 to 1865*. Edited by Robert E. L. Krick. Tuscaloosa: University of Alabama Press, 2010.

Chamberlayne, John Hampden. *Ham Chamberlayne—Virginian: Letters and Papers of an Artillery Officer in the War for Southern Independence, 1861-1865*. Edited by C. G. Chamberlayne. Richmond, Va.: Dietz, 1932.

Clemson, Floride. *A Rebel Came Home: The Diary and Letters of Floride Clemson, 1863-1866*. Edited by Charles M. McGee Jr. and Ernest M. Lander Jr. 1961. Rev. ed., Columbia: University of South Carolina Press, 1989.

Clark, Walter, ed. *Histories of the Several Regiments and Battalions from North Carolina in the Great War 1861-'65; Written by Members of the Respective Commands*. Vol. 1. Raleigh, N.C.: E. M. Uzzell, printer, 1901.

———. *The Papers of Walter Clark*. Vol. 1, *1857-1901*, edited by Aubrey Lee Brooks and Hugh Talmage Lefler. Chapel Hill: University of North Carolina Press, 1948.

Clarke, Mary Bayard. *Live Your Own Life: The Family Papers of Mary Bayard Clarke, 1854-1886*. Edited by Terrell Armistead Crow and Mary Moulton Barden. Columbia: University of South Carolina Press, 2003.

Confederate States of America, Secretary of War. *Regulations for the Army of the Confederate States, and for the Quartermaster's and Pay Departments*. New Orleans: Bloomfield and Steel Publishers, 1861.

———. *Uniforms and Dress of the Army of the Confederate States*. 1861. Reprint, New Hope, Penn.: Ray Riling and Robert Halter, 1952.

Cook, Walter Henry. *Secret Political Societies in the South during the Period of Reconstruction: An Address before the Faculty and Friends of Western Reserve University, Cleveland, Ohio*. Cleveland: Evangelical Publishing House, [1914].

D. Appleton and Company. *Appleton's Complete Letter Writer: The Useful Letter Writer: Comprising a Succinct Treatise on the Epistolary Art; and Forms of Letters for All the Ordinary Occasions of Life*. New York: D. Appleton, 1854.

Davis, Jefferson. *The Papers of Jefferson Davis*. Vol. 2. Edited by Lynda L. Crist, Barbara J. Rozek, and Kenneth H. Williams. Baton Rouge: Louisiana State University Press, 2003.

Dooley, John. *John Dooley, Confederate Soldier: His War Journal*. Edited by Joseph T. Durkin. Notre Dame, Ind.: University of Notre Dame Press, 1963.

Duncan, Malcolm C. *Duncan's Masonic Ritual and Monitor, or, Guide to the Three Symbolic Degrees of the Ancient York Rite and to the Degrees of Mark Master, Past Master, Most Excellent Master, and the Royal Arch*. New York: Crown, n.d.

Eggleston, George Cary. "A Rebel's Recollections." *Atlantic Monthly* 34, no. 206 (June-December 1874).

———. *A Rebel's Recollections*. 1874. Reprint, Bloomington: Indiana University Press, 1959.

Elliott, William. *William Elliott's Carolina Sports by Land and Water: Including Incidents of Devil-Fishing, Wild-Cat, Deer and Bear-Hunting, Etc*. 1864. Reprint, Columbia: University of South Carolina Press, 1994.

Fitzpatrick, Marion Hill. *Letters to Amanda: The Civil War Letters of Marion Hill Fitzpatrick, Army of Northern Virginia*. Edited by Jeffrey C. Lowe and Sam Hodges. Macon, Ga.: Mercer University Press, 1998.

Fletcher, William A. *Rebel Private: Front and Rear, Memoirs of a Confederate Soldier*. New York: Dutton Books, 1995.

Fremantle, Arthur Lyon. *Three Months in the Southern States, April-June 1863*. 1864. Reprint, Bedford, Mass.: Applewood Books, 2008.

Gorgas, Josiah. *The Journals of Josiah Gorgas*. Edited by Sarah Woolfolk Wiggins. Tuscaloosa: University of Alabama Press, 1995.

Graham, James Augustus. *The James A. Graham Papers, 1861-1884*. Edited by Henry McGilbert Wagstaff. Chapel Hill: University of North Carolina Press, 1928.

Grant, Ulysses S. *Grant: Memoirs and Selected Letters*. New York: Literary Classics of the United States, 1990.

Green, John Patterson. *Recollections of the Inhabitants, Localities, Superstitions, and Ku Klux Outrages of the Carolinas*. Documenting the American South, University of North Carolina at Chapel Hill, 2004. http://docsouth.unc.edu/southlit/green/green.html.

Hammond, James Henry. *Secret and Sacred: The Diaries of James Henry Hammond, a Southern Slaveholder*. Edited by Carol K. Rothrock Bleser. New York: Oxford University Press, 1988.

Harris, Essic. "Testimony." July 1, 1871. In *Testimony Taken by the Joint Select Committee to Inquire into the Condition of Affairs in the Late Insurrectionary States, Part 2: North Carolina*, 1:86-102. Washington, D.C.: Government Printing Office, 1872.

Hoyle, Joseph J. *"Deliver Us from This Cruel War": The Civil War Letters of Lieutenant Joseph J. Hoyle, 55th North Carolina Infantry*. Edited by Jeffrey M. Girvan. Jefferson, N.C.: McFarland, 2010.

Jackman, John S. *Diary of a Confederate Soldier: John S. Jackman of the Confederate Brigade*. Edited by William C. Davis. Columbia: University of South Carolina Press, 1990.

Lawson, John. *A New Voyage to Carolina*. Edited by Hugh Talmage Lefler. 1714. Reprint, Chapel Hill: University of North Carolina Press, 1967.

McCarthy, Carlton. *Detailed Minutiae of Soldier Life in the Army of Northern Virginia, 1861-1865*. 1882. Reprint, Richmond, Va.: B. F. Johnson, 1899.

Merrill, Samuel H. *The Campaigns of the First Main and First District of Columbia Cavalry*. Portland, Me.: Bailey and Noyes, 1866.

"New Light on the Ku Klux Klan." *Century* 28, no. 3 (July 1884): 461-62.

North Carolina, Hanover County. 1860 U.S. Census, population schedule.

———. 1860 U.S. Slave Census.

North Carolina General Assembly. *Public Laws of the State of North-Carolina, Passed by the General Assembly at Its Adjourned Session of 1863*. Raleigh, N.C.: W. W. Holden, printer to the state, 1863.

Redwood, A. C. "The Fortunes and Misfortunes of Co. 'C.'" *Scribner's Monthly* 17, no. 4 (February 1879): 528-36.

Reid, Whitelaw, and A. J. L. Fremantle. *Two Witnesses at Gettysburg: The Personal Accounts of Whitelaw Reid and A. J. L. Fremantle*. Edited by Gary W. Gallagher. Saint James, N.Y.: Brandywine, 1994.

Robuck, J. E. *My Own Personal Experience and Observation as a Soldier in the Confederate Army during the Civil War, 1861-1865 Also during the Period of Reconstruction*. 1911. Reprint, Memphis: Burke's Book Store, n.d.

Schenck, Nicholas W. *The Diary of Nicholas W. Schenck*. Accessed April 5, 2009. http://library.uncw.edu/web/collections/schenck/schenck-full.html.

Semmes, Raphael. *Memoirs of Service Afloat, during the War between the States*. Baltimore: Kelly, Piet, 1869.

Shotwell, Randolph Abbott. *The Papers of Randolph Abbott Shotwell*. 2 vols. Edited by J. G. de Roulhac Hamilton and Rebecca Cameron. Raleigh: North Carolina Historical Commission, 1931.

———. *Three Years in Battle and Three in Federal Prisons*. Edited by J. G. de Roulhac Hamilton. Raleigh: North Carolina Historical Commission, 1929.

Simpson, Richard Wright, and Taliferro N. Simpson. *"Far, Far from Home": The Wartime Letters of Dick and Tally Simpson, Third South Carolina Volunteers*. Edited by Guy R. Everson and Edward H. Simpson Jr. New York: Oxford University Press, 1994.

Smedes, Aldert. *"She Hath Done What She Could," or the Duty and Responsibility of Woman: A Sermon, Preached in the Chapel of St. Mary's School, by the Rector, and Printed for the Pupils at Their Request*. Raleigh, N.C.: printed by Seaton Gales, 1851.

Spears, Arabella, and William Beverley Pettit. *Civil War Letters of Arabella Spears and William Beverley Pettit of Fluvanna County, Virginia, March 1862-March 1865*. 2 vols. Edited by Charles W. Turner. Roanoke: Virginia Lithography and Graphics, 1988.

Thompson, James Thomas. "A Georgia Boy with 'Stonewall' Jackson: The Letters of James Thomas Thompson." Edited by Aurelia Austin. *Virginia Magazine of History and Biography* 70, no. 3 (July 1962): 314-31.

Torrence, Leonidas. "The Road to Gettysburg: The Diary and Letters of Leonidas Torrence of the Gaston Guards." Edited by Haskell Monroe. *North Carolina Historical Review* 36 (October 1959): 476-517.

Tourgée, Albion Winegar. *The Invisible Empire*. Edited by Otto H. Olsen. Baton Rouge: Louisiana State University Press, 1989.

United States Congress, Joint Select Committee. *Report of the Joint Select Committee to Inquire into the Condition of Affairs in the Late Insurrectionary States*. Washington, D.C.: Government Printing Office, 1871. [Klan Trials]

United States War Department. *The War of the Rebellion: A Compilation of the Official Records of the Union and Confederate Armies*. 128 vols. Washington, D.C.: Government Printing Office, 1880-1901. [OR]

Vance, Zebulon Baird. *The Duties of Defeat: An Address Delivered before the Two Literary Societies of the University of North Carolina, June 7th, 1866*. Raleigh, N.C.: William B. Smith, 1866.

Williams, James M. *From That Terrible Field: Civil War Letters of James M. Williams, Twenty-First Alabama Infantry Volunteers*. Edited by John Kent Folmar. Tuscaloosa: University of Alabama Press, 1981.

Secondary Sources

Abbott, Edith. "The Civil War and the Crime Wave." In *The Civil War Veteran: A Historical Reader*, edited by Larry M. Logue and Michael Barton, 65-79. New York: New York University Press, 2007.

Adams, Michael C. C. *Living Hell: The Dark Side of the Civil War*. Baltimore: Johns Hopkins University Press, 2014.

Adler, Jeffrey S. "Murder, North and South: Violence in Early-Twentieth-Century Chicago and New Orleans." *Journal of Southern History* 74, no. 2 (May 2008): 297-324.

Albright, James W. *Greensboro, 1808-1904*. Greensboro, N.C.: Jos. J. Stone, 1904.

Anderson, Benedict. *Imagined Communities: Reflections on the Origins and Spread of Nationalism*. 1983. Reprint, London: Verso, 2002.

Andrew, Rod, Jr. *Wade Hampton: Confederate Warrior to Southern Redeemer*. Chapel Hill: University of North Carolina Press, 2008.

Ash, Stephen V. *A Year in the South: Four Lives in 1865*. New York: Palgrave Macmillan, 2002.

Ayers, Edward L. *Vengeance and Justice: Crime and Punishment in the 19th-Century American South*. New York: Oxford University Press, 1984.

Bailey, Fred Arthur. *Class and Tennessee's Confederate Generation*. Chapel Hill: University of North Carolina Press, 1987.

Baker, Bruce E. *What Reconstruction Meant: Historical Memory in the American South*. Charlottesville: University of Virginia Press, 2007.

Ballard, Michael B. *A Long Shadow: Jefferson Davis and the Final Days of the Confederacy*. Jackson: University Press of Mississippi, 1986.

Baptist, Edward E. *Creating an Old South: Middle Florida's Plantation Frontier before the Civil War*. Chapel Hill: University of North Carolina Press, 2002.

Baptist, Edward E., Stephen Berry, Orville Vernon Burton, Kenneth S. Greenberg, and Mark M. Smith. "Looking Back on Bertram Wyatt-Brown's *Southern Honor*: A Roundtable." *Historically Speaking: The Bulletin of the Historical Society* 9, no. 6 (July/August 2008): 13-18.

Barney, William L. *The Making of a Confederate: Walter Lenoir's Civil War*. New York: Oxford University Press, 2008.

Barrett, John G. *The Civil War in North Carolina*. Chapel Hill: University of North Carolina Press, 1963.

Barry, Craig L., and David C. Burt. *Suppliers to the Confederacy II: S. Isaac Campbell & Co., London, Peter Tait & Co., Limerick*. Fairfield, Ohio: Stainless Banner, 2014.

Barton, Michael. *Goodmen: The Character of Civil War Soldiers*. University Park: Pennsylvania State University Press, 1981.

Baumgarten, Linda R. "Leather Stockings and Hunting Shirts." In *American Material Culture: The Shape of the Field*, edited by Ann Smart Martin and J. Ritchie Garrison, 251-76. Knoxville: University of Tennessee Press, 1997.

Bederman, Gail. *Manliness and Civilization: A Cultural History of Gender and Race in the United States, 1880-1917*. Chicago: University of Chicago Press, 1995.

Beilein, Joseph M., Jr. *Bushwhackers: Guerrilla Warfare, Manhood, and the Household in Civil War Missouri*. Kent, Ohio: Kent State University Press, 2016.

———. "The Guerrilla Shirt: A Labor of Love and the Style of Rebellion in Civil War Missouri." *Civil War History* 58, no. 2 (June 2012): 151-79.

Benn, S. I., and G. F. Gaus, eds. *Public and Private in Social Life*. New York: St. Martin's, 1983.

Bercaw, Nancy D. *Gendered Freedoms: Race, Rights, and the Politics of Household in the Delta, 1861-1875*. Gainesville: University Press of Florida, 2003.

Berry, Stephen W., II. *All That Makes a Man: Love and Ambition in the Civil War South*. New York: Oxford University Press, 2005.

———, ed. *Princes of Cotton: Four Diaries of Young Men in the South, 1848-1860*. Athens: University of Georgia Press, 2007.

Blackford, W. W. *War Years with Jeb Stuart*. New York: Charles Scribner's Sons, 1945.

Blair, William. *Cities of the Dead: Contesting the Memory of the Civil War in the South, 1865-1914*. Chapel Hill: University of North Carolina Press, 2004.

Bledsoe, Andrew S. *Citizen-Officers: The Union and Confederate Volunteer Junior Officer Corps in the American Civil War*. Baton Rouge: Louisiana State University Press, 2015.

Blight, David. "No Desperate Hero: Manhood and Freedom in a Union Soldier's Experience." In *Divided Houses: Gender and the Civil War*, edited by Catherine Clinton and Nina Silber, 55-75. New York: Oxford University Press, 1992.

———. *Race and Reunion: The Civil War in American Memory*. Cambridge, Mass.: Harvard University Press, 2001.

Blum, Edward. *Reforging the White Republic: Race, Religion, and American Nationalism, 1865-1898*. Baton Rouge: Louisiana State University Press, 2007.

Bohannon, Keith S. "Dirty, Ragged, and Ill-Provided For: Confederate Logistical Problems in the 1862 Maryland Campaign and Their Solutions." In *The Antietam Campaign*, edited by Gary W. Gallagher, 101-42. Chapel Hill: University of North Carolina Press, 1999.

Bourdieu, Pierre. *The Field of Cultural Production: Essays on Art and Literature*. Translated by Randal Johnson. New York: Columbia University Press, 1993.

———. *Language and Symbolic Power*. Cambridge: Polity, 2011.

Bradley, Mark L. *The Army and Reconstruction, 1865-1877*. Washington, D.C.: Center of Military History, United States Army, 2015.

———. *Bluecoats and Tar Heels: Soldiers and Civilians in Reconstruction North Carolina*. Lexington: University Press of Kentucky, 2009.

———. *This Astounding Close: The Road to Bennett Place*. Chapel Hill: University of North Carolina Press, 2000.

Brasher, Glenn David. *The Peninsula Campaign and the Necessity of Emancipation: African Americans and the Fight for Freedom*. Chapel Hill: University of North Carolina Press, 2012.

Broomall, James J. "'We Are a Band of Brothers': Manhood and Community in Confederate Camps." *Civil War History* 60, no. 3 (September 2014): 270-309.

Brown, Richard Maxwell. *The South Carolina Regulators*. Cambridge, Mass.: Harvard University Press, 1963.

Brown, Russell K. "Post-Civil War Violence in Augusta, Georgia." *Georgia Historical Quarterly* 90, no. 2 (Summer 2009): 196-213.

Brown, Thomas J., ed. *Reconstructions: New Perspectives on the Postbellum United States*. New York: Oxford University Press, 2006.

Brubaker, Rogers, and Frederick Cooper. "Beyond 'Identity.'" *Theory and Society* 29, no. 1 (February 2000): 1-47.

Bruce, Dickson D., Jr. *Violence and Culture in the Antebellum South*. Austin: University of Texas Press, 1979.

Brundage, W. Fitzhugh. *The Southern Past: A Clash of Race and Memory*. Cambridge, Mass.: Belknap Press of Harvard University Press, 2005.

Burton, Orville Vernon. *In My Father's House Are Many Mansions: Family and Community in Edgefield, South Carolina*. Chapel Hill: University of North Carolina Press, 1985.

Butler, Judith. "Performative Acts and Gender Constitution: An Essay in Phenomenology and Feminist Theory." *Theatre Journal* 40, no. 4 (1988): 519-31.

Butler, Leslie. "Reconstructions in Intellectual and Cultural Life." In *Reconstructions: New Perspectives on the Postbellum United States*, edited by Thomas J. Brown, 172-205. New York: Oxford University Press, 2006.

Calkins, Chris M. *The Final Bivouac: The Surrender Parade at Appomattox and the Disbanding of the Armies, April 10-May 20, 1865*. Lynchburg, Va.: H. E. Howard, 1988.

Cantwell, Robert. *Ethnomimesis: Folklife and the Representation of Culture*. Chapel Hill: University of North Carolina Press, 1993.

Cardyn, Lisa. "Sexualized Racism/Gendered Violence: Outraging the Body Politic in the Reconstruction South." *Michigan Law Review* 100, no. 4 (February 2002): 675-867.

———. "Sexual Terror in the Reconstruction South." In *Battle Scars: Gender and Sexuality in the American Civil War*, edited by Catherine Clinton and Nina Silber, 140-67. New York: Oxford University Press, 2006.

Carmichael, Peter S. *The Last Generation: Young Virginians in Peace, War, and Reunion*. Chapel Hill: University of North Carolina Press, 2005.

———. "Soldier-Speak." In *Weirding the War: Stories from the Civil War's Ragged Edges*, edited by Stephen Berry, 272-81. Athens: University of Georgia Press, 2011.

Carnes, Mark C. *Secret Ritual and Manhood in Victorian America*. New Haven, Conn.: Yale University Press, 1989.

Carney, Charity R. *Ministers and Masters: Methodism, Manhood, and Honor in the Old South*. Baton Rouge: Louisiana State University Press, 2011.

Carter, Dan T. *When the War Was Over: The Failure of Self-Reconstruction in the South, 1865-1867*. Baton Rouge: Louisiana State University Press, 1985.

Cash, W. J. *The Mind of the South*. 1941. Reprint, New York: Vintage Books, 1991.

Cashin, Joan E. Introduction to "Special Issue on Gender in the Early Republic." *Journal of the Early Republic* 15, no. 3 (Autumn 1995): 353-58.

Catton, Bruce. *A Stillness at Appomattox*. Garden City, N.Y.: Doubleday, 1953.

Cauble, Frank P. *The Surrender Proceedings, April 9th, 1865 Appomattox Court House*. Lynchburg, Va.: H. E. Howard, 1987.

Cecelski, David S., and Timothy B. Tyson, eds. *Democracy Betrayed: The Wilmington Race Riot of 1898 and Its Legacy*. Chapel Hill: University of North Carolina Press, 1998.

Clarke, Frances M. *War Stories: Suffering and Sacrifice in the Civil War North*. Chicago: University of Chicago Press, 2011.

Clawson, Mary Ann. *Constructing Brotherhood: Class, Gender, and Fraternalism*. Princeton, N.J.: Princeton University Press, 1989.

Clinton, Catherine, and Nina Silber, eds. *Divided Houses: Gender and the Civil War*. New York: Oxford University Press, 1992.

Cobb, James C. *Away Down South: A History of Southern Identity*. New York: Oxford University Press, 2005.

Coddington, Edwin B. *The Gettysburg Campaign: A Study in Command*. 1963. Reprint, New York: Charles Scribner's Sons, 1968.

Collins, Darrell L. *46th Virginia Infantry*. Lynchburg, Va.: H. E. Howard, 1992.

Costa, Dora L., and Matthew E. Kahn. *Heroes and Cowards: The Social Face of War*. Princeton, N.J.: Princeton University Press, 2008.

Cott, Nancy F. *The Bonds of Womanhood: "Woman's Sphere" in New England, 1780-1835*. 2nd ed. 1977. Reprint, New Haven, Conn.: Yale University Press, 1997.

Crawford, Martin. *Ashe County's Civil War: Community and Society in the Appalachian South*. Charlottesville: University Press of Virginia, 2001.

Dailey, Jane, Glenda Elizabeth Gilmore, and Bryant Simon, eds. *Jumpin' Jim Crow: Southern Politics from Civil War to Civil Rights*. Princeton, N.J.: Princeton University Press, 2000.

Daniel, John W. *The Campaign and Battles of Gettysburg*. Lynchburg, Va.: Bell, Browne, printers, 1875.

Davis, Natalie Zemon. "The Reasons of Misrule: Youth Groups and Charivaris in Sixteenth-Century France." *Past and Present* 50 (February 1971): 41-75.

Davis, Susan L. *Authentic History, Ku Klux Klan, 1865-1877*. New York: American Library Service, 1924.

Davis, William C. *An Honorable Defeat: The Last Days of the Confederate Government*. New York: Harvest Books, 2001.

Davis, William C., and James I. Robertson Jr., eds. *Virginia at War, 1865*. Lexington: University Press of Kentucky, 2011.

Dean, Eric T., Jr. *Shook over Hell: Post-traumatic Stress, Vietnam, and the Civil War*. Cambridge, Mass.: Harvard University Press, 1997.

Deetz, James. *In Small Things Forgotten: An Archaeology of Early American Life*. New York: Doubleday, 1996.

DeGruccio, Michael. "Letting the War Slip through Our Hands." In *Weirding the War: Stories from the Civil War's Ragged Edges*, edited by Stephen Berry, 15-35. Athens: University of Georgia Press, 2011.

Ditz, Toby L. "The New Men's History and the Peculiar Absence of Gendered Power: Some Remedies from Early American Gender History." *Gender and History* 16, no. 1 (April 2004): 1-35.

Dollar, Kent T. "'Strangers in a Strange Land': Christian Soldiers in the Early Months of the Civil War." In *The View from the Ground: Experiences of Civil War Soldiers*, edited by Aaron Sheehan-Dean, 145-70. Lexington: University Press of Kentucky, 2007.

Donald, David Herbert. "A Generation of Defeat." In *The Civil War Veteran: A Historical Reader*, edited by Larry M. Logue and Michael Barton, 327-53. New York: New York University Press, 2007.

Downs, Gregory P. *After Appomattox: Military Occupation and the Ends of War*. Cambridge, Mass.: Harvard University Press, 2015.

Edwards, Laura. *Gendered Strife and Confusion: The Political Culture of Reconstruction*. Urbana: University of Illinois Press, 1997.

Ellis, Michael. *North Carolina English, 1861-1865: A Guide and Glossary*. Knoxville: University of Tennessee Press, 2013.

Ely, Melvin Patrick. *Israel on the Appomattox: A Southern Experiment in Black Freedom from the 1790s through the Civil War*. New York: Vintage Books, 2004.

Escott, Paul D. *After Secession: Jefferson Davis and the Failure of Confederate Nationalism*. Baton Rouge: Louisiana State University Press, 1978.

———. *Many Excellent People: Power and Privilege in North Carolina, 1850-1900*. Chapel Hill: University of North Carolina Press, 1985.

Eustace, Nicole. "AHR Conversation: The Historical Study of Emotions." *American Historical Review* 117, no. 5 (December 2012): 1487-531.

———. *Passion Is the Gale: Emotion, Power, and the Coming of the American Revolution*. Chapel Hill: University of North Carolina Press, 2008.

Evans, William McKee. *Ballots and Fence Rails: Reconstruction on the Lower Cape Fear*. 1966. Reprint, Athens: University of Georgia Press, 1995.

———. *To Die Game: The Story of the Lowry Band, Indian Guerrillas of Reconstruction*. 1971. Reprint, Syracuse, N.Y.: Syracuse University Press, 1995.

Faust, Drew Gilpin. "Altars of Sacrifice: Confederate Women and the Narratives of War." *Journal of American History* 76, no. 4 (March 1990): 1200-1228.

———. "Christian Soldiers: The Meaning and Revivalism in the Confederate Army." *Journal of Southern History* 53, no. 1 (February 1987): 63-90.

———. *James Henry Hammond and the Old South: A Design for Mastery*. Baton Rouge: Louisiana State University Press, 1982.

———. *Mothers of Invention: Women of the Slaveholding South in the American Civil War*. New York: Vintage Books, 1997.

———. *Southern Stories: Slaveholders in Peace and War*. Columbia: University of Missouri Press, 1992.

———. *This Republic of Suffering: Death and the American Civil War*. New York: A. Knopf, 2008.

Feis, William B. "Jefferson Davis and the 'Guerrilla Option.'" In *The Collapse of the Confederacy*, edited by Mark Grimsley and Brooks D. Simpson, 104-28. Lincoln: University of Nebraska Press, 2001.

Fleming, Walter Lynwood. *The Sequel of Appomattox: A Chronicle of the Reunion of the States*. New Haven, Conn.: Yale University Press, 1919.

Flynn, Thomas. *Sartre, Foucault, and Historic Reason: Toward an Existentialist Theory of History*. 2 vols. Chicago: University of Chicago Press, 1997.

Foner, Eric. *Reconstruction: America's Unfinished Revolution, 1863-1877*. New York: Harper and Row, 1988.

Foote, Lorien. *The Gentlemen and the Roughs: Manhood, Honor, and Violence in the Union Army*. New York: New York University Press, 2010.

Ford, Lacy K., Jr. *Origins of Southern Radicalism: The South Carolina Upcountry, 1800-1860*. New York: Oxford University Press, 1988.

Forth, Christopher E. *Masculinity in the Modern West: Gender, Civilization, and the Body*. New York: Palgrave Macmillan, 2008.

Fossett, Judith Jackson. "(K)night Riders in (K)night Gowns: The Ku Klux Klan, Race, and Constructions of Masculinity." In *Race Consciousness: African American Studies for the New Century*, edited by Judith Jackson Fossett and Jeffrey A. Tucker, 35-49. New York: New York University Press, 1997.

Foster, Gaines M. *Ghosts of the Confederacy: Defeat, the Lost Cause, and the Emergence of the New South, 1865 to 1913*. New York: Oxford University Press, 1987.

Foucault, Michel. *The Order of Things: An Archaeology of the Human Sciences.* 1970. Reprint, New York: Vintage Books, 1994.

Fox-Genovese, Elizabeth. "The Anxiety of History: The Southern Confrontation with Modernity." *Southern Cultures* 1 (1993): 65-82.

Franklin, John Hope. *The Militant South, 1800-1861.* 1956. Reprint, Urbana: University of Illinois Press, 2002.

———. *Reconstruction after the Civil War.* 2nd ed. Chicago: University of Chicago Press, 1994.

Frassanito, William A. *Gettysburg: A Journey in Time.* New York: Charles Scribner's Sons, 1975.

Fredrickson, George M. *Racism: A Short History.* Princeton, N.J.: Princeton University Press, 2002.

Friend, Craig Thompson, ed. *Southern Masculinity: Perspectives on Manhood in the South since Reconstruction.* Athens: University of Georgia Press, 2009.

Friend, Craig Thompson, and Lorri Glover, eds. *Southern Manhood: Perspectives on Masculinity in the Old South.* Athens: University of Georgia Press, 2004.

Friend, Craig Thompson, and Lorri Glover, "Rethinking Southern Masculinity: An Introduction." In *Southern Manhood: Perspectives on Masculinity in the Old South*, edited by Craig Thompson Friend and Lorri Glover, vii-xvii. Athens: University of Georgia Press, 2004.

Fry, Gladys-Marie. *Night Riders in Black Folk History.* Knoxville: University of Tennessee Press, 1975.

Fussell, Paul. *The Great War and Modern Memory.* 1974. Reprint, New York: Sterling, 2009.

———. *Uniforms: Why We Are What We Wear.* New York: Houghton Mifflin, 2005.

Gaines, W. Craig. *The Confederate Cherokees: John Drew's Regiment of Mounted Rifles.* Baton Rouge: Louisiana State University Press, 1989.

Gallagher, Gary W., ed. *The Antietam Campaign.* Chapel Hill: University of North Carolina Press, 1999.

———. *The Confederate War: How Popular Will, Nationalism, and Military Strategy Could Not Stave Off Defeat.* Cambridge, Mass.: Harvard University Press, 1997.

———. "Lee's Army Has Not Lost Any of Its Prestige: The Impact of Gettysburg on the Army of Northern Virginia." In *The Third Day at Gettysburg and Beyond*, edited by Gary W. Gallagher, 1-30. Chapel Hill: University of North Carolina Press, 1994.

Gallagher, Gary W., and Kathryn Shively Meier. "Coming to Terms with Civil War Military History." *Journal of the Civil War Era* 4, no. 4 (December 2014): 487-508.

Gallagher, Gary W., and Alan T. Nolan, eds. *The Myth of the Lost Cause and Civil War History.* Bloomington: Indiana University Press, 2000.

Gannon, Barbara A. *The Won Cause: Black and White Comradeship in the Grand Army of the Republic.* Chapel Hill: University of North Carolina Press, 2011.

Gaston, Paul M. *The New South Creed: A Study of Southern Mythmaking.* 1970. Reprint, Montgomery, Ala.: NewSouth Books, 2002.

Geertz, Clifford. "Deep Play: Notes on the Balinese Cockfight." In *The Interpretation of Cultures: Selected Essays*, 56-86. 1973. Reprint, New York: Basic Books, 2000.

———. *The Interpretation of Cultures: Selected Essays*. 1973. Reprint, New York: Basic Books, 2000.

Genovese, Eugene D. *Roll, Jordan, Roll: The World the Slaves Made*. 1972. Reprint, New York: Vintage Books, 1976.

Glatthaar, Joseph T. "The Common Soldier's Gettysburg Campaign." In *The Gettysburg Nobody Knows*, edited by Gabor S. Boritt, 3-30. New York: Oxford University Press, 1997.

———. *General Lee's Army: From Victory to Collapse*. New York: Free Press, 2009.

Glover, Lorri. "'Let Us Manufacture Men.'" In *Southern Masculinity: Perspectives on Manhood in the South Since Reconstruction*, edited by Craig Thompson Friend, 22-48. Athens: University of Georgia Press, 2009.

———. *Southern Sons: Becoming Men in the New Nation*. Baltimore: Johns Hopkins University Press, 2007.

Glymph, Thavolia. *Out of the House of Bondage: The Transformation of the Plantation Household*. New York: Cambridge University Press, 2008.

Grant, Susan-Mary. "The Lost Boys: Citizen-Soldiers, Disabled Veterans, and Confederate Nationalism in the Age of People's War." *Journal of the Civil War Era* 2, no. 2 (June 2012): 233-59.

Green, Jennifer. *Military Education and the Emerging Middle Class in the Old South*. New York: Cambridge University Press, 2008.

Greenberg, Amy S. *Manifest Manhood and the Antebellum American Empire*. New York: Cambridge University Press, 2005.

Greenberg, Kenneth S. *Honor and Slavery: Lies, Duels, Noses, Masks, Dressing as a Woman, Gifts, Strangers, Humanitarianism, Death, Slave Rebellions, the Proslavery Argument, Baseball, Hunting, and Gambling in the Old South*. Princeton, N.J.: Princeton University Press, 1996.

Greenough, Mark K. "Aftermath at Appomattox: Federal Military Occupation of Appomattox County May-November 1865." *Civil War History* 31, no. 1 (March 1985): 5-23.

Guelzo, Allen C. *Fateful Lightning: A New History of the Civil War and Reconstruction*. New York: Oxford University Press, 2012

———. *Gettysburg: The Last Invasion*. New York: Alfred A. Knopf, 2013.

Guterl, Matthew Pratt. *American Mediterranean: Southern Slaveholders in the Age of Emancipation*. Cambridge, Mass.: Harvard University Press, 2008.

Hackney, Sheldon. "Southern Violence." *American Historical Review* 74, no. 3 (February 1969): 906-25.

Hadden, Sally E. *Slave Patrols: Law and Violence in Virginia and the Carolinas*. Cambridge, Mass.: Harvard University Press, 2001.

Hahn, Steven. *A Nation under Our Feet: Black Political Struggles in the Rural South from Slavery to the Great Migration*. Cambridge, Mass.: Harvard University Press, 2003.

———. *The Roots of Southern Populism: Yeoman Farmers and the Transformation of the Georgia Upcountry, 1850-1890*. New York: Oxford University Press, 1983.

Harcourt, Edward John. "The Whipping of Richard Moore: Reading Emotion in Reconstruction America." *Journal of Social History* 36, no. 2 (Winter 2002): 261-82.

———. "Who Were the Pale Faces? New Perspectives on the Tennessee Ku Klux." *Civil War History* 51, no. 1 (March 2005): 23-66.
Harris, Trudier. *Exorcising Blackness: Historical and Literary Lynching and Burning Rituals*. Bloomington: Indiana University Press, 1984.
Hesseltine, William B., ed. *The Tragic Conflict: The Civil War and Reconstruction*. New York: George Braziller, 1962.
Hodes, Martha. *The Sea Captain's Wife: A True Story of Love, Race, and War in the Nineteenth Century*. New York: W. W. Norton, 2006.
Hoffman, Ronald, Mechal Sobel, and Fredrika J. Teute, eds. *Through a Glass Darkly: Reflections on Personal Identity in Early America*. Chapel Hill: University of North Carolina Press, 1997.
Hogue, James K. *Uncivil War: Five New Orleans Street Battle and the Rise and Fall of Radical Reconstruction*. Baton Rouge: Louisiana State University Press, 2006.
Holberton, William B. *Homeward Bound: The Demobilization of the Union and Confederate Armies, 1865-1866*. Mechanicsburg, Pa.: Stackpole Books, 2001.
Holt, Michael F. *The Fate of Their Country: Politicians, Slavery Extensions, and the Coming of the Civil War*. New York: Hill and Wang, 2004.
Horn, Stanley F. *Invisible Empire: The Story of the Ku Klux Klan, 1866-1871*. Boston: Houghton Mifflin, 1939.
Hundley, Daniel Robinson. *Social Relations in Our Southern States*. New York: Henry B. Price, 1860.
Isaac, Rhys. "Ethnographic Method in History: An Action Approach." In *Material Life in America, 1600-1860*, edited by Robert Blair St. George, 39-61. Boston: Northeastern University Press, 1988.
———. *Landon Carter's Uneasy Kingdom: Revolution and Rebellion*. New York: Oxford University Press, 2004.
———. "Stories and Constructions of Identity: Folk Tellings and Diary Inscriptions in Revolutionary Virginia." In *Through a Glass Darkly: Reflections on Personal Identity in Early America*, edited by Ronald Hoffman, Mechal Sobel, and Fredricka J. Teute, 206-37. Chapel Hill: University of North Carolina Press, 1997.
———. *The Transformation of Virginia, 1740-1790*. 1982. Reprint, Chapel Hill: published for the Omohundro Institute of Early American History and Culture by the University of North Carolina Press, 1999.
Jabour, Anya. *Marriage in the Early Republic: Elizabeth and William Wirt and the Companionate Ideal*. Baltimore: Johns Hopkins University Press, 1998.
Janiewski, Dolores. "The Reign of Passion: White Supremacy and the Clash between Passionate and Progressive Emotional Styles in the New South." In *An Emotional History of the United States*, edited by Peter N. Stearns and Jan Lewis, 126-54. New York: New York University Press, 1998.
Janney, Caroline E. *Burying the Dead but Not the Past: Ladies' Memorial Associations and the Lost Cause*. Chapel Hill: University of North Carolina, 2008.
———. *Remembering the Civil War: Reunion and the Limits of Reconciliation*. Chapel Hill: University of North Carolina Press, 2013.

Jensen, Leslie D. "A Survey of Confederate Central Government Quartermaster Issue Jackets." Pt. 1. *Military Collector and Historian*, Fall/Winter 1989. http://www.military-historians.org/company/journal/confederate/confederate-1.htm.

Jerome, Roy, ed. *Conceptions of Postwar German Masculinity*. Albany: State University of New York Press, 2001.

Johnson, Walter. *Soul by Soul: Life inside the Antebellum Slave Market*. Cambridge, Mass.: Harvard University Press, 1999.

Jordan, Brian Matthew. "'Living Monuments': Union Veteran Amputees and the Embodied Memory of the Civil War." *Civil War History* 57, no. 2 (June 2011): 121-52.

Jordan, Winthrop. *White over Black: American Attitudes toward the Negro, 1550-1812*. 2nd ed. Chapel Hill: University of North Carolina Press, 2012.

Kantrowitz, Stephen. *Ben Tillman and the Reconstruction of White Supremacy*. Chapel Hill: University of North Carolina Press, 2000.

———. "One Man's Mob Is Another Man's Militia: Violence, Manhood, and Authority in Reconstruction South Carolina." In *Jumpin' Jim Crow: Southern Politics from Civil War to Civil Rights*, edited by Jane Dailey, Glenda Elizabeth Gilmore, and Bryant Simon, 67-87. Princeton, N.J.: Princeton University Press, 2000.

———. "The Two Faces of Domination in North Carolina, 1800-1898." In *Democracy Betrayed: The Wilmington Race Riot of 1898 and Its Legacy*, edited by David S. Cecelski and Timothy B. Tyson, 95-111. Chapel Hill: University of North Carolina Press, 1998.

Kars, Marjoleine. *Breaking Loose Together: The Regulator Rebellion in Pre-revolutionary North Carolina*. Chapel Hill: University of North Carolina Press, 2002.

Katz, Jonathan Ned. *Love Stories: Sex between Men before Homosexuality*. Chicago: University of Chicago Press, 2003.

Keegan, John. *The Face of Battle*. New York: Viking, 1976.

Kerby, Robert L. *Kirby-Smith's Confederacy: The Trans-Mississippi South, 1863-1865*. New York: Columbia University Press, 1972.

Kierner, Cynthia A. *Beyond the Household: Women's Place in the Early South, 1700-1835*. Ithaca, N.Y.: Cornell University Press, 1998.

Kimmel, Michael. *Manhood in America: A Cultural History*. New York: Free Press, 1996.

Klein, Rachel N. *Unification of a Slave State: The Rise of the Planter Class in the South Carolina Backcountry, 1760-1808*. Chapel Hill: University of North Carolina Press, 1990.

Kleinman, Arthur, Veena Das, and Margaret Lock, eds. *Social Suffering*. Berkeley: University of California Press, 1997.

Kohn, Richard H. "The Social History of the American Soldier: A Review and Prospectus for Research." *American Historical Review* 86, no. 3 (June 1981): 553-67.

Krick, Robert K. Foreword to *Huts and History: The Historical Archaeology of Military Encampment during the American Civil War*, edited by Clarence R. Geier, David G. Orr, and Matthew B. Reeves, xv-xviii. Gainesville: University Press of Florida, 2006.

Laskin, Elisabeth Lauterbach. "'The Army Is Not Near So Much Demoralized as the Country Is': Soldiers in the Army of Northern Virginia and the Confederate Home Front." In *The View from the Ground: Experiences of Civil War Soldiers*, edited by Aaron Sheehan-Dean, 91-120. Lexington: University Press of Kentucky, 2007.

———. "Good Old Rebels: Soldiering in the Army of Northern Virginia, 1862-1865." PhD diss., Harvard University, 2003.

Laver, Harry S. "Refuge of Manhood: Masculinity and Militia Experience in Kentucky." In *Southern Manhood: Perspectives on Masculinity in the Old South*, edited by Craig Thompson Friend and Lorri Glover, 1-21. Athens: University of Georgia Press, 2004.

Lears, T. J. Jackson. "The Concept of Cultural Hegemony: Problems and Possibilities." *American Historical Review* 90, no. 3 (June 1985): 567-93.

———. *No Place of Grace: Antimodernism and the Transformation of American Culture, 1880-1920*. New York: Pantheon, 1981.

———. *Rebirth of a Nation: The Making of Modern America, 1877-1920*. New York: HarperCollins, 2009.

Lebsock, Suzanne. *The Free Women of Petersburg: Status and Culture in a Southern Town, 1784-1860*. New York: W. W. Norton, 1984.

Lefebvre, Henri. *The Production of Space*. Translated by Donald Nicholson-Smith. 1991. Reprint, Malden, Mass.: Blackwell, 2003.

Lemann, Nicholas. *Redemption: The Last Battle of the Civil War*. New York: Farrar, Straus and Giroux, 2006.

Lester, J. C., and D. L. Wilson. *Ku Klux Klan: Its Origin, Growth, and Disbandment*. 1884. Reprint with new introduction by Walter L. Fleming. New York: Neale, 1905.

Levin, Kevin. "'When Johnny Comes Marching Home': The Demobilization of Lee's Army." In *Virginia at War, 1865*, edited by William C. Davis and James I. Robertson Jr., 85-101. Lexington: University Press of Kentucky, 2011.

Lewis, Jan. *The Pursuit of Happiness: Family and Values in Jefferson's Virginia*. 1983. Reprint, New York: Cambridge University Press, 2003.

Lewis, Jan, and Peter N. Stearns, eds. *An Emotional History of the United States*. New York: New York University Press, 1998.

Linderman, Gerald F. *Embattled Courage: The Experience of Combat in the American Civil War*. New York: Free Press, 1987.

Litwack, Leon F. *Been in the Storm So Long: The Aftermath of Slavery*. New York: Vintage Books, 1980.

Logue, Larry M. *To Appomattox and Beyond: The Civil War Soldier in War and Peace*. Chicago: I. R. Dee, 1996.

Logue, Larry M., and Michael Barton, eds. *The Civil War Veteran: A Historical Reader*. New York: New York University Press, 2007.

Lumpkin, Katharine Du Pre. *The Making of a Southerner*. 1946. Reprint, Athens: University of Georgia Press, 1991.

Lynn, John A. *Battle: A History of Combat and Culture from Ancient Greece to Modern America*. 2003. Reprint, New York: Basic Books, 2009.

Maddex, Jack P. *The Reconstruction of Edward A. Pollard: A Rebel's Conversion to Postbellum Unionism*. Chapel Hill: University of North Carolina Press, 1974.

Manarin, Louis H., Weymouth T. Jordan, Matthew M. Brown, and Michael W. Coffey. *North Carolina Troops, 1861-1865: A Roster*. Raleigh, N.C.: State Department of Archives and History, 1966.
Manning, Chandra. *What This Cruel War Was Over: Soldiers, Slavery, and the Civil War*. New York: Alfred A. Knopf, 2007.
Marks, Stuart A. *Southern Hunting in Black and White: Nature, History, and Ritual in a Carolina Community*. Princeton, N.J.: Princeton University Press, 1991.
Marten, James. "Fatherhood in the Confederacy: Southern Soldiers and Their Children." *Journal of Southern History* 63, no. 2 (May 1997): 269-92.
———. *Sing Not War: The Lives of Union and Confederate Veterans in Gilded Age America*. Chapel Hill: University of North Carolina Press, 2011.
Martin, Brian Joseph. *Napoleonic Friendship: Military Fraternity, Intimacy, and Sexuality in Nineteenth-Century France*. Durham: University of New Hampshire Press, 2011.
Marvel, William. *Lee's Last Retreat: The Flight to Appomattox*. Chapel Hill: University of North Carolina Press, 2002.
McClurken, Jeffrey W. *Take Care of the Living: Reconstruction Confederate Veteran Families in Virginia*. Charlottesville: University of Virginia Press, 2009.
McConnell, Stuart. *Glorious Contentment: The Grand Army of the Republic, 1865-1900*. Chapel Hill: University of North Carolina Press, 1992.
McCurry, Stephanie. *Confederate Reckoning: Power and Politics in the Civil War South*. Cambridge, Mass.: Harvard University Press, 2010.
———. *Masters of Small Worlds: Yeoman Households, Gender Relations, and the Political Culture of the Antebellum South Carolina Low County*. New York: Oxford University Press, 1995.
McPherson, James M. *Battle Cry of Freedom*. New York: Ballantine, 1988.
———. *For Cause and Comrades: Why Men Fought in the Civil War*. New York: Oxford University Press, 1997.
McPherson, James M., and William J. Cooper Jr., eds. *Writing the Civil War: The Quest to Understand*. Columbia: University of South Carolina Press, 1998.
McWhiney, H. Grady, and Perry D. Jamieson. *Attack and Die: Civil War Military Tactics and the Southern Heritage*. Tuscaloosa: University of Alabama Press, 1984.
McWhiney, H. Grady, and Francis B. Simkins. "The Ghostly Legend of the Ku-Klux Klan." *Negro History Bulletin* 14 (February 1951): 109-12.
Meier, Kathryn Shively. *Nature's Civil War: Common Soldiers and the Environment in 1862 Virginia*. Chapel Hill: University of North Carolina Press, 2013.
Melville, Herman. *Moby Dick*. Edited by Tony Tanner. 1851. Reprint, New York: Oxford University Press, 1998.
Menand, Louis. *The Metaphysical Club: A Story of Ideas in America*. New York: Farrar, Straus and Giroux, 2001.
Mitchell, Reid. *Civil War Soldiers: Their Expectations and their Experiences*. New York: Simon and Schuster, 1998.
———. *The Vacant Chair: The Northern Soldier Leaves Home*. New York: Oxford University Press, 1993.
Myers, Robert Manson. *The Children of Pride: A True Story of Georgia and the Civil War*. New Haven, Conn.: Yale University Press, 1972.

Neely, Mark E., Jr., Harold Holzer, and Gabor S. Boritt. *The Confederate Image: Prints of the Lost Cause*. Chapel Hill: University of North Carolina Press, 1987.

Nelson, Dean E. "'Right Nice Little House[s]': Winter Camp Architecture of the American Civil War." In *Huts and History: The Historical Archaeology of Military Encampment during the American Civil War*, edited by Clarence E. Geier, David Gerald Orr, and Matthew Reeves, 79-93. Gainesville: University Press of Florida, 2006.

Nelson, Megan Kate. *Ruin Nation: Destruction and the American Civil War*. Athens: University of Georgia Press, 2012.

Nelson, Scott Reynolds. *Iron Confederacies: Southern Railways, Klan Violence, and Reconstruction*. Chapel Hill: University of North Carolina Press, 1999.

Noe, Kenneth W. *Reluctant Rebels: The Confederates Who Joined the Army after 1861*. Chapel Hill: University of North Carolina Press, 2010.

Nudelman, Franny. *John Brown's Body: Slavery, Violence, and the Culture of War*. Chapel Hill: University of North Carolina Press, 2004.

Nye, Robert A. "Western Masculinities in War and Peace." *American Historical Review* 112, no. 2 (April 2007): 417-38.

Nylander, Jane C. "Everyday Life on a Berkshire County Hill Farm: Documentation from the 1794-1835 Diary of Sarah Snell Bryant of Cummington, Massachusetts." In *The American Home: Material Culture, Domestic Space, and Family Life*, edited by Eleanor McD. Thompson, 95-118. Winterthur, Del.: Henry Francis du Pont Winterthur Museum, 1998.

Olsen, Otto H. "North Carolina: An Incongruous Presence." In *Reconstruction and Redemption in the South*, edited by Otto H. Olsen, 156-201. Baton Rouge: Louisiana State University Press, 1980.

Ownby, Ted. *Subduing Satan: Religion, Recreation, and Manhood in the Rural South, 1865-1920*. Chapel Hill: University of North Carolina Press, 1990.

Paludan, Phillip Shaw. *Victims: A True Story of the Civil War*. 1981. Reprint, Knoxville: University of Tennessee Press, 2004.

Parratt, Cartriona M. "Athletic 'Womanhood': Exploring Sources for Female Sport in Victorians and Edwardian England." *Journal of Sport History* 16, no. 2 (Summer 1989): 140-57.

Parsons, Elaine Frantz. *Ku-Klux: The Birth of the Klan during Reconstruction*. Chapel Hill: University of North Carolina Press, 2015.

———. "Midnight Rangers: Costume and Performance in the Reconstruction-Era Ku Klux Klan." *Journal of American History* 92, no. 3 (December 2005): 811-36.

Perry, Aldo S. *Civil War Courts-Martial of North Carolina Troops*. Jefferson, N.C.: McFarland, 2012.

Pfanz, Harry W. *Gettysburg—Culp's Hill and Cemetery Hill*. Chapel Hill: University of North Carolina Press, 1993.

Phillips, Jason. "Battling Stereotypes: A Taxonomy of Common Soldiers in the Civil War History." *History Compass* 6, no. 6 (September 2008): 1407-25.

———. *Diehard Rebels: The Confederate Culture of Invincibility*. Athens: University of Georgia Press, 2007.

Piersen, William D. *Black Legacy: America's Hidden Heritage*. Amherst: University of Massachusetts Press, 1993.

Poole, W. Scott. *Never Surrender: Confederate Memory and Conservatism in the South Carolina Upcountry*. Athens: University of Georgia Press, 2004.

———. "Religion, Gender, and the Lost Cause in South Carolina's 1876 Governor's Race." *Journal of Southern History* 68, no. 3 (August 2002): 573-98.

Powell, William S. "Clarke, William John." *NCpedia*, January 1, 1979. http://www.ncpedia.org/biography/clarke-william-john.

Power, J. Tracy. *Lee's Miserables: Life in the Army of Northern Virginia from the Wilderness to Appomattox*. Chapel Hill: University of North Carolina Press, 1998.

Prince, Stephen K. *Stories of the South: Race and the Reconstruction of Southern Identity, 1865-1915*. Chapel Hill: University of North Carolina Press, 2014.

Pritchard, Russ A., Jr., and C. A. Huey. *The English Connection: Arms, Material and Support Furnished to the Confederate States of America by Great Britain*. Gettysburg, Penn.: Thomas, 2014.

Proctor, Nicolas W. *Bathed in Blood: Hunting and Mastery in the Old South*. Charlottesville: University Press of Virginia, 2002.

Prost, Antoine. *In the Wake of War: "Les Anciens Combattants" and French Society, 1914-1939*. Translated by Helen McPhail. Providence, R.I.: Berg, 1992.

Prown, Jules David. *Art as Evidence: Writings on Art and Material Culture*. New Haven, Conn.: Yale University Press, 2001.

Pryor, Elizabeth Brown. *Reading the Man: A Portrait of Robert E. Lee through His Private Letters*. New York: Viking, 2007.

Rable, George C. *But There Was No Peace: The Role of Violence in the Politics of Reconstruction*. Athens: University of Georgia Press, 1984.

———. *Civil Wars: Women and the Crisis of Southern Nationalism*. Urbana: University of Illinois Press, 1989.

Reardon, Carol. *Pickett's Charge in History and Memory*. Chapel Hill: University of North Carolina Press, 1997.

Reddy, William M. "Against Constructionism: The Historical Ethnography of Emotions." *Current Anthropology* 38, no. 3 (June 1997): 327-51.

———. *The Navigation of Feeling: A Framework for the History of Emotions*. New York: Cambridge University Press, 2001.

Reeves, Matthew B., and Clarence R. Geier. "Under the Forest Floor: Excavations at a Confederate Winter Encampment, Orange, Virginia." In *Huts and History: The Historical Archaeology of Military Encampment during the American Civil War*, edited by Clarence E. Geier, David Gerald Orr, and Matthew Reeves, 194-215. Gainesville: University Press of Florida, 2006.

Reid, Whitelaw. *After the War: A Tour of the Southern States, 1865-1866*. Edited by C. Vann Woodward. 1866. Reprint, New York: Harper and Row, 1965.

———. "Excluding the Rebel." In *The Tragic Conflict: The Civil War and Reconstruction*, edited by William B. Hesseltine, 464-471. New York: George Braziller, 1962.

Richardson, Heather Cox. "North and West of Reconstruction: Studies in Political Economy." In *Reconstructions: New Perspectives on the Postbelllum United States*, edited by Thomas J. Brown, 66-90. New York: Oxford University Press, 2006.

Rister, Carl Coke. "Carlota, a Confederate Colony in Mexico." *Journal of Southern History* 11, no. 1 (February 1945): 33-50.

Roach, Mary Ellen, and Joanne B. Eicher. *The Visible Self*. Englewood Cliffs, N.J.: Prentice Hall, 1973.

Roark, James L. *Masters without Slaves: Southern Planters in the Civil War and Reconstruction*. New York: Norton, 1977.

Rolle, Andrew F. *The Lost Cause: The Confederate Exodus to Mexico*. 1965. Reprint, Norman: University of Oklahoma Press, 1992.

Rose, Anne C. *Victorian America and the Civil War*. New York: Cambridge University Press, 1992.

Rosen, Hannah. *Terror in the Heart of Freedom: Citizenship, Sexual Violence, and the Meaning of Race in the Postemancipation South*. Chapel Hill: University of North Carolina Press, 2009.

Rosenburg, R. B. *Living Monuments: Confederate Soldiers' Homes in the New South*. Chapel Hill: University of North Carolina Press, 1993.

Rosenwein, Barbara H. "Worrying about Emotions in History." *American Historical Review* 107, no. 3 (June 2002): 812-45.

Rotundo, E. Anthony. "Learning about Manhood: Gender Ideals and the Middle-Class Family in Nineteenth-Century America." In *Manliness and Morality: Middle-Class Masculinity in Britain and America, 1800-1940*, edited by J. A. Mangan and James Walvin, 35-51. New York: St. Martin's, 1987.

Rubin, Anne Sarah. *A Shattered Nation: The Rise and Fall of the Confederacy, 1861-1868*. Chapel Hill: University of North Carolina Press, 2007.

Scarry, Elaine. *The Body in Pain: The Making and Unmaking of the World*. New York: Oxford University Press, 1985.

Schantz, Mark S. *Awaiting the Heavenly Country: The Civil War and America's Culture of Death*. Ithaca, N.Y.: Cornell University Press, 2008.

Schivelbusch, Wolfgang. *The Culture of Defeat: On National Trauma, Mourning, and Recovery*. Translated by Jefferson Chase. New York: Metropolitan, 2003.

Schlereth, Thomas J., ed. *Material Culture Studies in America*. Lanham, Md.: AltaMira, 1999.

Scott, James C. *Domination and the Arts of Resistance: Hidden Transcripts*. New Haven, Conn.: Yale University Press, 1990.

Sheehan-Dean, Aaron, ed. *The View from the Ground: Experiences of Civil War Soldiers*. Lexington: University Press of Kentucky, 2007.

———. *Why Confederates Fought: Family and Nation in Civil War Virginia*. Chapel Hill: University of North Carolina Press, 2007.

Shelley, Percy Bysshe. *The Major Works*. Edited by Zachary Leader and Michael O'Neill. New York: Oxford University Press, 2003.

Shils, Edward A., and Morris Janowitz. "Cohesion and Disintegration in the Wehrmacht in World War II." *Public Opinion Quarterly* 12, no. 2 (1948): 280-315.

Silber, Nina. *Gender and the Sectional Conflict*. Chapel Hill: University of North Carolina Press, 2008.

Silkenant, David. *Moments of Despair: Suicide, Divorce, and Debt in Civil War Era North Carolina*. Chapel Hill: University of North Carolina Press, 2011.

Singal, Daniel Joseph. *The War Within: From Victorian to Modernist Thought in the South, 1919-1945*. Chapel Hill: University of North Carolina Press, 1982.

Snay, Mitchell. *Fenians, Freedman, and Southern Whites: Race and Nationality in the Era of Reconstruction*. Baton Rouge: Louisiana State University Press, 2007.

Sommerville, Diane Miller. "'A Burden Too Heavy to Bear': War Trauma, Suicide, and Confederate Soldiers." *Civil War History* 59, no. 4 (December 2013): 453-91.

———. "'Will They Ever Be Able to Forget?': Confederate Soldiers and Mental Illness in the Defeated South." In *Weirding the War: Stories from the Civil War's Ragged Edges*, edited by Stephen Berry, 321-39. Athens: University of Georgia Press, 2011.

Stearns, Carol Zisowitz, and Peter N. Stearns. *Anger: The Struggle for Emotional Control in America's History*. Chicago: University of Chicago Press, 1989.

Sternhell, Yael A. "Revisionism Reinvented? The Antiwar Turn in Civil War Scholarship." *Journal of the Civil War Era* 3, no. 2 (June 2013): 239-56.

———. *Routes of War: The World of Movement in the Confederate South*. Cambridge, Mass.: Harvard University Press, 2012.

Stevens, John W. *Reminiscences of the Civil War: A Soldier in Hood's Texas Brigade, Army of Northern Virginia*. Hillsboro, Tex.: Hillsboro Mirror Print, 1902.

Stewart, George R. *Pickett's Charge: A Microhistory of the Final Attack at Gettysburg, July 3, 1863*. 1959. Reprint, Boston: Houghton Mifflin, 1987.

Stiles, T. J. *Jesse James: Last Rebel of the Civil War*. New York: Vintage Books, 2003.

Stowe, Steven M. *Intimacy and Power in the Old South: Ritual in the Lives of the Planters* Baltimore: John Hopkins University Press, 1987.

Struna, Nancy L. "Beyond Mapping Experience: The Need for Understanding in the History of American Women's Sports." *Journal of Sport History* 11, no. 1 (Spring 1984): 120-33.

Styple, William B., ed. *Writing and Fighting in the Army of Northern Virginia*. Kearney, N.J.: Belle Grove, 2003.

Sutherland, Donald E. "Exiles, Emigrants, and Sojourners: The Post-Civil War Confederate Exodus in Perspective." *Civil War History* 31, no. 3 (September 1985): 237-56.

Syrett, Nicholas L. *The Company He Keeps: A History of White College Fraternities*. Chapel Hill: University of North Carolina Press, 2009.

Taylor, Karen. "Reconstructing Men in Savannah, Georgia, 1865-1876." In *Southern Masculinity: Perspectives on Manhood in the South since Reconstruction*, edited by Craig Thompson Friend, 1-24. Athens: University of Georgia Press, 2009.

Thompson, E. P. *Customs in Common: Studies in Traditional Popular Culture*. New York: New Press, 1991.

Trelease, Allen W. *White Terror: The Ku Klux Klan Conspiracy and Southern Reconstruction*. New York: Harper and Row, 1971.

Tripp, Steven E. *Yankee Town, Southern City: Race and Class Relations in Civil War Lynchburg*. New York: New York University Press, 1999.

Trudeau, Noah Andre. *Out of the Storm: The End of the Civil War, April-June 1865*. Boston: Little, Brown, 1994.

Turner, Victor. *Process, Performance, and Pilgrimage*. New Delhi: Concept, 1979.

Ulrich, Laurel Thatcher. *A Midwife's Tale: Martha Ballard from Her Diary, 1785-1812*. New York: Vintage, 1990.

Ural, Susannah J. *Hood's Texas Brigade: The Soldiers and Families of the Confederacy's Most Celebrated Unit*. Baton Rouge: Louisiana State University Press, 2017.

Varon, Elizabeth R. *Disunion! The Coming of the American Civil War, 1780-1859*. Chapel Hill: University of North Carolina Press, 2008.

Waugh, Joan. *U. S. Grant: American Hero, American Myth*. Chapel Hill: University of North Carolina Press, 2009.

Weaver, Blanche Henry Clark. "Confederate Emigration to Brazil." *Journal of Southern History* 27, no. 1 (February 1961): 33-53.

Wert, Jeffry D. "Shotwell, Randolph Abbott." *NCpedia*, January 1, 1994. http://www.ncpedia.org/biography/shotwell-randolph.

Whites, LeeAnn. *The Civil War as a Crisis in Gender: Augusta, Georgia, 1860-1890*. Athens: University of Georgia Press, 1995.

———. *Gender Matters: Civil War, Reconstruction, and the Making of the New South*. New York: Palgrave Macmillan, 2005.

Wickberg, Daniel. "What Is the History of Sensibilities? On Cultural Histories, Old and New." *American Historical Review* 112, no. 3 (June 2007): 661-84.

Wiley, Bell Irvin. *The Life of Johnny Reb*. 1943. Reprint, Baton Rouge: Louisiana State University Press, 1992.

Williams, Raymond. *Marxism and Literature*. New York: Oxford University Press, 1977.

Williams, Timothy J. "Intellectual Manhood: Becoming Men of the Republic at a Southern University, 1795-1861." PhD diss., University of North Carolina at Chapel Hill, 2010.

———. *Intellectual Manhood: University, Self, and Society in the Antebellum South*. Chapel Hill: University of North Carolina Press, 2014.

Wilson, Charles Reagan. *Baptized in Blood: The Religion of the Lost Cause, 1865-1920*. Athens: University of Georgia Press, 1980.

Wilson, Harold S. *Confederate Industry: Manufacturers and Quartermasters in the Civil War*. Jackson: University Press of Mississippi, 2002.

Winik, Jay. *April 1865: The Month That Saved America*. New York: Harper Perennial, 2001.

Winter, Hans-Gerd. "Brutal Heroes, Human Marionettes, and Men with Bitter Knowledge: On the New Formulation of Masculinity in the Literature of the 'Young Generation' after 1945." In *Conceptions of Postwar German Masculinity*, edited by Roy Jerome, 191-218. Albany: State University of New York Press, 2001.

Woods, Michael E. *Emotional and Sectional Conflict in the Antebellum United States*. New York: Cambridge University Press, 2014.

Woodward, C. Vann. *The Burden of Southern History*. Rev. ed. Baton Rouge: Louisiana State University Press, 1991.

———. *Origins of the New South: 1877-1913*. Baton Rouge: Louisiana State University Press, 1951.

———. *Tom Watson: Agrarian Rebel*. 1938. Reprint, New York: Oxford University Press, 1963.

Woodworth, Steven E. *While God Is Marching On: The Religious World of Civil War Soldiers*. Lawrence: University Press of Kansas, 2001.

Wyatt-Brown, Bertram. *Hearts of Darkness: Wellspring of a Southern Literary Tradition.* Baton Rouge: Louisiana State University Press, 2003.

———. *The Shaping of Southern Culture: Honor, Grace, and War, 1760s-1890s.* Chapel Hill: University of North Carolina Press, 2001.

———. *Southern Honor: Ethics and Behavior in the Old South.* New York: Oxford University Press, 1982.

Zuczek, Richard. *State of Rebellion: Reconstruction in South Carolina.* Columbia: University of South Carolina Press, 1996.

Index

African Americans: depictions in art, 56; enslavement, 48; and hunting, 27–28; and Ku Klux Klan, 142, 143–45, 147, 148–50, 151; and postbellum violence against, 96, 97, 102–4, 106, 107, 110, 148–49; white people's thoughts on, 43, 47, 113
Akerman, Amos T., 147
Albright, James, 46, 52
Alexander, Edward Porter: and gun ownership, 29; military service, 53, 68; postbellum life, 86, 96
Appomattox Court House, Va.: in memory, 88, 90; surrender at, 10, 86, 89, 96, 104
Army of Northern Virginia, 68, 69, 85; demobilization of, 87, 88–94, 96, 99, 100; and masculinity, 10, 60; and soldiers' loyalty to, 1, 38–39, 44, 55, 62, 67–68; and uniforms, 39–41, 42, 43
Army of Tennessee, 86, 99–100, 101
Avery, C. W., 83

Barringer, Rufus, 108
Battle, George, 35, 65
Biggerstaff, Aaron, 150
black codes, 105, 106
Blackford, W. W., 40
Boyd, James E., 135–36, 149
Brownlow, William G., 141
Buford, Munson 128, 129

Campbell, J. A., 103
Chamberlayne, John "Ham," 96, 97, 109
Chapman, Conrad Wise, 55, 56, 57, 57–58

Chapman, John Gadsby, 55–56
Chapman, Kena King, 90–91
Clarke, Mary Bayard, 4, 123–25
Clarke, William J., 3–5, 15–16, 123–24
clothes, 33, 41, 59–60, 72, 73, 98; civilian clothes, meanings of, 40–41, 106–7; government issued, 39–40, 42, 43; home production, 33–39; and Ku Klux Klan violence, 149, 150; repair of, 49; theft of, 99, 100
Cocke, John, 38, 39, 83
Collier, Elizabeth, 101
commutation system, 35–36, 38, 39
Confederacy: collapse of, 86, 87–88, 94–95, 96, 98; loyalty to, 70, 85, 89, 108, 111, 113, 119; material culture of, 42; revival by Ku Klux Klan, 140, 144, 145–46; trade with Great Britain, 42

Daniel, John Warwick, 30–31, 74, 79, 83
Danville, Va., 98, 100
Davis, Jefferson, 37, 181n72
death: and African Americans, 47–48; and family members, 17, 22, 25, 156; and Ku Klux Klan rituals, 134–37; and memory, 128, 153; and military service, 51, 53, 61, 65, 68, 74, 75, 76, 77, 79–80, 81–82, 83, 84, 154, 175–76n94; one's own, 17, 24, 38, 63; and postbellum violence, 100, 103; and religious faith, 64. *See also* Good Death
demobilization, 86–91, 94–95; alternatives to, 87, 91, 93–94, 96, 97; and emotions, 88–89, 99, 102; and lawlessness, 94, 97–102, 103, 104; and social order, 102–4, 105, 106. *See also* Appomattox Court House, Va.

223

diaries, 12, 13, 14–18, 23, 26, 129; and death, 25, 156; during war, 47, 52, 63, 66, 69–70, 90, 108; and emotions, 24, 31, 154; functions of, 10, 19, 20, 21, 22, 25; and postbellum, 114, 121, 122, 128; secret diaries, 18; and women, 16–17, 24, 25–26

Dooley, John: camp life, 45, 50; Gettysburg campaign, 61, 71, 77, 78; postbellum life, 96–98, 123; slaves, 48

Doyle, John, 51

Eaves, J. B., 147

Eggleston, George Cary, 104

Elliott, William, 28–30

emotional communities, 2, 8, 43–44, 52, 62, 127, 132, 151

emotions, 2–3, 5, 6, 154–55; in battle, 61–62, 66, 67, 74–77; and defeat, 88, 89, 113, 118; emotional detachment, 47–48; and hunting, 28, 29; and Ku Klux Klan, 134, 137, 146–47, 148, 151–52; and manliness, 11, 12–13, 18, 22, 148; postbellum expressions of, 95, 97, 99, 104, 109, 121, 122, 124, 131; and soldiers, 32, 33, 36, 43, 44, 49, 51, 60, 69–70, 90; written expressions of, 9, 14, 15, 17, 24–25, 78–79, 80–82, 83–84, 108, 125, 156. *See also* emotional communities

encampments, 1, 9, 32–34, 43–52, 53, 54, 56, 56, 57, 57, 59, 59, 69; bed sharing, 50; and boredom, 52, 53; and disease, 64, 65; and domesticity, 43, 44, 48, 49, 50, 55, 57–58, 62; and isolation, 51; and slave labor, 47–48; winter quarters, 46–47, 50, 65. *See also* Army of Northern Virginia; messmates

Finch, Ned, 150

Fishburne, Clement Daniel, 14–15, 17, 20

Fitzpatrick, Hill, 37–38, 39–40, 49, 72, 73

food: and hunting, 28; lack of, 70, 78, 94; and military life, 32, 48, 53, 58, 59, 60, 80; necessity of, 97, 101; preparation of, 47, 48, 56; theft of, 100

Forrest, Nathan Bedford, 140–41

Fraley, W. C., 127–28

Fremantle, Arthur Lyon, 42

Futch, Charles ("Charley"), 74, 76–77, 79–82

Futch, John: on brother's death, 79–83; Gettysburg Campaign, 70, 74, 76–77

Gaines, John Charles, 49

Gary, Martin Witherspoon, 18

Gettysburg Campaign, 41, 61–62, 68, 69, 70, 72, 73; aftermath, 83–85; battle accounts, 74–78; and death, 79–82; and the march north, 69–70, 71. *See also* Lee, Robert E.; Shotwell, Randolph A.; Simpson, Tally (Taliaferro N.)

Goldsboro, N.C., 105

Good Death, 64, 76, 82

Gorgas, Josiah: as Chief of Ordnance, 42; diary of, 17, 19, 20, 22, 23–25, 122; and postbellum life, 101, 114, 115, 122

Graham, James A., 40, 49, 50, 72

Green, John Patterson, 145, 149

Greensboro (N.C.) Patriot, 100

Greensboro, N.C., 88, 100

Grimes, Bryan, 107, 128

Grimes, Charlotte E., 106–7

guns, 183n109; and African Americans, 27; and hunting, 26; and Ku Klux Klan, 131, 144, 148, 149, 150, 151, 192n35; and white supremacy, 29, 30

Harris, Essic, 147, 149, 150

Harriss, T. W., 60, 65

Hix, William D., 104–5

Hoke, William Alexander, 89

home, 1, 10, 28, 103; camp as, 43–48, 50, 55, 58; home production, 33, 36, 49; journeys home, 88–91; men leaving, 23, 24, 38, 71; postbellum, 3–4, 5, 44,

104, 108; and self-identity, 39, 49; writing to, 2, 39, 53, 62, 65, 67, 70, 73, 111, 112, 122
Hoyle, Joseph J., 70, 71, 73, 78, 83, 85
hunting, 12, 13, 26–30, 31

Intelligencer (Atlanta, Ga.), 89

Jackman, John S., 52, 57
Johnson, Reverdy, 147
Johnston, Joseph E., 99–100; surrender of, 86, 87, 108
Jones, Cadwallader ("Wad"), 126
Jordan, Daniel, 149
Joyner, Joseph D., 45–46, 55, 72–73, 79
Joyner, Julia, 38, 40–41
Joyner, William H., 36, 40

Keitt, Ellison Summerfield, 143
Kirby-Smith, Cassie, 92
Kirby-Smith, Edmund: and demobilization, 87; diary of, 17, 18, 19–20, 21–22, 24; postbellum life, 91–93
Ku Klux Klan, 4, 7, 11, 105; advertisements, 142–43; and African Americans, 142, 143–45, 147, 148–50, 151; costumes, 136, 141–42; as emotional communities, 132, 151–52; existence questioned, 143; as ghosts of Confederate dead, 131, 137, 140, 143–44, 145; organization of, 131, 134; and ritual, 132, 133, 135, 137, 138–39, 143; scholarly interpretations of, 133; use of violence, 147–50. *See also* African Americans; clothes; death; emotions; masculinity; Shotwell, Randolph A.; women

Lee, Robert E.: antebellum life, 20; Gettysburg campaign, 68; surrender of, 86, 87, 88, 96, 179n28
Leigh, Stuart (pseud.). *See* Clarke, Mary Bayard
Lenoir, Julia, 37
Lester, John C., 137, 143, 146

Lindsey, J. B., 128
Lineback, Julius A., 89, 129
Lost Cause, 2, 40, 43, 56, 94, 103, 120, 130, 133, 145
Lumpkin, Katharine Du Pre, 144
Lynchburg, Va., 74, 99
Lynchburg College, 30–31, 75

MacRae, John Burgwyn, 18
manhood. *See* masculinity
Martinsburg, W.V., 80
masculinity, 1, 12–13, 14, 19, 94, 107, 154; emasculation, 112, 138; and hunting, 26, 28–29, 31; and Ku Klux Klan, 127, 131, 139, 141, 146, 147, 148, 151–52; masculine achiever, 19; masculine domesticity, 23; militant masculinity, 96, 131; and military life, 33, 34, 62, 67, 81; and postbellum life, 111, 129, 132, 145, 147; and self-improvement, 22
McAlister, A. C., 100
McCarthy, Carlton, 43, 107, 129
McIntosh, David G., 96, 97
McLean, William, 72
Mendenhall, E. B., 44–45, 64
Mercer, George Anderson: diary of, 12–13, 14, 16, 17, 18, 21, 24, 25, 156; and family, 13, 118; and the natural world, 26; and postbellum life, 114, 115, 121–22, 139, 153–54, 155
Merrill, Samuel H., 97
messmates, 46, 48–53, 58, 60, 78, 80. *See also* encampments
Mexico, exile in, 91–93
Milwaukee Daily Sentinel, 96
Mitchell, James B., 118–19

Narrative of Andersonville (Spencer), 147
Ned (enslaved man), 48
New York Evening Post, 143

O'Daniel, W. J., 38, 83–84
Omenhauser, John J., 58, 59

Peninsula Campaign, 36, 45, 66
Perry, Benjamin Franklin, 105
Pettit, William Beverley, 69, 70, 79
Preston (enslaved man), 48

"Rebel's Recollection, A" (Eggleston), 104
Regulations for the Army of the Confederate States, 33, 34, 48, 57
religion, 16, 17, 22, 24, 25, 45, 52, 55, 64–65
Republicans, 4, 110, 131, 132, 144, 147, 148; attacks on, 106, 139, 141, 155
reunions, postbellum, 126–28, 129, 130, 183n111
Reynolds, Thomas Caute, 93
Richardson, Eunice, 113
Richardson, Henry Brown, 110–11, 112–13, 114, 117–18, 119
Rodes, Robert E., 71
Roxboro, N.C., 100
Ruffin, Thomas, Jr., 33–34, 36
Ruffin, Thomas, Sr., 36

Schenck, David, 103, 141–42, 148
self-improvement, efforts at, 16, 19–22
Semmes, Raphael, 98
sewing, 36, 37–38, 49, 117
Shand, Robert Wallace, 63–64
Shepherdstown, W.V., 1
shoes, 33, 35, 38, 40, 43, 99
Shotwell, Randolph A., 35, 45, 51, 69, 107; Gettysburg campaign, 71–73; and Ku Klux Klan, 131, 133–34, 135, 136, 139, 143, 192n35
Simpson, Dick (Richard Wright), 50, 72
Simpson, Tally (Taliaferro N.), 38, 48–49, 52, 54, 68; Gettysburg campaign, 70, 71, 72–73
sleep and sleeplessness, 46, 48, 50, 52, 126
Smart, Henry W., 65
Smedes, Aldert, 23
Smith, Job B., 126
soldiers' bodies, transformation of, 70–71, 73
soldier's heart, 82

Spencer, Cornelia Phillips, 25, 101
Steel, Gadsden, 149–50
Stevens, John H., 46

Tenella (pseud.). *See* Clarke, Mary Bayard
Terry, Alfred H., 141
Thompson, James Thomas, 55, 60, 64–65
Thomson, Ruffin, 32, 39, 45, 46, 47, 48, 49, 50, 52, 59–60, 68, 73, 118
Thomson, William H., 68
Timons, Andy, 143
Torrence, Leonidas, 39, 46, 50, 51, 66–67, 69–70, 83–84
Tripp, William Henry, 126–27
Trollinger, Nathan, 150
Turner, John W., 99

Vance, Zebulon Baird, 102, 103, 120–21, 125
Vann, T. E., 127

Waddy, George M., 39
Waldrop, Richard W., 40, 46, 47, 50, 90, 91
Waller, Nancy C., 17, 24, 25–26
Walton, James Burdge, 110–12, 115–16, 119
Waring, Joseph Frederick, 88–89
Wells, Harrison, 1
White Brotherhood. *See* Ku Klux Klan
Whitehorne, J. E., 88–91
Wills, Charles A., 68
Wilson, Dick, 143–44
Wilson, D. L., 137, 143
winter quarters. *See* encampments
women, 4, 5, 23, 49, 57, 67, 70, 79–80, 90; and home production, 37–39; and hunting, 27, 30; and Ku Klux Klan, 133, 139, 147, 149, 150; and postbellum identity, 103, 118, 124–25, 183n111; and religion, 16–17; and writing, 15, 16, 24
Wood, John Taylor, 94
Worth, Jonathan, 101

Yorkville (S.C.) Enquirer, 120, 142

www.ingramcontent.com/pod-product-compliance
Lightning Source LLC
Chambersburg PA
CBHW030647230426
43665CB00011B/992